The SCORE
Takes Care
of Itself

The SCORE Takes Care of Itself

My Philosophy of Leadership

BILL WALSH

with Steve Jamison and Craig Walsh

PORTFOLIO

PORTFOLIO

Published by the Penguin Group

Penguin Group (USA) Inc., 375 Hudson Street, New York, New York 10014, U.S.A. • Penguin Group (Canada), 90 Eglinton Avenue East, Suite 700, Toronto, Ontario, Canada M4P 2Y3 (a division of Pearson Penguin Canada Inc.) • Penguin Books Ltd, 80 Strand, London WC2R 0RL, England • Penguin Ireland, 25 St. Stephen's Green, Dublin 2, Ireland (a division of Penguin Books Ltd) • Penguin Books Australia Ltd, 250 Camberwell Road, Camberwell, Victoria 3124, Australia (a division of Pearson Australia Group Pty Ltd) • Penguin Books India Pvt Ltd, 11 Community Centre, Panchsheel Park, New Delhi – 110 017, India • Penguin Group (NZ), 67 Apollo Drive, Rosedale, North Shore 0632, New Zealand (a division of Pearson New Zealand Ltd) • Penguin Books (South Africa) (Pty) Ltd, 24 Sturdee Avenue, Rosebank, Johannesburg 2196, South Africa

Penguin Books Ltd, Registered Offices: 80 Strand, London WC2R 0RL, England

First published in 2009 by Portfolio, a member of Penguin Group (USA) Inc.

10 9 8 7 6 5 4 3 2 1

ISBN: 978-1-59184-266-8

Printed in the United States of America

Acknowledgments

Craig Walsh

My father would want to acknowledge and thank Eddie DeBartolo Jr., the only owner who had the foresight and courage to give Bill Walsh a chance to be a head coach in the NFL.

He would also want to express his deep dedication and appreciation to all the people who wore the San Francisco 49er uniform both on the field or off—the entire organization who helped make a dream come true.

I would also like to dedicate our book to my children, Nate and Samantha. I know their grandfather is very proud of them just as they are proud of him. This book is also dedicated to my mother, Geri, my sister, Elizabeth, and the memory of my brother, Steve.

Steve Jamison

The Score Takes Care of Itself is dedicated with a lot of love to my mother, Mary Jean Edstrom. And, to my father, Everett, his brother, Harold, and their friend Roger Busdicker who created magic when they created Hal Leonard Publishing—my introduction to the world of publishing. Also, to Bill Walsh, Coach John Wooden, Uncle Roy Stark, David Varner, Aunt Jo Edstrom. And, lest we forget, the great publishing mind of Jeffrey Krames made it all happen.

Running a football franchise is not unlike running any other business: You start first with a structural format and basic philosophy and then find the people who can implement it.

—BILL WALSH

A Leader's Book for Leaders

Craig Walsh

My father, Bill Walsh, was one of the NFL's pivotal figures, a leader, head coach, and general manager whose innovations changed the way football is played and whose San Francisco 49er dynasty—five Super Bowl championships in fourteen years—ranks among the great achievements in sports history. *The Score Takes Care of Itself* is his very personal and, at times, painful account of the leadership lessons he learned during his life as well as his conclusions on how they might be useful in overcoming your own challenges as a leader.

Obviously, every profession has many elements unique unto itself. Nevertheless, when it comes to the fundamentals of effective leadership in the context of human nature and managing people, there are great parallels among the NFL, corporate America, or a grocery store with twelve employees. At least, Bill Walsh thought so.

The applicability of what he did in the NFL to the world of business is attested to by the fact that many CEOs in Silicon Valley and elsewhere not only were among his friends but also sought his advice and invited him to speak about leadership to their executive teams. After his retirement as head coach of the San Francisco 49ers, he did the same at Stanford University, where he gave lectures on leadership to graduate students at the business school. The *Harvard Business Review, Forbes,* and other magazines and business publications regularly came to him for ideas on team building and leadership beyond the context of football.

You might wonder about the origins of the title. *The Score Takes Care of*

Itself was one of my dad's oft-told sayings. Do all the right things to precision and "the score will take care of itself" sums up my father's philosophy, which is why we thought it the perfect title for his book.

It is the ultimate guidebook to the Bill Walsh philosophy and methodology of leadership and is drawn from my father's revealing and extensive conversations on the subject with best-selling author Steve Jamison. We have also utilized my father's private notes, including those for his lectures at the Stanford Graduate School of Business and video- and audiotapes of talks that he gave to the 49ers, as well as intimate conversations I had with him over his years as head coach about how he was doing it—and what *it* was doing to him.

Additionally, we've included concise but revealing and frank opinions about my father from five key "players" in his professional life, each chosen for a specific reason:

1. Joe Montana was the quarterback whom my father drafted in his first year as head coach at San Francisco. Joe was at the helm for all of the Super Bowl championships coached by my father, and his comments on how Bill Walsh could make dreams come true, "His Standard of Performance," is a master's analysis of a master and the foreword for the book.

2. John McVay, vice president and director of football operations for my father, offers insights into the great skills Bill Walsh exhibited when it came to getting the right people on the same page of the same book—a book written by Bill Walsh. "The Organization Man" is John's overview of the superb organization he saw put in place very quickly by the new coach, who could see a connection between wearing a tie and winning a Super Bowl.

3. Mike White was one of my father's true pals, a fellow assistant coach at the University of California–Berkeley who later worked for him in the beginning at San Francisco. Mike labored with Bill Walsh professionally at those two crucial points in his career and understood him inside and out. "The Problem Solver" is his description of the "spectacular" creative and analytical skills he saw demonstrated right from

the beginning. Bill Walsh had very few intimate friends, but Mike White was one of those guys.

4. Bill McPherson was a defensive assistant coach through the entire decade that Bill Walsh was at the helm of the 49ers, an insider who saw firsthand how my father came in and cleaned house. If you didn't "get with the program," as defined by Bill Walsh, you were gone. "The House Cleaner" is Bill McPherson's description of those rough early months when Bill Walsh started building a dynasty by dismantling a disaster.

5. Randy Cross, a great offensive lineman and now a top CBS football analyst, was a member of the San Francisco 49ers for thirteen years, including his first three, which were *pre*–Bill Walsh seasons. He was chosen because he experienced, as a player, what life was like on the worst team in the NFL and how Bill Walsh transformed it into the best. "The Fog Cutter" is Randy's keen perspective on the tumultuous events that were part of the creation of a dynasty by his new head coach and general manager.

These five, all important figures in my father's life, were asked to contribute their analyses of the leadership philosophy of Bill Walsh to complement and expand on the comprehensive lessons my father offers in *The Score Takes Care of Itself.* Others certainly were well qualified, but these five were asked and kindly accepted the invitation to more fully explain the "genius" of Bill Walsh.

Nevertheless, there is only one person who can fully articulate what he did, why it worked, and how it may benefit you as a leader; namely, Bill Walsh. In his own words, this book is his explanation.

My father's journey was arduous, but his dream was big: Bill Walsh wanted to be a successful head coach in the NFL more than anything else in the world. As he moved his family back and forth across the country, he chased his dream, from the Oakland Raiders and the San Jose Apaches to the Cincinnati Bengals, San Diego Chargers, and Stanford University. Ultimately, the dream came true: head coach of the San Francisco 49ers. The lessons he learned he wanted to share. My father is no longer with us, but I know he would be proud that his hard-earned lessons are now available in his book, *The Score Takes Care of Itself.*

His Standard of Performance

Joe Montana

I never saw a regular-season NFL game in person until I was a player in the NFL—watching from the sidelines as a rookie backup quarterback for the San Francisco 49ers during a game against the Minnesota Vikings. It was my first game as a pro. Bill Walsh was my coach.

We lost that game to the Vikings (28–22) as well as thirteen of our next fifteen games; fans were unhappy, and critics were howling and having a field day at our expense because all they could see was our 2–14 won-lost record. But I had my own opinion: Bill Walsh was special.

His mind for technical football was extraordinary, but beyond that was his ability to organize and manage his staff, players, everybody—to get the whole organization on exactly the same page. *On* that page he set the standard for how he wanted things done, and his standard was simple: perfection. That's what he taught us individually and as a group—to believe it could be achieved and then achieve it (or come close). He had in his mind this ideal—an image of perfect football—coupled with the nuts-and-bolts details of how to accomplish it, which he then taught.

That, in my opinion, was his primary leadership asset: his ability to teach people how to think and play at a different and much higher, and, at times, perfect level. He accomplished this in three ways: (1) he had a tremendous knowledge of all aspects of the game and a visionary approach to offense; (2) he brought in a great staff and coaches who knew how to coach, how to complement his own teaching of what we needed to know to rise to his standard of performance; and (3) he taught us to hate mistakes.

Bill got all of us striving to be perfect in games *and* practice. (You didn't want to see any balls on the ground, no fumbles, no mistakes, no turnovers.) Without all the screaming that coaches usually do, he was very focused and demanding because he was making you test yourself, take yourself to different limits. He said that if you aim for perfection and miss, you're still pretty good, but if you aim for mediocre and miss? Well, he didn't allow us to think like that.

That was the thing about his perspective: Being really good wasn't good enough. He taught us to want to be perfect and instilled in the team a hunger for improvement, a drive to get better and better. We saw his own hunger for perfection, and it was contagious.

In fact, that was the biggest challenge in playing for Bill—trying to be perfect. It applied to everyone on the team, everyone in the organization, but it seemed like it especially applied to his quarterback. He expected a lot from his quarterback.

Bill just assumed I was supposed to be great and didn't praise me routinely. The quarterback didn't get the game ball, didn't get a load of compliments. Win a Super Bowl? Yes, then you'd get praise from Bill, but otherwise he didn't believe his starting quarterback needed a lot of praise for doing what he was being paid to do.

You might think that trying to meet his extremely high expectations would tighten you up, but Bill didn't jump on you for a mistake; he came right in with the correction: "Here's what was wrong; this is how to do it right." Over and over, without getting all upset, he taught the smallest details of perfecting performance.

He had this little way of taking the pressure off with a comment or, on occasion, some sarcasm. Humor was one of his assets. One time, to emphasize the dress code, he had all the assistant coaches come into a meeting wearing outfits that were ridiculous. One was dressed like a bum, another like a hippie, and somebody was wearing tights, a dress, and falsies—that may have been Bill. He said something like, "Now, we don't want to look like this on the road, do we?" He made a serious point with humor.

He was extremely demanding without a lot of noise. He was supportive. Bill and I both knew what we were trying to achieve, and his approach with me was simply to teach what was necessary to get there. He was great at making people great students.

The first time Bill ever saw me throw a football in person was across from Los Angeles International Airport at a little public park. He and his assistant coach, Sam Wyche, had flown down from San Francisco to work out James Owens, a receiver, and me. It wasn't even a football field, just a little park with a playground for kids.

Bill and Sam had me throw to Owens for about thirty minutes. I was struck by Bill's easy manner. He was friendly, but there was another air about him too. I could sense he was very knowledgeable, and later, when he drafted me, it was apparent that he wanted things a very specific way and that he had logical reasons for it. He had this self-assurance—not cocky, just very confident. And that didn't change, even when we went 2–14 that first season.

Bill ran a pretty tight ship, but he knew when to let up. He didn't beat up players mentally or physically in practice. In fact, his approach was unique because often we didn't even wear pads in practice—there was no contact—especially as the season went on. Word got around the league, and other players wanted to be 49ers because Bill had this enlightened approach: He wanted us healthy on Sunday, so he didn't work us to death on Wednesday like most other coaches. And that was just the start of his advanced way of thinking. Everything he did was well thought out and ahead of the curve.

Bill raised everybody's standard, what we defined as acceptable. Perfection was his acceptable norm, and he got us thinking we could achieve it by teaching us what perfection was and how to reach it—not just how to locate a receiver, but every other aspect of doing your job at the top level, whatever that job was in the organization. It was something special, teaching a person, a whole team, an entire organization, to want to be perfect, to want to get to the next level, and the next one. And then *do* it.

The place you dreamed of but didn't know you could reach? Bill Walsh taught me how to reach it. He taught all of us how to reach it.

Contents

Part I: My Standard of Performance: An Environment of Excellence

PART II: Success Is Not Spelled G-E-N-I-U-S: Innovation, Planning, and Common Sense

Part III: Fundamentals of Leadership: Concepts, Conceits, and Conclusions

Part IV: Essentials of a Winning Team: People, Priorities, and Performance

Part V: Thin Skin, Baloney, and "The Star-Spangled Banner": Looking for Lessons in My Mirror

Bill's Final Lecture on Leadership

Steve Jamison

The phone rang four times before somebody picked it up: "This is Bill
Walsh," a voice announced. I was startled. After my calling and leaving
messages on his answering machine or with secretaries many times over
many months, the creator of one of the NFL's legendary dynasties, the San
Francisco 49ers (five Super Bowl championships!), the man who is perhaps
the greatest coach in football history, had picked up the phone *himself.*

"This is Bill Walsh. Hello. Hello?" he repeated.

Briefly, I was thrown off; fortunately, he didn't hang up.

And that's how this book began. It was that sudden and that simple.

I started talking, explaining to him my idea for a book about his philosophy of leadership as it applied beyond football—to management, business, and corporate life. And that I would like to collaborate with him in
writing it. "I think I saw one of your letters," he said. "Sounds okay." (Yes,
I had written several letters to him over the course of those many months.)
"Can you meet me here at 9 A.M. tomorrow?" he continued. I got there at
eight.

His office was located on the second floor of an expansive and expen-
sive office complex right next to the exclusive Sharon Heights Golf and
Country Club, just two minutes from Stanford University on Sand Hill
Road. The complex, forty minutes south of San Francisco in Silicon Valley, was populated by a host of technology-related companies and some of
the most successful venture capitalists in the world, including the most
famous, Kleiner Perkins Caufield and Byers (friends of Bill's).

The parking areas—beautifully designed and landscaped—looked like the crowded showroom of a Lexus or Mercedes-Benz dealer. I found an open space and parked, eager to meet Bill—nervous, in fact.

At 8:30 A.M. I walked up to his second floor office and knocked. No answer. I began staring directly down at the staircase I had just climbed, in anticipation of his grand arrival. Bill's arrival wasn't so grand. At exactly 9 A.M. I saw the top of a head—white hair, neatly trimmed and combed. Bill was walking up the stairs rather deliberately. Sandals (no socks), freshly pressed khaki Bermudas, a red and gold golf shirt (49ers colors). In his left hand a cup of Dunkin' Donuts coffee; in his right, a bag of Dunkin' Donuts.

"Steve? C'mon in. I got some doughnuts on the way over," he said as an introduction. He opened up the bag of doughnuts, and we started talking. Here's exactly what he told me in the first minute: "I came to the San Francisco 49ers with a specific goal—to implement what I call the Standard of Performance. It was a way of doing things, a leadership philosophy, that has as much to do with core values, principles, and ideals as with blocking, tackling, and passing; more to do with the mental than with the physical."

Bill talked about the need for character as a component of leadership (as well as the elements of character as he saw it); the evolution of the NFL's most significant change in fifty years—the pass-oriented offense he created—and the lesson it offers beyond football; how he taught the intricacies of high performance to players such as Joe Montana and how they apply to high performance elsewhere.

"Hey, wait a minute," he said at one point. "I've got some old videotapes in the closet that might help you get the idea of what we did in practice to get all the moving parts moving in the right direction. I'll get some for you." Bill put his coffee down, walked to the closet behind his desk, and after a couple of minutes came out with an armful of videotapes. "Here. Take these home. They might help you get the idea. When I put all the pieces together, it looked complicated, but each piece is simple. Most big things are simple in the specific, much less so in the general." Bill was a genius at making the complex comprehensible, the comprehensible achievable.

I asked him about the years with the Cincinnati Bengals when he began to emerge as a quarterback coach and offensive strategist whom others around the league started to take notice of. "I got fooled at Cincinnati," he chuckled. "Taken right down the primrose path by Paul Brown. But here's the lesson I learned." And he told me the lesson. He talked about winning his first Super Bowl and how it destroyed the next season: "But here's the lesson I learned." And he told me the lesson. Bill talked about his final game as an assistant coach with the Bengals, when he became flummoxed in the last moments of a game against the Oakland Raiders: "But here's the lesson I learned." All those lessons, all that accumulating leadership expertise.

This went on for three hours until he called our conversation—a lecture on leadership—to a halt because of a scheduled lunch with friends at the Sundeck Restaurant across the parking lot. Our discussions in that office continued for several months as he expanded on his core concepts of leadership—with accompanying anecdotes—for this book. Along the way there were more videotapes, notes, lessons of all sorts that he had learned along the way.

We would talk. I would write. He would review. We would talk some more. That's how we worked. Quickly, this book developed. Along the way I came to better understand Bill and how and why he did things as a leader, who he was as a person. Let me share a few observations.

Bill Walsh was brilliant almost beyond comprehension. His ability to analyze an intractable problem and come up with a solution (the West Coast Offense, for example) was stunning. It applied not only to touchdowns but also to managing and organizing individuals. Of course, how he did the latter facilitated the former. He was a master at it. Bill's analytical intelligence was coupled with an immense creativity that allowed him to see things differently. The result moved NFL football, in many ways, from the Stone Age to the twenty-first century. If there is such a thing as a Renaissance coach, he was it: truly enlightened when it came to directing an organization's attention and best effort to achieving goals he defined.

Bill Walsh held the need to treat individuals within his organization fairly almost sacrosanct (in return, those individuals were expected to consistently work at their most productive level). It stemmed from his own professional experience of being treated unfairly, which he describes here in detail. This did not preclude harsh—at times, seemingly ruthless—action when someone in the organization behaved in a manner contrary to the team's best interests.

He did not view the organization and the individuals within it as two separate entities, but as one and the same: "People are the heart of your organization," he instructed me. This perspective affected his leadership profoundly.

Bill Walsh loved lists, viewed them as a road map to results. That may sound simplistic, but I believe it was an important part of his astounding deductive-reasoning ability. When confronted with a "problem"—for example, how do we score touchdowns without a good running game or a strong passer? what is our communication process on the sidelines during a game when crowd noise becomes overwhelming? what are the specific duties of my executive vice president for football operations? and hundreds and hundreds more—Bill Walsh dissected the issue into its relevant parts, found a solution, and then taught the solution to the appropriate individuals. His creative and commonsense brilliance as a problem solver was unsurpassed and a major component in the installation of what he called the Standard of Performance.

I kidded him once that he was so obsessive about lists that he probably had lists of the lists in his file cabinet. He didn't deny it. I found a list of directives for his speech to receptionists at 49er headquarters that was two pages long with bullet point after bullet point. Here's bullet point number seventeen: "Your job is not civil service or even big corporate business. We exist to support and field a football team. In other words, we don't 'exist for the sake of existing.' We are not *maintaining*." He told me this addressed his concern that most people simply go through the motions at their jobs, just putting in time—existing—with a "business as usual" attitude. Not if you're on *his* team.

The meticulous manner in which he detailed specific actions and attitudes of his Standard of Performance as applied to secretaries and receptionists was true throughout the organization but in increasingly exponential quantities.

Bill Walsh was cautious in part because he was savvy. One day I started asking him about the leadership characteristics of other outstanding coaches—first Tom Landry, then Mike Holmgren, next Jimmy Johnson. Initially, he was open and insightful (as you'll read later). But then, suddenly, he decided this was a subject he did not like, namely, talking about his peers—that I was taking him down a path that could cause problems for him. And *that* was the end of that discussion. The atmosphere in his small office chilled: "I've got to make some calls," he said brusquely as he broke off his description of Bill Parcells and picked up the phone. And without his saying so, I knew he had dismissed me for the day. (I noticed as I was leaving that he put the phone down, never made a call.)

Bill had sensed, incorrectly, that I was looking for some dirt or critical comments on other coaches. He was a very careful man.

Bill Walsh was an educator—a teacher. He accumulated great knowledge because he was a Grade A student of leadership, paying close attention along the way to some of football's most outstanding and forward-thinking coaches, most of all Paul Brown (of the Cincinnati Bengals). Bill absorbed their good ideas, learned from their bad ones, applied his own even more advanced concepts, and then *reveled* in the process of teaching what he knew to his teams. I came to believe that the part of football he enjoyed best was teaching, or more accurately, identifying outstanding talent and teaching that player, assistant coach, or staff member how to be great. He loved it.

Bill Walsh was without pretense, almost soft-spoken. While his comportment was never chummy—there was a reserve to his manner—he was easy to talk to and be with unless I hit a nerve. For all the attention and glory that had been heaped on him during and especially after the dynasty years, he was normal—coffee-and-doughnuts normal; although not laid-back or casual, he was unaffected. You'd think you were talking to a very successful and focused midlevel corporate executive unless you noticed the picture on the wall of Bill standing next to Joe Montana holding a Super Bowl trophy, or the picture on the other wall of Bill standing next to Joe Montana holding a different Super Bowl trophy.

All of the above became apparent to me as we proceeded to write this book revealing Bill's leadership philosophy. Along the way, I secured a generous offer from a publisher eager to share the "wisdom of Walsh"— when it came to building a top team in business or elsewhere. And then, boom! Just as simply and suddenly as it had begun, it stopped. No book.

Bill—retired from the NFL for ten years—had accepted an offer to return in an executive capacity to the San Francisco 49ers. On the same day that I received a lengthy contract from a publisher, he called with the news that he was going back to the NFL. I knew what that meant, because in our earliest conversations he had laid out only one stipulation: "If I go back to the NFL, I don't want this book coming out. I don't need the headache." It was a handshake deal. And so, no book.

As writers do, I put my writing and notes and tapes and collected articles and interviews and research material into boxes, put the boxes into storage, and then forgot about it—or tried to. It was great stuff on leadership that Bill had shared in our conversations, and it seemed a shame to pack it up and move on. But that's what happened.

Bill lent a hand to resuscitating the moribund 49ers for several years (his towering San Francisco 49er dynasty had fallen into disrepair and he was called back to duty) and I continued work with UCLA's legendary basketball coach, John Wooden. A book we had written earlier was becoming a best seller, and it led us to a productive professional association and friendship, including more books, television presentations, seminars, and even a best-selling publication for children.

My boxes marked "Bill Walsh Leadership" were collecting dust. And then one day my phone rang. "Hello, this is Bill Walsh," the voice said. "I'm very interested in getting that book finished up, Steve." As with our first phone call, I was almost at a loss for words. He was no longer working for the 49ers and, in fact, was lecturing on a regular basis to corporate groups and students at Stanford University about leadership. It was time, he said, to get his book on leadership published. Ten years had gone by.

I was delighted: "If you've got some time next week, I'll meet you at Stanford and you can review the manuscript again before I go back to publishers." That sounded good to him: "Fine! Oops, wait a minute. I'm going into the hospital for some tests next week. But if you want, it's probably okay to meet me there."

I don't like hospitals and didn't particularly want to impose on Bill while he was wearing a gown: "No, no. Let's wait a week. Is it anything to be worried about, the tests?" I asked. He assured me that it was routine, nothing serious, just a series of tests to check on something that had been going on for a while. I said, "Okay, I'll talk to you after you finish up at the hospital. Good luck." He replied, "I'll see you then."

Not long after that, Bill was dead—leukemia. The greatest coach in football's history was seventy-five.

I had come to feel close to him over the years, first as a fan watching Bill lead the 49ers to multiple Super Bowl championships; later working with him on this book; and still later watching him from afar as he wrestled once again with the problems of a struggling team. Through it all he had exhibited poise, intelligence, and a basic decency.

Bill and I certainly were not buddies, but from the start he treated me right. (I learned recently that Bill had plenty of friends, associates, and a ton of great working relationships but almost no buddies, intimates with whom he could bare his soul.) He was unpretentious, forthright, no BS; his composure and presence were so unique and appealing. As Joe Montana told me, "You knew immediately there was something special about him."

And I had grown to appreciate—be astonished by—his incredible story of overcoming impossible odds in the NFL with the singularity of his leadership brilliance, management acumen, and football creativity and the force of his will.

There also was his willingness to talk about the personal issues, his emotional meltdown in the second season, the toll of not just getting to the top, but staying there, triumph and burnout, and, of course, all the insights into leadership—"but here's the lesson I learned."

I had, in my own small way, gotten to know and greatly respect Bill, and his death hurt; it knocked the wind out of my sails for the book; I'm not sure why. He was a good guy, a real guy. So, sadly, once again I put our manuscript back in boxes. This time for good. Or so I thought.

Several months after the public tributes and a big memorial service at Candlestick Park (where Bill had worked his leadership genius) had been concluded, a friend of mine, Peter Fatooh, a successful local executive and big-time fan of the 49ers, started telling me how much he respected Bill Walsh as a leader, how far ahead of everybody he had been in his thinking. I mentioned casually that I had been working on a book with Bill at the time of his death but wasn't going to publish it now—that I had kind of lost heart, gotten the wind knocked out of me by his death. "Would you mind if I read it?" Peter asked. "I'd like to know what Bill says about leadership."

I offered to let him read the manuscript if he promised not to pass it around. "It's just for you to read," I told him. He agreed. One week later I saw him again at the San Francisco Tennis Club (where Bill used to play a frustrating game of tennis occasionally), and Peter was eager to tell me the following: "Steve, you've got to get Bill's book published. It's great. Just great." He returned the manuscript and said, "Now I know why he was so exceptional. I've already started using some of his ideas myself." Somehow, Peter's honest and positive opinion got me back up and running.

A few weeks later, I contacted Bill's only surviving son, Craig, who agreed to meet me and listen to the history of his father's book on leadership. We met for lunch at the Fish Market Restaurant in Foster City, California, not too far from 711 Nevada Street, where Bill had begun his work building the 49er dynasty more than twenty-five years earlier. I gave Craig the manuscript for this book and told him that if he didn't like it I would withhold it from publication. With his father's death, he was the one who should now decide whether or not the book merited publication.

A few days later, Craig called: "I think you've really got something special here, Steve. I see why Dad wanted this available to the public." And then he added that he had access to additional lecture notes by his father, as well as tapes and other material that might be useful. He could also supply original notes and information from a book for football coaches that Bill had written but withdrawn from publication. Also, and most important, he could offer his own insider's perspective on his father's incredible journey.

And so Bill's book was back on track once again, this time without Bill, but with the blessing and participation of his son. I contacted Jeffrey Krames, one of the publishing world's foremost editors in the field of management and leadership (also the author of books on the leadership lessons of Jack Welch, Peter Drucker, Lou Gerstner, and others), who saw the deep value of the Bill Walsh philosophy of leadership when it came to management and team building. He, in turn, brought the great creative resources of Portfolio Publishing into play and gave us the green light. And that, in a big nutshell, is how Bill's book on leadership got published. Looking back, it seems almost impossible.

It has been an extraordinary experience for me. So many unusual happenings: Bill picking up the phone *himself* that day many years ago because his secretary was away on a family emergency (if he hadn't, I doubt we would have gotten together for this book); his return to the NFL, which stopped the book in its tracks; Bill's call to me years later saying he wanted to get this book published (nudged, it turns out, by my friend UCLA coach John Wooden); soon after, Bill's final, fatal diagnosis of leukemia; his death; the mourning; the encouragement from Peter Fatooh; the blessing and full participation of Craig Walsh and the great perception of Jeffrey Krames and his boss at Portfolio, Adrian Zackheim. All I can figure is that Bill's book was meant to be.

Through it all there has been one fundamental and powerful constant: the substantive leadership wisdom of football's legendary coach, Bill Walsh. His brilliance was evident in the first minute of our conversation in that little office on Sand Hill Road, and it continued every time he spoke.

Bill Walsh loved to teach. This is his final lecture on leadership.

The SCORE
Takes Care
of Itself

To Succeed You Must Fail

I would never write anything that suggests the path to success is a continuum of positive, even euphoric experiences—that if you do all the right things everything will work out. Frequently it doesn't; often you crash and burn. This is part and parcel of pursuing and achieving very ambitious goals. It is also one of the profound lessons I have learned during my career, namely, that even when you have an organization brimming with talent, victory is not always under your control. Rather, it's like quicksilver—fleeting and elusive, not something you can summon at will even under the best circumstances. Almost always, your road to victory goes through a place called "failure."

That reality was present throughout my career, from coaching the Huskies of Washington Union High School in Fremont, California, to the San Francisco 49ers, and all the stops along the way—San Jose State, Stanford University and the University of California–Berkeley, the Oakland Raiders, the Cincinnati Bengals, and the San Diego Chargers. Always the same principle was present: There is no guarantee, no ultimate formula for success.

However, a resolute and resourceful leader understands that there are a multitude of means to increase the *probability* of success. And that's what it all comes down to, namely, intelligently and relentlessly seeking solutions that will increase your chance of prevailing in a competitive environment. When you do that, the score will take care of itself.

Professional football, in my opinion, is the moral equivalent of war. The stress, wear and tear, and assault on a person's spirit and basic self-esteem are incredible. It takes an individual to the outer limits of his capabilities and may provide one of the ultimate studies of people because it is such a cruel, volatile, and emotionally and physically dangerous activity.

I also believe that NFL football, absent the extreme physical component, is the intellectual equivalent of business as it pertains to the fundamental task of leadership; specifically, organizing and managing a group of individuals to achieve difficult goals in an extremely competitive world.

The ideas, experiences, and conclusions I offer here are drawn from my own search for success in the context of my profession—football—and intended to add to your own knowledge of leadership in your profession, to give you insights on what a fellow traveler experienced during my own competitive journey.

Pursuing your ambitions, especially those of any magnitude, can be grueling and hazardous, and produce agonizing failure along the way, but achieving those goals is among life's most gratifying and thrilling experiences. The ability to survive and overcome the former to attain the latter is a fundamental difference between winners and losers.

I've observed that if individuals who prevail in a highly competitive environment have any one thing in common besides success, it is failure— and their ability to overcome it. "Crash and burn" is part of it; so are recovery and reward. As you're about to see, I experienced more than my share of both. In the process, I've discovered a few things worth sharing, a few lessons worth learning.

PART I

My Standard of Performance: An Environment of Excellence

The ability to help the people around me self-actualize their goals underlines the single aspect of my abilities and the label that I value most—teacher.

—BILL WALSH

How to Know if You're Doing the Job

When I give a speech at a corporate event, I often ask those in attendance, "Do you know how to tell if you're doing the job?" As heads start whispering back and forth, I provide these clues: "If you're up at 3 A.M. every night talking into a tape recorder and writing notes on scraps of paper, have a knot in your stomach and a rash on your skin, are losing sleep *and* losing touch with your wife and kids, have no appetite or sense of humor, and feel that everything might turn out wrong, then you're probably doing the job."

This always gets a laugh, but not a very big one. Those executives in the audience recognize there is a significant price to pay to be the best. That price is not something they laugh at.

Coaches Aren't Supposed to Cry: Survive One Minute at a Time

In my second year as head coach of the San Francisco 49ers, we were preparing to play the defending AFC East champions, Don Shula's powerful Miami Dolphins, a team that was formidable, especially at home in the Orange Bowl.

The showdown came in week eleven of our schedule and at the worst possible moment for me because after a great start to my second season—three straight wins against the New Orleans Saints, St. Louis Cardinals, and New York Jets—we had lost seven consecutive games. Our year was imploding. (The previous season, my first as head coach, our record had been 2–14, which meant that since I had taken over leadership of the 49ers we had won five games and lost twenty-one, the worst record in the NFL.)

A loss to Miami on Sunday would be our eighth in a row and likely have enormous consequences, including the possibility of my being terminated or at least being put on a "death watch" by the media—an unofficial lame duck and powerless coach.

Conversely, I recognized that a victory against the Dolphins would stop the hemorrhaging and provide hope for salvaging the last part of our season, which, in turn, could have a positive impact on the following year. Huge stakes were on the table. I was somewhat hopeful, perhaps even optimistic.

Nevertheless, the professional and personal magnitude of the upcoming Miami–San Francisco game clouded the entire week's practice for me and created a brittleness in my behavior that was out of character. I was brusque, short-tempered, and not as tuned in as I should have been.

The game itself—played in suffocating Florida heat and humidity—turned into a bruising battle in front of over seventy-five thousand screaming Dolphin fans who had packed themselves into the stadium. For the 49ers it was like going to a wild party to which you are uninvited and unwelcome—everybody tries to throw you out the window.

Miami's tropical sun had pushed daytime temperatures into the nineties, and dusk didn't bring them down. In fact, the heat seemed to get worse, as if we were playing in a swamp, trying to move in quicksand. None of this appeared to affect Coach Shula's team. They built an early lead and held onto it throughout the game. It seemed evident that we were headed for our eighth straight defeat—a potentially disastrous event.

However, with time running down—less than two minutes remaining—49er kicker Ray Wersching, perhaps the league's best field goal specialist, calmly nailed a winner to get us within a point: 17–16. Immediately, the entire San Francisco bench leaped up, pumping their fists and yelling wildly. You could feel this huge surge in momentum erupt.

Unfortunately, it was a short-lived surge; our field goal did not count. To my dismay, a holding penalty was called against us and the score was nullified. Quickly, I again nodded at Ray, who strapped on his helmet, trotted out, and calmly kicked another field goal from five yards farther back. Again, raucous cheers erupted on our bench, but immediately *another* flag was thrown and another penalty called against us.

Now the line of scrimmage put us out of field-goal range and forced us into a passing situation; we needed a first down to retain possession of the ball. Quickly, we completed a pass that gave us just enough yards to pick up the first down. The 49ers had survived for the moment, stayed alive. Or so it seemed.

As I watched in disbelief, a linesman raced in and gave Miami a spot so friendly it could have gotten him elected to local public office. Our drive had been stopped three times in a row under increasingly outrageous circumstances. What made it maddening was that Shula had been berating officials throughout the game whenever they made a call against the Dolphins. This seemed to be his reward—a spot he had to love and two penalties against us on the previous plays. As bad as the 49er season had become, nothing this agonizing and damaging had happened to us before. And the crowd loved it.

Sensing the imminent kill, fans went into a stadium-wide uproar as we silently turned the ball back to Miami—the game essentially over as the Dolphins extended our losing streak to eight games with their 17–13 victory. The pain of that loss haunts me even now as I think about those final seconds ticking off the clock.

It was a horrible and numbing defeat, overwhelming for me because of its potential impact—a job I had worked for my entire adult life was in jeopardy—but also because of the stupid, self-inflicted, almost suicidal way in which we lost. As the crowd roared its approval and Miami players and fans swarmed over the field, I stood alone on the sideline in a cocoon of grief, emotionally gutted, wondering if I had the strength to even get back to our locker room.

Unless you've experienced this type of emotional shock and the bleak interior landscape it creates, it's hard to comprehend the impact. The memory never leaves you and acts as both a positive and negative force, spurring you to work harder and harder while also creating a fear inside that it might happen again. (For me, that fear eventually became more than I could handle.)

Now Shula trotted briskly across the field to shake hands and offer a few perfunctory words of condolence. I have no clue as to what he said, but even though I was in some state of shock, instincts took over. I offered my hand; he shook it, shouted something in my ear, and disappeared back into the public pandemonium and celebration at midfield.

The next few hours—until we got out of the stadium complex and arrived at the Miami airport—remain a blur. I can't remember what, if anything, I said to the players and coaches in the locker room or reporters in the press room. Probably I was on some kind of automatic pilot and experiencing what victims of violence go through when they blot out the memory of the assault.

While the moments immediately following that game are missing in my mind, the long trip home is vivid. Coaches aren't supposed to cry, but I'm not ashamed to admit that on the night flight back to San Francisco I sat in my seat in the first row of the plane and broke down sobbing in the darkness. I felt like a casualty of war being airlifted away from the battlefield.

Bill McPherson, Neal Dahlen, John McVay, Norb Hecker, and some of the other San Francisco assistant coaches and staff understood the grief I was experiencing and shielded me from any players who might come into the area—they huddled around my seat, blocking off view of me, while making small talk and eating peanuts, acting like we were all involved in the conversation.

Believe me, I was not participating in whatever it was they said or eating peanuts as I slumped down, depressed, in my dark little space, contemplating whether I should offer my resignation. Most debilitating of all—devastating—was a gnawing fear that I didn't have what it takes to be an NFL head coach. At one point I actually decided to hand in my resignation the next morning; then I changed my mind.

I have tried to describe my anguish, but the words come up short. Everything I had dreamed of professionally for a quarter of a century was in jeopardy just eighteen months after being realized. And yet there was something else going on inside me, a "voice" from down deeper than the emotions, something stirring that I had learned over many years in football and, before that, growing up; namely, I must stand and fight again, stand and fight or it was all over.

And that was the instinct that slowly prevailed as we headed home in the middle of a very dark night. I knew that in a matter of seven days the New York Giants were coming to town with the sole intent of making sure that neither I nor the San Francisco 49ers would stand and fight again.

In my mind—or gut—and in spite of the pain, I knew I had to force myself to somehow start looking ahead—to overcome my grief over the debacle in Miami—or it would severely damage our efforts to prepare properly for the battle with New York; my comportment would directly affect the attitudes and performance of everyone who looked to me for answers and direction. I had to do what I was being paid to do: be a leader.

I wish I could tell you that's what happened—that I simply turned a switch and was magically transformed from an emotional basket case into an invincible field general. It wasn't that way. It took time for me to stop despairing and regain some composure, to settle down and start thinking straight, but gradually, during those hard hours on the flight back to California, I began pulling myself together.

In the NFL events occur—hit you—at supersonic speeds with volcanic force during the regular season. There aren't months or weeks to recover, not even days. Usually only hours or minutes. While you're throwing a wolf out the back door, another is banging on your front door and two more are trying to crawl through the windows. I could hear the New York Giants at our front door.

I can say with some pride that by the time we landed at San Francisco International Airport at 3:15 A.M. after a six-hour flight, I had pulled myself out of the hopelessness and begun working on the strategy we would employ against the Giants when they arrived in a week. I was wobbly but back up on my feet again. I even ate a couple of bags of peanuts and drank some orange juice.

Those awful feelings brought on by the events in Miami were in retreat because I was able to summon strength enough to pull my *focus*, my thinking, out of the past and move it forward to our next big problem. It does take strength to shift your attention off the pain when you feel as though your soul has been stripped bare.

At times like that I would think back to my days as an amateur boxer, when I'd see a guy knocked flat on his back and then awkwardly struggle to one shaky knee. Everything is blurry, his balance is gone, consciousness is tenuous, he's bleeding and bruised, but as bad as things are there is one message he hears ringing inside his head: "Stand up, boy; stand up and fight." I know because as a young man I was that boxer.

NFL football is no different from any professional endeavor, boxing or business or anything where the stakes are significant and the competition extreme: When knocked down, you must get up; you must stand and fight.

When the inevitable setback, loss, failure, or defeat comes crashing down on you—losing a big sale, being passed over for a career-making promotion, even getting fired—allow yourself the "grieving time," but then recognize that the road to recovery and victory lies in having the strength to get up off the mat and start planning your next move.

This is how you must think if you want to win. Otherwise you have lost.

For me, on that flight back home after the Miami loss, it meant working one minute at a time—literally—to regain composure, confidence, and direction.

Failure is part of success, an integral part. Everybody gets knocked down. Knowing it will happen and what you must do when it does is the first step back. It's what got me up after being knocked down and almost out in Miami. I knew I had to stand and start facing the imminent challenge of a battle with the New York Giants.

One other thing about that upcoming game: On Sunday we defeated the Giants 12–0 at Candlestick Park and regained a little equilibrium, even momentum. A week later we beat New England 21–17; the next week the 49ers engineered one of the greatest comebacks in NFL history. Trailing at the half, 35–7, we defeated New Orleans in overtime, 38–35.

In fact, in spite of losing to the Atlanta Falcons and Buffalo Bills in our last two games to finish with a 6–10 record, the worst was over. Unbeknownst to me, we had hit rock bottom against the Dolphins. Sixteen months after I spent part of a transcontinental flight experiencing an emotional meltdown, the San Francisco 49ers became world champions, defeating the Cincinnati Bengals 26–21 at the Silverdome in Pontiac, Michigan, in Super Bowl XVI. In fact, a football dynasty was in the works.

During the ensuing fourteen years, the San Francisco 49ers won five Super Bowls. It happened only because at the moment of deepest despair I had the strength to stand and confront the future instead of wallowing in the past. Many can't summon the strength; they can't get up; their fight is over. Victory goes to another, a stronger competitor.

Competition at the highest level in sports or business produces gut-ripping setbacks. When you're fighting for your survival professionally, struggling when virtually no one else knows or cares, and there's nobody to bail you out, that's when you might remind yourself of my own dark night of despair.

When you stand and overcome a significant setback, you'll find an increasing inner confidence and self-assurance that has been created by conquering defeat. Absorbing and overcoming this kind of punishment engenders a sober, steely toughness that results in a hardened sense of independence and a personal belief that you can take on anything, survive and win.

The competitor who won't go away, who won't stay down, has one of the most formidable competitive advantages of all. When the worst happens, as it did to me, I was helped by knowing what it took to be that kind of competitor—to not go away, to get up and fight back.

The Miami game was not the last time I faced a grim situation as head coach, but when downturns occurred during the upcoming years, I tried to adhere to some simple dos and don'ts for mental and emotional equilibrium in my personal and professional life; nothing profound, just a few plain and uncomplicated reminders that helped me manage things mentally and stay afloat:

MY FIVE DOs FOR GETTING BACK INTO THE GAME:

1. **Do expect defeat.** It's a given when the stakes are high and the competition is working ferociously to beat you. If you're surprised when it happens, you're dreaming; dreamers don't last long.

2. **Do force yourself to stop looking backward and dwelling on the professional "train wreck" you have just been in.** It's mental quicksand.

3. **Do allow yourself appropriate recovery—grieving—time.** You've been knocked senseless; give yourself a little time to recuperate. A keyword here is "little." Don't let it drag on.

4. **Do tell yourself, "I am going to stand and fight again," with the knowledge that often when things are at their worst you're closer than you can imagine to success.** Our Super Bowl victory arrived less than sixteen months after my "train wreck" in Miami.

5. **Do begin planning for your next serious encounter.** The smallest steps—plans—move you forward on the road to recovery. Focus on the fix.

MY FIVE DON'TS:

1. Don't ask, "Why me?"
2. Don't expect sympathy.
3. Don't bellyache.
4. Don't *keep* accepting condolences.
5. Don't blame others.

My Standard of Performance: High Requirements for Actions and Attitudes

People asked me over the years, "Bill, when you became head coach and general manager of the 49ers, did you have a timetable for winning the Super Bowl?" My answer is succinct: "No."

Things were in such bad shape when I arrived that talk of a Super Bowl championship for San Francisco would have sounded delusional; people would have thought I was crazy. (In fact, some did think I was crazy for leaving a job at Stanford University, where I had been comfortably ensconced as head coach of a team that had just won two consecutive postseason bowl games—the Bluebonnet Bowl and the Sun Bowl. Additionally, I felt very much at home in the academic environment at Stanford.)

In the two years before I joined San Francisco, my predecessor as 49ers general manager, Joe Thomas, had basically gutted the entire 49er organization, forcing out head coach Monte Clark, whose 8–6 record had been the 49ers' first winning season in four years; hiring and firing three head coaches in twelve months; impetuously and vindictively firing—humiliating—players in front of the team; trading away or releasing quality talent, including quarterback Jim Plunkett to the Oakland Raiders, whom he would soon take to two Super Bowl championships; and removing all "success" memorabilia from previous years (including trophies for three divisional championships, banners, plaques, game programs, photographs of teams, and even MVP awards).

Perhaps the highlight of Thomas's mismanagement was his acquisition of O. J. Simpson from the Buffalo Bills when the superstar was at the end of his career—overweight, arthritic, and out of gas. Thomas had concluded that Simpson would attract fans simply because he was a local kid from San Francisco's Potrero Hill neighborhood.

Fans thought otherwise and decided that seeing Simpson sitting bored on the bench with a bag of ice on his knee was not worth the price of admission. The cost to the organization was extreme: Thomas gave Buffalo draft picks that included first-, second- (two of them), third-, and fourth-round choices over three years and appeared to have mortgaged away the future of the franchise. All of the above was part of his plan to start a "new era of 49er football." It certainly was.

What remained was a demoralized, chaotic, and near-mutinous organizational culture of failure that was epitomized by a team that produced a 2–14 record the year prior to my arrival (and was even worse than that record suggests). One writer declared that the San Francisco 49ers were the worst franchise in all of professional sports. Not just football—*all* professional sports.

Joe Thomas was summarily fired; I was hired.

That's what I faced on my first day of work—an organization in turmoil; a team whose roster of talent was paper-thin and tattered; a future that seemed dismal, in part because in spite of that 2–14 season the year before I arrived, I didn't even have a first-round draft pick.

Emblematic of the organizational dysfunction were the organization's substandard headquarters and training facility. There wasn't enough space for a regulation-size football field, so the team used two "semifields" in Redwood City, California. The weight room was sparsely furnished with rusting weights, the showers ran cold if somebody flushed a toilet, and our offices were worn, sparse, and cramped.

Consequently, I approached building the 49er organization with an agenda that didn't include a timetable for a championship or even a winning season. Instead, I arrived with an urgent timetable for installing an agenda of specific behavioral norms—actions and attitudes—that applied to every single person on our payroll.

To put it bluntly, I would teach each person in the organization what to do and how to think. The short-term results would contribute both symbolically and functionally to a new and productive self-image and environment and become the foundation upon which we could launch our longer-term goal, namely, the resurrection of a football franchise.

For me to do this I had to have autonomy, the power to quickly make decisions in all relevant areas. Team owner Eddie DeBartolo understood this and named me general manager soon after I became head coach. Equally important, he let everyone in the organization know that I was the boss and that he would not undercut my authority. Without this power and support my task would have been virtually impossible given the abysmal situation.

While the media eventually and inappropriately labeled me "the Genius," the 49ers' subsequent turnaround—from a 2–14 record my first season to Super Bowl champions twenty-four months later (becoming the first and only team in NFL history to go from the worst to the best in two seasons), from organizational chaos to praise from the *Harvard Business Review* for organizational excellence—was due in large part to many quantifiable, even nuts-and-bolts, skills available to you or anyone with drive and intelligence.

There was innovation and expertise, yes; force of will, certainly; and occasional good fortune, of course. But my organizational and managerial starting point was something else. I came to the San Francisco 49ers with an overriding priority and specific goal—to implement what I call the Standard of Performance. It was a way of doing things, a leadership philosophy that has as much to do with core values, principles, and ideals as with blocking, tackling, and passing; more to do with the mental than with the physical. While I prized preparation, planning, precision, and poise, I also knew that organizational ethics were crucial to ultimate and ongoing success.

It began with this fundamental leadership assertion: Regardless of your specific job, it is vital to our team that you do that job at the highest possible level in *all* its various aspects, both mental and physical (i.e., good talent with bad attitude equals bad talent).

An Organization Has a Conscience

Beyond the mechanical elements of doing jobs correctly, I assisted coaches, players, staff, and others in assimilating the values within my Standard of Performance, including what I believed regarding personal accountability among the organization and its personnel. This is consistent with my conviction that an organization is not just a tool like a shovel, but an organic entity that has a code of conduct, a set of applied principles that go beyond a company mission statement that's tacked on the wall and forgotten. In fact, we had no mission statement on the wall. My mission statement was implanted in the minds of our people through teaching.

Great teams in business, in sports, or elsewhere have a conscience. At its best, an organization—your team—bespeaks values and a way of doing things that emanate from a source; that source is you—the leader. Thus, the dictates of your personal beliefs should ultimately become characteristics of your team.

You must know what needs to be done and possess the capabilities and conviction to get it done. Several factors affect this, but none is more important than the dictates of your own personal beliefs. Collectively, they comprise your philosophy. A philosophy is the aggregate of your attitudes toward fundamental matters and is derived from a process of consciously thinking about critical issues and developing rational reasons for holding one particular belief or position rather than another.

Many things shape your philosophy, including your background, experiences, work environment, education, aspirations, and more. By adhering to your philosophical tenets you are provided with a systematic, yet practical, method of deciding what to do in a particular situation.

It is a conceptual blueprint for action; that is, a perception of *what* should be done, *when* it should be done, and *why* it should be done. Your philosophy is the single most important navigational point on your leadership compass.

My Standard of Performance—the values and beliefs within it— guided everything I did in my work at San Francisco and are defined as follows: Exhibit a ferocious and intelligently applied work ethic directed at continual improvement; demonstrate respect for each person in the organization and the work he or she does; be deeply committed to learning and teaching, which means increasing my own expertise; be fair; demonstrate character; honor the direct connection between details and improvement, and relentlessly seek the latter; show self-control, especially where it counts most—under pressure; demonstrate and prize loyalty; use positive language and have a positive attitude; take pride in my effort as an entity *separate* from the result of that effort; be willing to go the extra distance for the organization; deal appropriately with victory and defeat, adulation and humiliation (don't get crazy with victory nor dysfunctional with loss); promote internal communication that is both open and substantive (especially under stress); seek poise in myself and those I lead; put the team's welfare and priorities ahead of my own; maintain an ongoing level of concentration and focus that is abnormally high; and make sacrifice and commitment the organization's trademark.

These are also the basic characteristics of attitude and action—the new organizational ethos—I tried to teach our team, to put into our DNA. Of course, for this to happen the person in charge—whether a head coach, CEO, manager, or assembly-line foreman—must exhibit the principles, code of conduct, and behavior he or she is asking others to emulate. I believe I did this.

Make no mistake about it; my first commitment was to nurture an organizational conscience with this very high internal code of ethics, ideals, and attitudes. Concurrently, I was committed to identifying and hiring the best people I could find and teaching them what I deemed necessary to achieve the required levels of performance.

If you were lucky enough to receive a 49er paycheck, it meant you were part of an organization that had high expectations of itself and of you, whether you were a superstar or a secretary, manager or maintenance man, athlete, executive, or head coach. Those expectations, of course, went beyond ethics and attitude to specific performance standards and actions.

Specifics of My New Standards

For returning players, veterans acquired in trades, and rookies such as Notre Dame's Joe Montana and Clemson University receiver Dwight Clark, my Standard of Performance required not only maximum mental and physical effort, sacrifice, and commitment but also attention to such seemingly incidental requirements as "no shirttails out," "positive attitude," "promptness," "good sportsmanship (no strutting, no posturing, no cheap shots)," "never sit down while on the practice field," "no tank tops in the dining area," "control of profanity," "no fighting," "treat fans with respect and exhibit a professional demeanor," and many more, including "no smoking on premises," which applied to all of us. Much of this may seem trivial to you, but it adds up and changes the environment.

For example, how the players dressed at practice and the appearance they gave to others when taking the field was very important to me. I wanted our football team to look truly professional—impeccable. Thus, shirttails tucked in, socks up tight, and more were requirements.

Later, when Jerry Rice, our great receiver, joined the team, he would stand in front of a full-length mirror as he got dressed before a game, not because he was vain or adoring himself—maybe there was a little of that— but mostly because he was just looking at that uniform; he was looking at perfection; perfection was what was in his mind when he entered the arena.

Jerry Rice was a professional and looked like a professional. And it all helped him in some way to think and perform like a professional. That "perfect" appearance—"*appropriate* appearance" is more accurate—applied to others in the organization as well, because it is part of the motif that directs thinking into a mode I view as conducive to high performance. That perfect appearance was a predicate of perfect performance.

Of course, our coaching staff was meticulous and tenacious in analyzing and then teaching the requirements of each player's position—much more so than on any other team I knew of. Here's one very small example: After careful analysis, they identified thirty specific and separate physical skills— actions—that every offensive lineman needed to master in order to do his job at the highest level, everything from tackling to evasion, footwork to arm movement. Our coaches then created multiple drills for *each* one of those individual skills, which were then practiced relentlessly until their execution at the highest level was automatic—routine "perfection."

Linemen were taught multiple blocking techniques to capitalize on what they saw across the line of scrimmage; most teams taught far fewer. Quarterbacks were coached on the refined requirements of a three-step, five-step, and seven-step drop back; how to hold the ball; *where* to hold the ball (the tip of the football must never drop below waist level on a pass play); scanning the *entire* field for receivers; when to throw and not to throw; throwing the ball at different velocities and different trajectories; and hundreds of other elements, both mental and physical.

Passing routes were designed down to the inch and then practiced until receivers learned how to be at that exact inch at the exact moment the ball arrived. On paper my diagrams of plays resembled detailed architec-tural drawings. And they required the same exactness in construction— execution—that a good contractor brings to building a skyscraper. If he's sloppy in following the architectural schematic, the building falls down during the first stiff wind.

Our practices were organized to the minute—like a musical score for an orchestra that shows every musician what to play and when to play it. Our coaches then drilled the team so they could "play it" better and bet-ter. The specificity of detail and bombardment of information involved in doing this are mind-numbing to the casual observer—perhaps like the specifics of your own profession to an outsider.

My Standard of Performance applied to marketing, office personnel, and everyone else with the details applicable to their jobs, even to the extent of including specific instructions for receptionists on how to answer our telephones professionally. All of this increasingly demonstrated to others and to *ourselves* that we were on top of things, neither sloppy nor inatten-tive, and contributed to a greatly heightened sense of "this is who we are," even though a strong case could have been made that "who we are" wasn't much based on the initial won-lost records during my first two seasons: 2–14 and 6–10. Of course, that was part of my challenge—turning the self-image of the organization on its head, from toxic to top-notch.

More quickly than you might imagine, a transformation occurred in the quality of the team's attitudes and actions. An environment developed in which adherence to the details of my Standard of Performance became second nature as we worked to become absolutely first class in every possible way on and off the field.

Our groundskeepers raised their level of play to a point where Candlestick Park's football field was increasingly among those in the best shape of any natural surface in the NFL, despite its proximity to San Francisco Bay, which produced a soggy subsoil and a mushy topsoil, and the effects of our winter rainy season. They often succeeded in spite of having these tremendous obstacles to overcome.

Maintenance workers, ticket takers, parking lot attendants, and anyone receiving a paycheck with the emblem of the San Francisco 49ers on it were instructed as to the requirements of their own job's Standard of Performance and expected to measure up.

In fact, to encourage positive thinking, pride, and self-esteem, I insisted that specific equipment carrying the emblem of the San Francisco 49ers be treated with respect. For example, players were told their practice helmets, which carried our emblem, should never be tossed around, sat on, or thrown in the bottom of their lockers: "Wear it, hold it, or put it on the shelf in your locker." The same applied to their game helmets, of course.

The San Francisco 49er emblem, and the helmet it was affixed to, signified that they were members of an organization with pride and high behavioral expectations. It was similar to saluting the American flag: Show it respect, because it represents who you are and what you value.

Respect for the emblem was important because it represented something very significant, namely, respect within the organization for one another. I would tolerate no caste systems, no assumption of superiority by any coaches, players, or other personnel. Regardless of the size of an employee's check or the requirements of his or her job, I made it clear that he or she was 100 percent a member of our team, whether he or she was a superstar or secretary, black or white, manager or maintenance man.

In keeping with this philosophy, I forbade the traditional hazing of rookies and walk-ons—making them the butt of humiliation or physical punishment. When they arrived, I informed them, "You are a San Francisco 49er. As long as you're here, you will be treated like one." And it was true. They were respected, full-fledged members of our organization from day one and were treated as such until they proved otherwise. Of course, when they "proved otherwise" they were not subjected to hazing; they were subjected to termination.

Scouts, usually considered outliers who stopped by occasionally with information and opinions on prospects, were treated right by us. They came to feel like real members of our organization, rather than pizza delivery boys who showed up when called with hot tips about players.

The Prime Directive Was Not Victory

From the start, my prime directive, the fundamental goal, was the full and total implementation throughout the organization of the actions and attitudes of the Standard of Performance I described earlier. This was radical in the sense that winning is the usual prime directive in professional football and most businesses.

Thus, in the beginning our players, coaches, and staff heard little talk from me about winning anything, and certainly not by some arbitrary date. In fact, during our second season one of the staff members went to Eddie DeBartolo and complained that I was adrift in minutiae and had no stated goal for the 49ers when it came to winning games, conference titles, or Super Bowl championships.

The staff member was wrong. I had very profound and organization-changing goals, but he didn't accept my philosophy and was fired when I heard about what he had done behind my back. His betrayal was unacceptable. However, he was correct that I had no grandiose plan or timetable for winning a championship, but rather a comprehensive standard and plan for installing a level of proficiency—competency—at which our production level would become higher in all areas, both on and off the field, than that of our opponents. Beyond that, I had faith that the score would take care of itself.

In pursuing this ideal, I focused our personnel on the details of my

Standard of Performance—trying to achieve *it*—rather than how we measured up against a given team (i.e., the score). "Let the opponent worry about that" was my thinking. I sought to channel the concentration of the 49ers toward improving performance on the field and throughout the organization with as little force as possible from outside influences such as the media, fans, friends, or the standings. This was a formidable task, but in large part I accomplished it.

Consequently, the score wasn't the crushing issue that overrode everything else; the record didn't mean as much as the season progressed, because we were immersed in building the inventory of skills, both attitudinal and physical, that would lead to improved execution. That was the key. (The losses hurt, and the wins felt good. But neither was the primary focus of my effort or attention. At least, in the beginning. Unfortunately, that changed for me down the line.)

I directed our focus less to the prize of victory than to the process of improving—obsessing, perhaps, about the quality of our execution and the content of our thinking; that is, our actions and attitude. I knew if I did that, winning would take care of itself, and when it didn't I would seek ways to raise our Standard of Performance. At least, that was my plan. It may not sound very grandiose, but it was very comprehensive and was the platform from which I launched the turnaround.

During this early period I began hiring personnel with four characteristics I value most highly: talent, character, functional intelligence (beyond basic intelligence, the ability to think on your feet, quickly and spontaneously), and an eagerness to adopt my way of doing things, my philosophy. These included assistant coaches I was very familiar with—managers—to install and nurture my organizational values and job criteria.

I sought intelligence in employees, not just for the obvious reason, but also because a dull-witted staff member who's aggressive creates anarchy; when you have one of those who thinks he's intelligent in your midst, look out. The bull-headed know-it-all is a destructive force on your team.

In that regard I sought individuals who had the ability to work with others. A fundamental element in this is not only the ability of a person to understand his own role and how it fits into the organization's goal, but a knowledge or understanding of other people's roles. Part of my job was to facilitate this mutual understanding and appreciation.

Individuals who didn't measure up in various ways were removed without fanfare (usually), and those who challenged my authority did so at risk.

The Top Priority Is Teaching

In a very real way, everything I did was teaching in some manner or other. I would take out a calendar and plan when I would talk about different subjects with individual players, with a squad, with the entire team, with position coaches, staff members, and others. I would discuss a topic from every angle, every approach, never repeating it the same way, such as when I spoke on the subject of communication and *interdependence*—trying to keep the idea fresh and not become rote.

I was insisting that all employees not only raise their level of "play" but dramatically lift the level of their thinking—how they perceived their relationship to the team and its members; how they approached the vagaries of competition; and how willing they were to sacrifice for the goals I identified.

Much of this relates to the respect and sensitivity we accorded one another and to an appreciation of the roles each member of our organization fulfilled. Each player had a connection to and was an extension of his teammates.

On the field (and elsewhere) the assistant coaches and I were conscientious about educating players so they appreciated that when Jerry Rice caught a touchdown pass he was not solely responsible, but an extension of others—including those who blocked the pass rushers, receivers who meticulously coordinated their routes to draw defenders away from him, and the quarterback who risked being knocked unconscious attempting to throw the perfect pass. Jerry was taught the same. Likewise, Joe Montana understood that he was not some independent operator, but an extension of the left tackle's block and the efforts of many others.

This concept applied beyond the team itself. Players had a connection to—and were an extension of—the coaching staff, trainers, team doctor, nutritionists, maintenance crew, and, yes, the people who answered the phones. Everybody was connected, each of us an extension of the others, each of us with *ownership* in our organization. I taught this just as you should teach it in your own organization.

Victory is produced by and belongs to all. Winning a Super Bowl (or becoming number one in the marketplace, or reaching a significant quarterly production quota, or landing a big account) results from your whole team not only doing their individual jobs but perceiving that those jobs contributed to overall success. The trophy doesn't belong just to a superstar quarterback or CEO, head coach or top salesperson. And this organizational perception that "success belongs to everyone" is taught by the leader.

Likewise, failure belongs to everyone. If you or a member of your team "drops the ball," everyone has ownership. This is an essential lesson I taught the San Francisco organization: The offensive team is not a country unto itself, nor is the defensive team or the special teams, staff, coaches, or anyone in the organization separate from the fate of the organization. We are united and fight as one; we win or lose as one.

Leaders sometimes wonder why they or their organization fail to achieve success, never seem to reach their potential. It's often because they don't understand or can't instill the concept of what a team is all about at its best: connection and extension. This is a fundamental ingredient of ongoing organizational achievement. (Of course, incompetence as a leader is also a common cause of organizational failure.)

Combat soldiers talk about whom they will die for. Who is it? It's those guys right next to them in the trench, not the fight song, the flag, or some general back at the Pentagon, but those guys who sacrifice and bleed right next to them. "I couldn't let my buddies down," is what all soldiers say. Somebody they had never seen before they joined the army or marines has become someone they would die for. That's the ultimate connection and extension.

I nurtured a variation of that extreme attitude in our entire organization, most especially the players: "You can't let your buddies down. Demand and expect sacrifice from yourself, and they'll do the same for you." That is the measure, in my opinion, of any great organization, including a team of football players—that willingness to sacrifice for the team, to go the extra mile, the extra five or fifty miles. And it starts with the leader and your leadership staff.

It has a transformative effect. Bonding within the organization takes place as one individual and then another steps up and raises his or her level of commitment, sacrifice, and performance. They demand and expect a lot of one another. That's extremely important because when you know that your peers—the others in the organization—demand and expect a lot out of you and you, in turn, out of them, that's when the sky's the limit.

It's why egotism can hurt group pride and unity so much. An individual who acts like a big shot, as if he or she is solely responsible for what the team has accomplished, has taken over ownership of the group's achievement. You may remember basketball's Michael Jordan being interviewed after a game. The Chicago Bull would tell the media, "Scotty Pippen did a great job on defense; Dennis [Rodman] got a couple of key rebounds, and our bench really picked up the slack in the third quarter to give us a little breather. It was a great effort by everybody." What Jordan didn't mention might be the fact that he had scored fifty-five points, grabbed fifteen rebounds, and had twelve assists. As he matured as an on-court leader, he made everyone part of the victory.

The leader's job is to facilitate a battlefield-like sense of camaraderie among his or her personnel, an environment for people to find a way to bond together, to care about one another and the work they do, to feel the connection and extension so necessary for great results. Ultimately, it's the strongest bond of all, even stronger than money.

Winners Act Like Winners (Before They're Winners)

The commitment to, and execution of, the specific actions and attitudes embodied in my Standard of Performance—some picky, some profound—may seem far removed from Super Bowl victories, but they were crucial to creating and cementing a 49er level of professionalism that I viewed as the foundation on which future success could be constructed. (That's what the assistant coach who complained about my lack of focus on winning didn't understand.)

Consequently, the 49er organization increasingly became known for our businesslike and very professional behavior even when we were losing more games than we were winning. There was no showboating allowed after touchdowns, no taunting of opponents, no demonstrations to attract attention to oneself, because one individual shouldn't take credit for what our whole team had done. There was a minimum of whining, complaining, and backstabbing. And phones were answered in a professional manner: "San Francisco 49ers headquarters. How may I assist you?" All calls had to be returned within twenty-four hours.

Eventually—within months, in fact—a high level of professionalism began to emerge within our entire organization. The 49ers' *self*-perception was improving; individuals began acting and thinking in a way that reflected pride and professionalism, even as we continued to lose games. People want to believe they're part of something special, an organization that's exceptional. And that's the environment I was creating in the early months and years at San Francisco.

I moved forward methodically with a deep belief that the many elements of my Standard of Performance would produce that kind of mindset, an organizational culture that would subsequently be the foundation for winning games.

The culture precedes positive results. It doesn't get tacked on as an afterthought on your way to the victory stand. Champions behave like champions before they're champions; they have a winning standard of performance before they are winners.

It all sounds pretty simple, doesn't it? But it's a rough road. At the end of my first year, giving it everything I had, working more hours than seemed possible and after installing many of the elements of my Standard of Performance, this is what we had to show for it: the same miserable won-lost record as the year before I took over: 2–14. A cynic might have said, "Well, Bill, your switchboard operators answer the phones great, but your team stinks."

Nevertheless, my teaching in all areas was being implemented as the base for the future of the San Francisco 49ers. While the performance results were not good if measured strictly by the won-lost record, the organizational structure and environment were set in place to produce success. We lost most of our games, but we did not "stink."

In a way, an organization is like an automobile assembly line; it must be first class or the cars that come off it will be second rate. The exceptional assembly line comes first, before the quality car. My Standard of Performance was establishing a better and better "assembly line." We were becoming a first-class organization in all areas.

Proof of that existed although it was not evident in our 2–14 record. I needed to look for evidence elsewhere. Very talented individuals had been hired; malcontents, underachievers, and the unmotivated were being rooted out and replaced; learning was well under way, with very productive attitudes and behaviors becoming the norm; and statistical evidence—the internal metrics—showed improvement, including going from virtually the worst-ranked offensive team to one of the best: number one in passing offense and sixth in total offense. Additionally, we had lost five games during my first season by a touchdown or less—close, competitive games. We lost an additional seven games by two touchdowns or less. Both were improvements over the previous season. Before you can win the fight, you've got to be *in* the fight.

Even though my initial year as head coach produced the identical won-lost record, the resurrection of the San Francisco 49ers was under way; the organization's behavioral "infrastructure" was essentially built.

Achieving success takes patience, time, and fortitude. To demand the assimilation of my Standard of Performance throughout the organization, including the complex offensive plays and the specifics of player performance, when the roof is caving in—we lost thirteen of our first fourteen games—would have been challenging, even impossible, for many.

In the beginning, Eddie DeBartolo, the owner, had the patience and gave me the time to persevere. Tough days lay ahead, including that trip to Miami during my second season that was almost fatal, but our ship had found its mooring. We were no longer adrift and being tossed around with abandon by the competition and ourselves.

And in the turbulent and occasionally troubled times ahead it was indeed my Standard of Performance that kept us in contention or at the top for almost twenty years and produced five Super Bowl championships. This consistency of excellence and preeminence is difficult to achieve in professional sports—and equally hard in business.

Seek to Be Near the Summit

Within our organization the Standard of Performance served as a compass that pointed to true north. It embraced the individual requirements and expectations—benchmarks—required of our personnel in all areas *regardless* of whether things were going well or badly. That's the toughest thing—constancy amid chaos or presumed perfection.

If things are going well, points being scored and games won, your organization may be elated and lose focus; if things are going poorly, as they were when I arrived at San Francisco, people are likely to be despondent and start looking for the exit. Incredibly, both can exist at the same time, as you'll see later in a game we played against Kansas City. And, of course, between the ups and downs, the good times and bad, there are ongoing challenges to keep everyone firing on all cylinders at all times. Not to get too clever, but "consistent effort is a consistent challenge."

There's an ebb and flow, an up and down, in every significant endeavor at every level. I cut through that ebb and flow with the Standard of Performance. It was our point of reference, what we always returned to when things wobbled—deeply entrenched, ongoing, and stabilizing regardless of the final score. My high standards for actions and attitudes within our organization never wavered—regardless of whether we were winning or losing.

I envisioned it as enabling us to establish a near-permanent "base camp" near the summit, consistently close to the top, within striking distance, never falling to the bottom of the mountain and having to start all over again. Initially, it meant I had to drastically change the environment, raise the level of talent, and teach everyone what they needed to know to get to where I wanted us to go.

It also meant that as the years accrued, personnel had to be changed so that we remained near the summit. Players past their peak or near the end of their usefulness had to be taken out of the organization. And, yes, this is as cruel and hard to do as it sounds. It is perhaps the hardest task I faced, and I tried to execute it in a humane, direct, and honest manner. But it's impossible not to hurt an individual's deep self-respect when it's being done—when I had to look a great performer in the eye and say, "It's time for you to leave." There is perhaps no way you can do it without causing deep pain. But, the organization, our team, came first.

Losing and winning was only part of it; there was always another contest. If I didn't like the score, I would seek to step up the level of our Standard of Performance so that even in losing it was retained, but then elevated. It always went back to the requirements for actions and attitudes that I had formulated in my mind during the years before I took over as head coach of the San Francisco 49ers and then installed starting on my first day.

In many ways, it comes down to details. The intense focus on those pertinent details cements the foundation that establishes excellence in performance. The simplest correct execution of procedures represents the commitment of players and staff to the organization and the organization to them. Specifics such as "shirttails in," understanding and respecting the jobs of others in the organization, running exactly ten yards and not ten yards fifteen inches, exhibiting a positive attitude, answering the phones professionally, seeing the team as an extension of yourself—all contribute in varying degrees to a devotion to high standards visible to everyone. The self-image of the 49ers as a first-class professional outfit was nurtured and carefully developed in these incremental ways. That's what I focused on, knowing that if I did so, winning would take care of itself.

Establishing Your Standard of Performance

In quantifying and implementing your own version of the Standard of Performance, the following guidelines are a good reference point:

1. **Start with a comprehensive recognition of, reverence for, and identification of the *specific actions and attitudes* relevant to your team's performance and production.**
2. **Be clarion clear in communicating your expectation of high effort and execution of your Standard of Performance.** Like water, many decent individuals will seek lower ground if left to their own inclinations. In most cases you are

the one who inspires and demands they go upward rather than settle for the comfort of doing what comes easily. Push them beyond their comfort zone; expect them to give extra effort.

3. **Let all know that you expect them to possess the highest level of expertise in their area of responsibility.**

4. **Beyond standards and methodology, teach your beliefs, values, and philosophy.** An organization is not an inanimate object. It is a living organism that you must nurture, guide, and strengthen.

5. **Teach "connection and extension."** An organization filled with individuals who are "independent contractors" unattached to one another is a team with little interior cohesion and strength.

6. **Make the expectations and metrics of competence that you demand in action and *attitudes* from personnel the new reality of your organization.** You must provide the model for that new standard in your own actions and attitude.

How I Avoid Becoming a Victim of Myself

I have a terrible time closing out a set in tennis. Why? Because I tell myself to try harder and harder, to hit the ball better and better. I become a victim of myself and go into a kind of stupor because I'm trying so hard without really knowing what the heck I'm trying to do.

The same thing can happen to you professionally. Individuals or organizations can get almost mesmerized by pressure and stress and be unable to function as cleanly as they are capable of doing. It happens everywhere all the time. Have you noticed, however, that great players and great companies don't suddenly start hunching up, grimacing, and trying to "hit the ball harder" at a critical point? Rather, they're in a mode, a zone in which they're performing and depending on their "game," which they've mastered over many months and years of intelligently directed hard work.

There's only so much thinking you can isolate and focus on during that kind of extreme competitive pressure. It has to be tactical more than a conscious effort to really "try harder." You just want to function very well, up to your potential, effortlessly—do what you *already* know how to do at the level of excellence you've acquired—whether in making a presentation or coaching a game or anything else. That's why I'm no good in tennis at crunch time.

In football, I was a master at crunch time because I had put in years of smart hard work in mastering my craft and creating a comprehensive Standard of Performance for my organization. In tennis, I haven't done that, but it doesn't matter much because I'm playing just for fun. The business of football, however, was not something I did just for fun. It was deadly serious.

The key to performing under pressure at the highest possible level, regardless of circumstance, is preparation in the context of your Standard of Performance and a thorough assimilation by your organization of the actions and attitudes contained within your philosophy of leadership. With that comes the knowledge that you—and they—can step into that high-pressure arena and go about your work while the score works itself out. Rather than feel that somehow I had to get a supreme effort from our personnel—"try harder and harder"—I trusted that it was going to happen because we had prepared thoroughly.

Some leaders drive their team past being able to perform with poise and presence and into a state of anxiety where they're not thinking as clearly as they should. They pump them up so much for the "big game" that they can't perform well; it's like a balloon that bursts when you blow too much air into it.

By focusing strictly on my Standard of Performance, the 49ers were able to play the bigger games very well because it was basically business as usual—no "try harder" mentality was used. In fact, I believed it would be counterproductive.

I might do even less strategizing for a Super Bowl game, because in the midst of the extreme pressure I placed a premium on fundamentals, the skills and the execution ability the team already possessed as a result of our concentration and hard work going all the way back to day one of training camp and the previous training camp and the one before that.

Consequently, the San Francisco 49ers could function under tremendous stress and the forces that work on individuals in competitive situations. They were able to function under all the media hype and the absolute

intensity of the circumstances we were in. In that kind of environment—
your version of a big game—you must reach back and rely on your ability
to do things at a high level. There isn't much time to meditate or think
things through. The pressure of the situation can just wipe that all out,
and you're left with the raw bones.

When you get to Wimbledon you're not thinking, "Now I'm gonna
play well." You're operating on nerves, depending almost completely on
your game, how good it is. For us it meant I had to be sure our Standard of
Performance was so good that our opponents were the ones who would be
distracted by the intensity or importance of the game or what they might
have to do to win.

So while the opponents had to elevate their game, we did too, but it
was a very natural culmination of all our previous work. It's similar to a
wave that gathers force for many miles out at sea and eventually crashes
down with tremendous power on the beach.

Over the months—and years—the San Francisco 49ers acquired the
skill and proficiency to play right through extreme pressure and prevail.
In golf and tennis I am unable to do that. But in my professional world—
football—I became a master at it.

The Organization Man

John McVay, Vice President for Football Administration

I'd been in football a long time when Bill Walsh (and owner Eddie DeBartolo) hired me during his first few weeks at San Francisco. My résumé included being an assistant coach at Michigan State University, head coach at Dayton University, and assistant and then head coach of the New York Giants in the NFL and working in the old World Football League doing every job imaginable with the Memphis Southmen. Bill figured I brought something to him because of all that experience.

Technically, I was his vice president/director of football operations, or as I told people, "I'm in charge of everything that nobody else wants to do." Bill and I got along pretty good.

Over the next ten years, I was heavily involved with contract negotiations, player personnel, scouts, equipment—everything except his coaching. I had a front-row seat for how Bill, in conjunction with Eddie, made something—a dynasty—out of nothing.

What I saw when I arrived at San Francisco to work with him was organization and management that I had never seen done at the level Bill Walsh did it. It was comprehensive, meticulously detailed, and practical. At least, after awhile that's what I saw. Until Bill got it up and running the way he wanted it, things were rough. He had his work cut out for him.

Bill was a great observer and student who had the good fortune to work not only with the Oakland Raiders and San Diego Chargers but with one of the NFL's great masterminds, Paul Brown at Cincinnati. Brown was ahead of the rest of the league when it came to organization of time and management of people. I believe Bill liked what he saw at Cincinnati and then extended it, refined it in his own way, so that he developed an advanced organizational philosophy in his mind.

He liked tight management principles and wanted things *clear* and easily understood. This was important because Bill's overall system was complex. For it to work, people had to understand it. Consequently, he was explicit in his instructions: "Here's what we're going to do and here's how we're going to do it." Bill was very demanding in that respect, not just of players but of everyone in the organization.

He had written a series of lectures for each department detailing what he expected in all ways—appearance, attitude, performance, and more. He had it written out in detail for scouts, assistant coaches, equipment men, groundskeepers, and trainers. Even secretaries got specific and lengthy instructions from Bill himself. Did I mention the players? That's when he really got going.

Here's how comprehensive *and* detailed, big picture/little picture, he could be: I came to work my first day not wearing a tie. Bill liked to distinguish between coaches (no ties) and administration (ties). I was in administration, but I told him, "Bill, all of my ties have New York Giants helmets on them." He smiled and said, "John, I guess you're buying a new tie today." The small detail of wearing a tie was connected to his big concept of being a first-class operation, not just in point production, but in appearance and behavior, which he believed preceded scoring touchdowns; and he spelled it out word by word. I bought a new tie.

Meetings were held, and he would take an hour or two with every employee so they knew *exactly* what he expected of them, what he wanted them to do and how he wanted them to do it. He made it very clear. There was no confusion in their minds as to what he expected. And because he had such a marvelous background and such a keen eye for running things, he expected a lot. That included respect for one another within the organization—no cliques or hierarchy.

After he established his "organization"—got people in place and on the same page—he allowed department heads to function and intervened only if he became dissatisfied with something. Bill had set up an outstanding support mechanism of talented people, and he really had nothing to worry about except football. Of course, that was plenty to worry about, especially when he was taking over a 2–14 team.

Having said that, I will also say this: Bill Walsh was the king. And *we* knew it. He was the one in complete control. And *he* knew it. But the interesting thing about it was that he didn't act like a king, no bowing and scraping required. Bill wanted to be called Bill; everyone was on a first-name basis, but within that informality he simply did not allow for casual execution of your job. There was intensity and urgency, a focus all the time, a tight ship. He was friendly, but he held himself in a certain manner so that you knew he was in charge.

And why not? He took over a lousy situation. Eddie DeBartolo, the owner, needed somebody to come and grab that puppy by the throat and say, "Shape up or you're out of here!" Bill did it without always stomping and screaming. He was demanding and tough, but people loved him even though he was insistent, a real stickler not only about playing football but about raising the image of the franchise from within.

That's where he started—by raising the self-image of the San Francisco 49ers organization. In football that's tough to do when you're not winning games. My tie was a good example. What the heck did it have to do with a Super Bowl? Bill saw the connection. It was one of the tiny things—thousands of them—that he put in place that were part of eventually winning.

Communication within the organization was extremely important to Bill, especially between coaches and players. Even though our headquarters at 711 Nevada Street in Redwood City, California, weren't so good, he saw the cramped offices where we were almost sitting on top of each other as an asset.

When somebody was talking on the phone or having a conversation, everybody could hear what was going on. In a strange way, it meant that everybody on the staff was in the loop. In fact, eight years later when the DeBartolos built an ultramodern and spacious facility, Bill was very worried that it would not only create a "country club" mentality but hurt our communication process. We couldn't hear one another's phone calls anymore!

Bill Walsh was not afraid of talent. He hired assistant coaches who were extremely good, and he did it with the expectation that they would move on—up to head coaching positions. And in fact, about fifteen of them did. He didn't feel that you sold your soul to the company store. While you were a 49er, you were expected to give it your all, but Bill was very enlightened in the way he supported the lives and careers of employees beyond just what they could do for his team.

One thing that truly amazed me was his eye for talent when it came to football players. It was a gift that is hard to explain or overstate. He could see what others couldn't spot. Joe Montana, Jerry Rice, Steve Young, and more are among superstar Hall of Fame NFL players who didn't have a line of people knocking on their doors when Bill came calling. He was uncanny in that way.

Here's a good example. Early in Bill's coaching at San Francisco, he was desperate for good players and would hold tryouts for anybody and everybody. We had truck drivers coming in with high-top work shoes; big bruisers from local bars tried out. We were so lean on talent that Bill gave everybody a look.

One day it was ninety degrees and we had over a hundred prospects on the field going through the workout, trying to make the team, and I was standing up on the fire escape platform with Bill looking over this herd of guys. He said to me, "John, who's that blond kid down there?" At first I couldn't even tell who he was talking about. He pointed again: "Him, that kid over there with blond hair." I checked my chart. "Bill Ring," I replied. "Sign him," Bill said. That was the end of the discussion.

Bill Ring gave us six productive years and helped us win Super Bowl XVI and Super Bowl XIX, even though others thought he wasn't NFL material. Bill picked him out of a large pack of players with hardly a glance. He was simply unbelievable in the way he could spot potential in a person and then develop it.

He was extremely precise in how he ran not only the nonfootball end of things but the on-field execution. I doubt any coach in the NFL was bringing the precision to it that Bill did—drawing up plays almost to the inch and then teaching the players to perform with that same exactness. And that Standard of Performance permeated the whole organization in people's attitude and how they—we—did our jobs.

Bill Walsh was ahead of the times in many ways, but there was one thing he didn't like: He hated to fire someone. At times, he had to make brutal personnel decisions, and I think it hurt him inside knowing his action would change another person's life, and not necessarily for the better. Consequently, when it came to firing people, he was quick to assign that task to someone by the name of John McVay.

I saw him work himself so hard over those ten years, and the toll was increasingly terrible. It didn't have to be. Bill just had so much trouble letting up, getting out from under the increasingly crushing pressure of expectations that got sky-high as the decade rolled on. Burnout is what they call it, I guess; but who can argue with success?

PART II

Success Is Not Spelled G-E-N-I-U-S: Innovation, Planning, and Common Sense

Opportunity Is in the Eye of the Beholder

Creating gold from dross is alchemy; making lemonade when you're given lemons is leadership; making lemonade when you don't have any lemons is great leadership.

Here's a little example of it: Post-it notes are a multimillion-dollar product that began as an accident when a scientist working in the laboratory unintentionally created a glue that didn't stick very well. Obviously, nobody was looking for a glue that didn't stick, but then a creative leader saw a way to turn it into lemonade—Post-it Notes.

I witnessed a football version of Post-it Notes many years ago when I was an assistant coach with the Cincinnati Bengals. See if it applies to your own resourcefulness in evaluating situations and figuring out what to do with "glue that doesn't stick."

Early in the second half of our game with the Oakland Raiders, Bengals tight end Bob Trumpy (later a well-known announcer) came out of the huddle and lined up on the wrong end of the line of scrimmage—the left instead of the right side, as the play called for.

Trumpy recognized his mistake almost immediately and tried to correct it by sliding over to the right side before the ball snap. The Raiders were utilizing a complex pass defense at the time, so when they saw Bob shifting from one end of the line of scrimmage to the other—legal, but not done—all hell broke loose.

Oakland defensive backs began frantically flapping their arms and screaming, running around and creating havoc as they tried to react to the bizarre movement of Cincinnati's wandering tight end. Three of them actually collided in the middle of the field. The whole scene was kind of funny, although nobody was laughing on either bench. We lost yardage on the play, and when Bob trotted to the sidelines with a sheepish look on his face, he muttered to head coach Paul Brown, "Sorry, Coach. It won't happen again." He was wrong.

When we got back to Cincinnati and the assistant coaches looked at the Oakland game film, Bill Johnson, the offensive line coordinator, ran Trumpy's play over and over for us on the projector. At first the room was filled with laughter as we saw the mayhem Trumpy's mistake had precipitated. One man, however, wasn't laughing—Bill Johnson. He was thinking.

Finally, he stopped rerunning the play, turned to us, and asked, "Fellas, what would happen if we put Trumpy in motion intentionally and worked plays off it?"

There was silence in the room; everyone sitting in the darkness recognized the interesting possibilities this might offer. In fact, I was awake most of that night thinking up ideas that would let us capitalize on Bill Johnson's revelation, his crazy idea of how to turn a lemon into lemonade, an accident into an asset.

Putting the tight end in motion caught on quickly around the NFL because it created new problems for the defense. Soon every team in the league had added it to their playbook. And it all started with a botched play.

What's your own version of Trumpy's lemon and Johnson's lemonade? Is it right there in front of you, unseen because your thinking is rigid and resistant to originality and change? How effective are you at turning nothing into something, something into something that changes everything?

The West Coast Offense: From Checkers to Chess

Here's an example I'm proud of from my own coaching career. It profoundly—but unintentionally—changed the way NFL football is played. You may find in its genesis inspiration for extending your own receptiveness to innovation, for seeing what others don't see.

The West Coast Offense, considered by many to be one of the most dramatic changes in football during the last fifty years, was nothing more than my attempt to make the most out of what I had to work with as quarterback coach for the Cincinnati Bengals. And what I had wasn't much—a recent expansion franchise with perhaps the least overall talent of any team in the AFL (soon to merge with the NFL).

Among other things, the Bengals absolutely could not move the ball on the ground, because other teams were just too strong for us. That left the pass as our only option. Unfortunately, our quarterback, Virgil Carter, wasn't much of a passer in the traditional sense of having a strong arm capable of throwing deep with accuracy. In fact, somebody told him, "Virgil, if you want to throw the football more than twenty yards you better fill it with helium." (After he was released by Chicago, we acquired Carter on short notice to replace Greg Cook, a young quarterback with tremendous potential and a great arm. I have seen very few quarterbacks with his talent. Sadly, Greg tore his rotator cuff during his first season with the Bengals and never fully recovered.)

In studying films of Virgil and watching him in practice, I determined that while he didn't have much of an arm, he was composed under pressure and could read defenses and was nimble physically and quick mentally. Carter was very intelligent—a Scholastic All-American while at Brigham Young University. Additionally, he was able to throw short passes pretty well. But dependable long strikes? No, that wasn't him.

Virgil's skills weren't considered premium assets for an NFL starting quarterback, but that's all there was. Consequently, I began creating plays that tried to make the most of Virgil's "limited" abilities—first one play, then another and another.

What I came up with called for Carter to throw lots of short, quick-release, timed passes to any one of multiple receivers running exact routes, usually within twelve yards of the line of scrimmage. No helium was required, because Virgil seldom had to throw the football more than fifteen yards.

In designing appropriate plays I was constantly choosing and mixing receivers from a choice of running backs, wide receivers, and tight ends.

While each individual receiver's running route was not complicated—simple, by position—*collectively* it was complex and made almost dizzying to the defense by the fact that over the years I eventually began "hiding" the same play cosmetically by altering our formation at the line of scrimmage.

Thus, receivers for the Bengals (and later the Chargers, Stanford University, and the 49ers) could line up in different spots before the snap but run a route to the same location and be ready for the quarterback's pass, whether it came from Virgil Carter or Joe Montana. When you do this for scores of plays—and nobody in the NFL was doing it, in part because of the difficulty in creating, teaching, and executing the complexities of the system—you have an almost exponential multiplier of factors and "foolers" the defense has to figure out instantaneously; often they would think they were seeing something brand new while the quarterback was, in a sense, seeing something "old": his receivers in the same places seconds after the ball snap, even though the basic formation and routes run were quite different. (Conversely, I would also have receivers run routes to *different* locations off the same basic formation at the line of scrimmage.)

To make it all work, I "stretched" the field horizontally to create more room—used all available space from sideline to sideline—to avoid bunching our receivers and their defenders just beyond the line of scrimmage. (The width of a football field is much greater than most fans appreciate—53.3 yards. I used all of that width, slightly less than half the length of an NFL field, in designing plays, thus turning the approximately 15 yards of depth—Virgil's most effective range—and 53.3 yards of width into a wide-open war zone being hit not by long bombs but short ones. At least, that was the plan.)

Over the years, I created an array of pass options that the defense had to figure out, usually in less than 3.5 seconds. Often it was over—the lightning-quick short pass completed—before they knew what hit them.

Because the passes were often just beyond the line of scrimmage, slower linebackers and safeties were forced into coverage against quicker running backs whom I "converted" into potential receivers. This was a key to maximizing yardage on our pass plays, because I counted on the backs and tight ends to run for yardage after they caught the ball.

In the middle of this seeming bedlam, the quarterback's job—and

Virgil was the first of them—was to immediately scan the field, locate an open receiver among up to five possibilities amid an attacking pack of rushers, and throw a precise pass. Not an easy task.

Of course, that's where we capitalized on Carter's "limited" skills: great composure, nimble feet, good ability to read defenses, ability to throw short passes with accuracy. The skills necessary to run my offense were not lesser skills than those of the traditional strong-armed quarterback; they were different skills—equally valuable, perhaps more so, and uncommon. No strong arm? No problem. Perhaps the greatest quarterback of all time, Joe Montana, carried a résumé that lacked mention of a powerful throwing arm.

Of course, my many short-pass plays and their cosmetic variations— "looks"—would open up running and downfield passing opportunities, which we exploited. Ideally, we would present an ongoing assortment of plays that kept the defense off balance and vulnerable.

That's how NFL offensive football was changed from checkers to chess. A defense good at checkers but not chess was at a major competitive disadvantage. The Cincinnati Bengals offense started playing advanced checkers with my offensive designs. By the time I got to San Francisco, I was teaching teams how to play advanced chess. The media called it the West Coast Offense.

While all of this was initially being developed—and once I began it was in development throughout my career—there was never a thought in my mind that it would alter football in any radical way. Rather, I was looking at a situation that had little going for it and trying to get something going. I was forced to be innovative to a degree I didn't foresee.

It worked well enough to give us a fighting chance. In fact, with Virgil at the helm of my unorthodox but evolving offense, the Bengals won the AFC Central division that year with an 8–6 record in spite of losing six of our first seven games while I was thinking up and installing my new plays. In retrospect, this may be one of the more amazing feats I've ever been part of. Although we lost in the play-offs to the eventual Super Bowl champions, the Baltimore Colts, 17–0, the effectiveness of my new offensive scheme was startling.

By then I had spotted an unsung but promising quarterback at Minnesota's Augustana College, Ken Anderson. We drafted him, and his wider range of skills allowed me to expand my offensive ideas much further. When Virgil was injured, he soon became our starting quarterback.

Ken was a quick learner and eventually became so adept that he is the NFL's all-time leader for a season's completion percentage—70.60 percent. Another of my quarterbacks is in third place—San Francisco's Steve Young with 70.28 percent.

Quickly, what I had put together in a growing package of plays—short and less risky passes to multiple receivers flooding the secondary—became our stock in trade. Eventually, variations of it were incorporated by every team in the NFL and many at the college level. It was born of necessity, bred of innovation and creativity applied to existing—and so-called limited—assets.

And here's an interesting but very irritating footnote: For my effort in coming up with a successful new way of doing things, I received the disparagement of many in the NFL, especially old-timers who dismissively called it the nickel-and-dime, dink-and-dunk, fancy-pants, or finesse offense—even the swish-and-sway. Their condescension stemmed from the fact that my approach didn't rely on the traditional brute force, grinding ground game, or spectacular "long bomb" pass of old-time NFL football. It wasn't physical enough for them.

Mine was a different approach to gaining yardage, controlling the ball (and clock), and scoring touchdowns. In a sense, the naysayers were seeking victory, but only if it came the old-fashioned way. They were locked into the past and unwittingly locking themselves out of the future. Leaders do this to themselves and their organizations all the time.

My new system eventually became the media's vaunted West Coast Offense because it defined our teams in San Francisco and five of those teams won Super Bowl championships. However, a more accurate name would be the Cincinnati Offense, the Walsh Offense, or perhaps the Lemonade Offense—my response to being given lemons in the form of a team with no ground game and a quarterback without a strong arm.

Ironically, in San Francisco's first Super Bowl appearance we played Cincinnati. Their quarterback, Ken Anderson, threw for 300 yards with twenty-five completions, two touchdowns, and a 73.5 percent completion rate. Both the number of completions and percentage rate set Super Bowl records.

Anderson "outpassed" Joe Montana's 157 total passing yards, four-teen completions, and one touchdown, but Montana's nearly error-free performance earned him the title of Super Bowl MVP. Cincinnati got "nickel-and-dimed"—outscored 26–21—by an offensive scheme that was created, in part, while Anderson was my quarterback. They also were sty-mied by a tremendous San Francisco defensive effort, especially late in the second half of the game.

Later, in Super Bowl XXIII, we faced the Bengals again, this time coached by Sam Wyche, a former quarterback I had worked with during my Cincinnati days who later became one of my assistant coaches with the 49ers. And watching both of those San Francisco Super Bowl victo-ries against Cincinnati was the president of the Bengals, my former boss, Paul Brown, a man who had aggressively worked to prevent me from ever becoming a head coach in the NFL.

So that was the new direction I brought to NFL offensive playmaking—turning the concept of relying on the running game for yardage and ball control on its head, replacing it with a reliance on short passes to multiple receivers running exacting and intricate, precision-timed routes.

It was a change whose complexities were often misunderstood by observers. Howard Cosell once was critical of a call I made because he wasn't aware of just how complex and precise our receivers' routes were. He exclaimed with exasperation during the *Monday Night Football* broad-cast, "How could they [i.e., Bill Walsh] call for a twelve-yard pass play when they needed *fourteen* yards?"

Howard didn't understand the extraordinary precision required for successful execution of the play. We couldn't have the receiver running approximate routes and inexact distances each time; the route called for on that play was twelve yards *exactly*—not eleven, not thirteen, but twelve, and to an exact spot on the field. Additionally, what Howard and many others missed in the early days was that 60 percent of the yardage on our pass plays came through running after the catch. A twelve-yard pass was designed to produce an additional seven-yard gain on the ground.

One executive summed it up like this: "It's not real NFL football." He viewed it as gimmicky, smoke and mirrors, neither substantive nor long-lasting. He was wrong. The complexities of the offense I created as compared to his "real" way were as dissimilar as a Rolex to a sundial. (Few inventions are created out of nothing. What I was doing had its roots in the theories of others who had modernized the passing game, most notably the brilliant Sid Gillman.)

Those who were clinging to the past had apparently forgotten the past. Early in its evolution, football did not even allow the forward pass. In fact, it was brought into college football simply as a device to make the game safer. Eddie Cochems, head coach at Saint Louis University, immediately and enthusiastically embraced the new alternative to always running the ball. In 1906 his team went 11–0 and outscored opponents 407–11. He faced, I'm sure, traditionalists who looked down their noses at what he had incorporated as part of his search for victory. It's often the case that a "game changer" takes a while to change the way the game is played.

Lessons of the Bill Walsh Offense

My new short precision pass–oriented offense was ostensibly created out of nothing. In fact, it was created out of existing assets that only needed to be "seen" and then capitalized on in new ways. There are several elements in its evolution that are worth evaluating as they pertain to your own leadership.

1. **Success doesn't care which road you take to get to its doorstep.** The traditionalists—rigid and resistant in their thinking—who sneered at the new passing system I was creating were soon trying to figure out why it was beating them and how to copy it.

2. **Be bold. Remove fear of the unknown—that is, change—from your mind.** Respect the past without clinging to it: "That's the way we've always done it" is the mantra of a team setting itself up to lose to an organization that's *not* doing it that way any more. Paul Brown didn't flinch when I came to him with my revolutionary ideas—a completely new system of playing offensive football. By nature he was an innovator who wasn't afraid of change.

3. **Desperation should not drive innovation.** Here's a good

question to write on a Post-it Note and put on your desk: "What assets do we have right now that we're not taking advantage of?" Virgil Carter's "limited" skills, the 53.5 yards of width, and the availability of five potential receivers were all available assets even before desperation drove me to utilize them creatively. While waiting to get what you want—a "quarterback with a strong arm"—make the most of what you've got.

4. **Be obsessive in looking for the upside in the downside.** My evaluation of Virgil Carter's "weak" résumé, his so-called limited assets, led directly to utilizing them productively. Why? Instead of looking for reasons we couldn't make it work, I sought solutions that would make it succeed.

Welcome Skeptics to Your Team

There was a time, and perhaps still is in some organizations, when all hell would break loose if someone raised his or her hand during a staff meeting and asked, "What happens if this does not work? What then?" Others— usually the boss—would brand that person as a negative thinker, maybe even a loser. Today, of course, it's different. The marketplace is volatile, constantly changing with new products and competitors.

In your own challenges, are you receptive to new, even unorthodox ways of getting things done? Bill Johnson was when he perceived potential in a tight end who botched a play; so was the Post-it Notes guy who figured out how to sell glue that didn't stick; so was Cincinnati head coach Paul Brown when I started bringing him my new, unconventional, nontraditional ideas. He was a master at thinking both inside and outside the box.

Unfortunately, too often we find comfort in what worked before— even when it stops working. We get stuck there and resist the new, the unfamiliar, the unconventional.

If Virgil Carter had been a strong-armed, accurate quarterback, would I have had the inspiration to design the new offense? Had Greg Cook not been injured, would I have forged a short-pass system? Would Paul Brown have encouraged me to look for a new and even better way of doing things? It's impossible to know.

The fact that we had seemingly *no* options forced us to come up with new options—the West Coast Offense. But should desperation be the primary determinant for seeking new direction, innovative solutions?

Without any grand vision for changing NFL football, we changed it. It was made possible, in large part, because the brilliant leader of our team, Paul Brown, was a great facilitator. Paul Brown allowed me to be creative, encouraged and listened to my ideas (many of them counterintuitive), and put them into practice with the Cincinnati Bengals. Among his gifts, Paul Brown was a perceptive, astute, and shrewd listener who did not fear change.

Share the Glory

Here's a lesson for any leader interested in nourishing the spirit of the organization. Paul Brown, for all of his gifts, was not inclined to give credit for the new ideas I was bringing to his team. For a period of time, many on the outside assumed he was the one putting pencil to paper as architect of an emerging paradigm for offensive football in the NFL. He did not go out of his way to dissuade them; giving credit where credit was due was not something he liked to do, at least with me.

Brown was very protective of his public image as the one who made all the decisions—the boss. For example, he wanted it to look like he was calling the plays during a game, even though I was up in the booth making the decisions. For the sake of appearances, he set up a time-consuming and counterproductive process to accomplish this. I called the play down to an assistant coach on the sideline, who then relayed my decision to Brown. He would then pull aside a player and tell him what "he" had chosen, and the player would shuttle in the decision to our quarterback. Of course, the crowd thought Brown made the call himself. Obviously, this was an impediment to swift communication and hurt us from time to time. Brown was willing to pay that price to convey the impression that he was running the whole show.

When I became a head coach, the leader of my own organization, I tried to avoid his mistake and attempted to give ample credit to those working with me. Few things offer greater return on less investment than praise—offering credit to someone in your organization who has stepped up and done the job.

Write Your Own Script for Success: Flying by the Seat of Your Pants (Is No Way to Travel)

Here's a story to illustrate what can happen if you don't think things through, if you're a leader who doesn't have an appetite for looking perceptively into the future and then planning what to do when you get there.

The local fire department was called in to help rescue a cat stuck up in a tall tree. After a couple of hours, they got the cat down from the tree. During all the congratulations afterward, the fire truck drove off and ran over the cat. Despite their hard work, they had no plan for what to do after the cat was rescued.

Contingency planning is critical for a fire department, football team, or company and is a primary responsibility of leadership. You must continually be anticipating and preparing to deal with what management expert Peter Drucker characterized as "foul weather." He viewed it as the most important job of leadership. He may be right, but I would expand Drucker's category to include "fine weather"—what you'll do if the cat is rescued.

Having a well-thought-out plan ready to go in advance of a change in the weather is the key to success. I came to understand this when I realized that making decisions off the top of my head was a recipe for a bad decision—especially under pressure.

When I was the quarterback coach with the Cincinnati Bengals, this led me to start planning our first four offensive plays before the opening kickoff. In other words, I predetermined—wrote down—our first four plays. Head coach Paul Brown would ask, "What have you got for openers, Bill?" He wanted to know what I had come up with to get us going on our first possession, when nerves are on edge and clear thinking easily muddled in the middle of all the commotion.

I never really thought of taking it much beyond that until an event occurred in my final game with Cincinnati—an AFC play-off against the

Raiders in the Oakland Coliseum. The winner would advance to the AFC championship game with the Pittsburgh Steelers.

In the closing moments, we recovered a fumble on Oakland's forty-yard line. We were trailing by three points, 31–28; a field goal would send us into overtime. My job was to figure out how to get us within range of a field-goal attempt quickly. Unfortunately, the severe pressure and absolute pandemonium—thousands of Oakland's fans howling and throwing half-eaten hot dogs, half-empty cups of beer, crumpled-up game programs, and even clothes and shoes up at the booth where I was sitting—destroyed my thinking. Raiders fans in those days were rowdy.

I completely forgot the plays we had practiced that would have worked best under those circumstances, but equally important, I recognized (in retrospect) that I had no specific plan for what to do in that "foul-weather" circumstance. Thus, Oakland regained possession of the ball. Surprisingly, we still got one last chance to score with fifteen seconds to play.

But again, no plan. I was flying by the seat of my pants; we lost. "Never again," I vowed, "will that happen to me." That's when I got serious about scripting; never again would I walk into the future unprepared for foul weather.

Consequently the number of plays I planned out—scripted—increased substantially the following year when I was with the San Diego Chargers as Tommy Prothro's offensive coordinator. The next year, when I was head coach at Stanford University, the number increased again, and the impact was startling. In fact, during my second season, Stanford scored on our *first* possession eight times in eleven games. Typically during a season a team might score once or twice on the initial drive of a game.

This success wasn't an accident; I had written the script for our success. Informed preplanning—looking perceptively into the future and getting ready for it—gave the Stanford football team a distinct advantage. I took that advantage with me when I was hired by the 49ers.

At San Francisco our first twenty or twenty-five plays of the game would be scripted, along with a multitude of options, alternatives, and contingency plays depending on the situation and circumstance. Among other things, it plugged me into the future; I was visualizing the game ahead, "seeing" what would happen. I could close my eyes and literally see all twenty-two men running and responding to some specific play I had drawn up.

I was the first to employ scripting to this extent, and it gave us a stunning tactical offensive asset that no other teams were utilizing at that time. Scripting was a most effective leadership tool in fair and foul weather. In a very calculated way, I began calling the plays for the game before the game was played. It took years for other teams to fully implement the concepts I had been developing for a long time.

The motto of the Boy Scouts, "Be Prepared," became my modus operandi, and to be prepared I had to factor in every contingency: good weather, bad weather, and everything in between. I kept asking and answering this question: "What do I do if . . . ?"

It's the same for you, of course: "What do you do if . . . ?" Most leaders take this no deeper than the first level of inquiry. You must envision the future deeply and in detail—creatively—so that the unforeseeable becomes foreseeable. Then you write your script for the foreseeable.

I learned through years of coaching that far-reaching contingency planning gave me a tremendous advantage against the competition because I was no different from anyone else; it was almost impossible for me to make quick and correct decisions in the extreme emotional and mental upheaval that accompanied many situations during a game. I defy you to think as well—as clearly—under great stress as you do in normal circumstances. I don't care how smart or quick-witted you are, what your training or intellect is; under extreme stress you're not as good. Unless, that is, you've planned and thought through the steps you're going to take in all situations—your contingency plans.

With the 49ers I began asking my offensive coaches to give me their twenty-five scripted plays; then I'd revise and add my own to their ideas. We'd go over the new list with the team; they wanted those plays and would raid my office to get them. Randy Cross, a big offensive lineman and one of only a few to play on San Francisco's first three Super Bowl teams, would come in and say, "I want those plays, Bill, where are they?"

Randy and the others wanted them so they could start thinking about them. During a practice I'd tell them, "This is the first play of the game on Sunday." Right away the expectation level would pop up. Now they connected practice with the game. The scripted plays extended that.

The players and coaches could sleep a little better because I had alleviated some of the deep anxiety caused by uncertainty prior to the competition; they were somewhat relieved because they could anticipate what we'd do in the opening stages of the battle.

I took scripting very seriously; my preplanning was done in a clinical atmosphere on Thursday and Friday—sometimes Saturday, the day before a game. Planning even one day ahead was usually much better than trying to make a decision in the heat of the contest amid the clatter and chaos. In doing so, I reduced the possibility of panic-driven, ill-conceived decisions.

Developing the plays may have taken more energy from me than the game, but once the scripting was complete, I felt we could breathe easier; now all we had to do was perform. It made it possible for me to almost always get a good night's sleep before the opening kickoff—even a Super Bowl.

Scripting was a preprepared format, a *flexible* blueprint that I used to navigate through the turmoil, uncertainty, and stress of competition. "If this situation arises, we do this; if this happens, we do that." On and on. It was almost by the numbers; the minute those new situations came up, I'd go to the contingency play that I had worked up in advance and printed on the script on my clipboard.

If I'd done my work properly, little would arise that hadn't been anticipated; we'd seldom be caught off guard or have to come up with a plan in a panic. Of course, there's always something you can't anticipate, but you strive to greatly reduce the number of those unforeseeables. A good example of readiness for anything, one of many hundreds I could refer back to, occurred in the last moments of a game between San Francisco and my former team, the Cincinnati Bengals.

With two seconds remaining on the clock, trailing 26–20, the 49ers took possession of the ball on the Bengals' twenty-five-yard line. We had time to run one play. While this might suggest a last-ditch-effort mode, some version of a "Hail Mary pass," it was not. I had a contingency plan scripted for a situation exactly like this—time enough for one play, ball on the opponent's twenty-five- to thirty-yard line, needing a touchdown. (The scripted play was called "tandem left 76 all go." Three receivers lined up on the left side; a fourth, Jerry Rice, on the right. Joe Montana took the snap, dropped back five steps, looked left, pump faked, turned right, and threw to Rice, who was almost alone in the end zone.) Touchdown; point after; final score 27–26.

While I was ecstatic with the dramatic finish that produced victory, the manner in which we achieved it was almost routine because I had anticipated and prepared our team for that exact situation. Scripting did not lock me into a play or series of plays. Some observers didn't understand it: "You mean if you're on the two-yard line, you're still going to throw the long pass if it's next on the script?" Obviously, no. If Steve Young threw a completion that put us suddenly on the two-yard line, bang, I'd go to the play chosen earlier for that situation, which had factored in score, field position, conditions, time remaining, and more. It was not a robotic response system. Rarely did we go straight by the numbers, one through twenty-five. Usually it would be more like one through four; seven through ten; back to five and six; then perhaps a play from page three of my laminated sheets on the clipboard.

The contingency scripting provided a well-thought-out basis for situational decision making and action, but from start to finish our entire team, especially the assistant coaches, were intensely analyzing every single thing that happened on the field and looking for the right response, whether it was scripted or not. There was tremendous flexibility, creativity, and adaptability applied to what I had on the clipboard in front of me, just as there should be for you and your organization.

By analyzing, planning, and rehearsing in advance you can make a rational decision, the best choice for the situation at hand. And that still leaves room for those gut-instinct decisions you may want to make. This is true in the context of offensive strategy, a contract negotiation, a sales meeting, and a vast array of other business situations I can think of.

Michael Ovitz, a top talent agent in Hollywood for many years and later president of the Walt Disney Company, recognized the link between scripting and success: "Every detail is important. Where do you have a meeting? What is the surrounding environment? People who don't think about these things have a harder time in business. It's got to be the right place. It's got to be the right color. It's got to be the right choice. Everything has to be strategized. You have to know where you're going to come out before you go in. Otherwise you lose." *(New York Times, May 9, 1999.)* Scripting and strategizing are simply two different words for fair- and foul-weather leadership.

Instead of saying to myself, "Don't worry. I'll take care of it when it happens; I'll think of something even if it means drawing a play in the dirt with my finger," I had already carefully thought through the situation and come up with an answer.

I'd come to see that the intense pressure and confusion of the game could cloud my mind and I might start "swinging at shadows," so to speak—seeing things that weren't really there or were distorted in my mind by the chaos of the moment. Contingency planning cleared away the clouds and removed the shadows. It brought clarity to what could be a confusing situation.

Consequently, you must not only have a plan but also prepare for what happens if the plan works or fails or if an unexpected situation suddenly requires a completely different approach. What then? And what happens after that? And after that?

The military is known for doing this—war gaming, thinking through its response to all contingencies. The more thorough, the more extensive, the more rehearsed, the better you perform under the pressure of any situation that calls for an immediate decision.

Here is a very tiny sampling of the contingencies I would "war game": What if we fall behind by two or more touchdowns in the first quarter? What is the best defensive strategy with the wind at our back? What if the offense starts to sputter in the second half? What do we consider defensively when facing a strong wind? What if specific key players are injured? What if we are ahead by two touchdowns early in the fourth quarter? What is the best offensive strategy in a heavy rain? What precautions can be taken to ensure effective communications amid the noise of hostile spectators?

Those are a few of the general situational circumstances I wanted to have answers for before they arose in a game. I got more specific on the "script" I carried on a clipboard during the game, as evidenced by this sample of third-down situations from the open field (as opposed to the red zone) that would result in a package of plays tailored to the following down and distance situations: third down and short (i.e., two to four yards), third and medium (i.e., five to seven yards), third and long (i.e., eight to eleven yards). Within that third-down category, I also scripted what we would do against the nickel blitz and the nickel zone defense. Each had a specific scripted response on my clipboard.

I include those examples (knowing they're probably tedious to read) to illustrate how thorough I became in creating a response to every fore-seeable circumstance, how many levels of scrutiny I applied, how hard I worked at turning "unforeseeables" into "foreseeables."

Be prepared? I was prepared for almost anything, just as you should be. I never wanted to be in a situation where I would kick myself later and say, "Why didn't I *think* of that?" I didn't want a repeat of what had happened to me up in the booth near the end of the Bengals/Raiders play-off game.

What is the width and depth of the intellect you have applied to your own team's contingency planning? What is the extent of your own "script-ing"? What could happen tomorrow, next week, or next year that you haven't planned for, aren't ready to deal with, or have put in the category of "I'll worry about that when the time comes"? Planning for the future shouldn't be postponed until the future arrives.

When you're thorough in your preparation—"scripting" is a part of it—you can almost go on automatic pilot and reduce the chance of mak-ing emotional and ill-considered decisions. Scripting allowed me to take randomness and stress out of the decision-making process. The result is a very adaptable but intelligent plan for the future.

My planning was not limited to plays on the football field, of course, but also to the big picture. A leader must see the forest *and* the trees. In 1987, for example, the 49ers were very strong at the quarterback position. Future Hall-of-Famer Joe Montana's backup was the very capable Jeff Kemp. When Joe was injured and missed eight games during the season, I had to look at a foul-weather situation of a team minus Montana at some point in the future. At the conclusion of the season, we quickly moved to acquire Tampa Bay's Steve Young, a potentially great quarterback whose potential had not been realized. (This was done expeditiously because our owner, Eddie DeBartolo, was inclined to act fast when he deemed it nec-essary. When our decision was made, he simply picked up the phone and called Hugh Culverhouse, owner of the Tampa Bay Buccaneers. The deal was done in minutes.)

Young would be my "contingency plan" in the event that Joe faltered. This was a very controversial move that many, including Montana, were not very happy about. None of them, however, was charged with princi-pal responsibility for charting the future of the team. That was my job— planning for fair and foul weather.

Competition inevitably produces randomness that can leave you grasping at straws. I attempted to reduce the randomness of my responses. Hearing someone described as being able to "fly by the seat of his pants" always suggests to me a leader who hasn't prepared properly and whose pants may soon fall down.

When you're forced to go to some version of a "Hail Mary pass" on a recurring basis, you haven't done your job. Nevertheless, it's a macho attitude to believe, "I'm at my best when all hell breaks loose." But it's usually not true; you cannot think as clearly or perform as well when engulfed by stress, anxiety, fear, tension, or turmoil. You are not at your best. Believing you are creates a false sense of confidence that can lead to slipshod preparation. You think, "Don't worry, I'll be able to put it all together when it counts. I can just turn it on." When it counts is *before* all hell breaks loose.

Control What You Can Control: Let the Score Take Care of Itself

The final score of a football game is decided, on average, according to the following percentages: 20 percent is due to luck, such as a referee's bad call, a tricky bounce of the ball, an injury, or some other happenstance. I accepted the fact that I couldn't control that 20 percent of each game. However, the rest of it—80 percent—could be under my control with comprehensive planning and preparation.

What about the quantity and quality of talent on my team? Doesn't that override everything? Of course you need talent, but talent is not the only factor. And at the upper levels of competition, talent becomes much more evenly distributed. Thus, for working purposes my 80/20 ratio is quite good. Additionally, regardless of the level of talent in your organization, you have got to maximize the 80 percent when it matters most—on game day.

Those same numbers, in my opinion, applied not only to the San Francisco 49ers but to our competition, as well. I recognized that my job as a leader was to get more out of my 80 percent than the opposing coach and his staff could get out of their 80 percent. I believe a parallel phenomenon holds true in business. After all, in business, every day is game day.

Contingency planning is a major determinant of who gets closest to taking total control of their own 80 percent, the closest to maximizing their organization's assets. That explains why scripting eventually became the norm throughout the NFL, and college football as well. As you can see, it started modestly—Paul Brown asking me, "What have you got for openers, Bill?"—and gradually became a major component of my methodology.

There are many aspects of professional football that directly correspond to the subject of leadership in business. I believe scripting, adapted to your own environment in your own way, can have the same tremendous benefit for you that it did for me, and I offer this summary as a good point of reference:

1. Flying by the seat of your pants precedes crashing by the seat of your pants.

2. Planning for foul or fair weather, "scripting" as it applies to your organization, improves the odds of making a safe landing and is a key to success. When you prepare for everything, you're ready for anything.

3. Create a crisis-management team that is smart enough to anticipate and plan for crises. Being decisive isn't enough. A wrong call made in a decisive manner is still the wrong call. I *hadn't* planned for the "crisis" up in the booth against the Oakland Raiders, and we lost; I had planned for the "crisis" against Cincinnati when we got the ball with two seconds left on the clock and won. The former desperate situation was, indeed, desperate; the latter was *not*, because we were ready for it.

4. All personnel must recognize that your organization is adaptive and dynamic in facing unstable "weather." It is a state of mind. Situations and circumstances change so quickly in football or business that no one can afford to get locked into one way of doing things. You must take steps to prepare employees to be flexible when the situation and circumstances warrant it.

5. In the face of massive and often conflicting pressures, an organization must be resolute in its vision of the future and the *contingent* plans to get where it wants to go.

6. You bring on failure by reacting in an inappropriate manner to pressure or adversity. Your version of "scripting" helps ensure that you will offer the appropriate response in a professional manner, that you will act like a leader.

Protect Your Blind Side: The Leadership Two-Step: Move/Countermove

Things take longer to play out in business than in football. In the corporate world the wisdom of a personnel decision or a competitor's new initiative may take months or years to reveal itself. In the NFL time is compressed, and results are sometimes immediate. For example, within days of my hiring Fred Dean as a 49er defensive end, he wreaked havoc on Dallas and its quarterback as part of a 45–14 San Francisco victory. The quality of my decision—hiring Fred—was immediately evident. In fact, my hire was an important element in our success a few months later—a Super Bowl championship—during my third year as coach.

It rarely happens this fast and dramatically in business. Consequently, you may have to prompt yourself to continually and aggressively analyze not only your personnel but your organization's vulnerabilities: What's our blind side? What are the implications of the competition's recent initiative? What's our countermove to their move? Or is one even necessary?

Prompting myself was unnecessary because the hazards in football are usually evident and the consequences immediate. There is seldom subtlety on the field; results were produced fast and violently right in front me every Sunday. When one of our players was loaded onto a cart and lugged away—semiconscious from a concussion or in agony from cracked ribs or torn ligaments—it was a cue that perhaps something was amiss; maybe I hadn't seen something coming that I should have seen. Had I been blindsided?

Therefore, as you do in your profession, I worked hard to foresee the implications of what a competitor had done "last Sunday" for our team "next Sunday." My pass-based offense, for example, depended on a multitude of components operating with precision and timing in the midst of 250-pound defensive linemen seeking to disrupt our well-laid plans.

Our center had to be consistent in making a good snap; linemen had to block; receivers had to run exact routes and catch the ball in traffic. But most of all, the quarterback had to execute with precision. For this to occur, Joe Montana needed a precious few seconds of protection while he attempted to locate a receiver and throw the ball. And the protection he needed most of all was on his blind side (for a right-handed quarterback it was his left side). Montana was "blind" on his left side because he turned his back to it in stepping away from center after the snap to throw the ball; he virtually couldn't see what was coming from the left because of the mechanics of throwing right-handed. The quality of his production depended on the quality of his protection.

On his right side he could see and react to a defender bearing down on him—throw the football away, scramble, or at least cover up for the impending blow. The left side was another story. It's called the blind side for a reason.

Consequently, our blocker on the blind side became almost second in importance to the quarterback because he was Montana's de facto personal security guard, the lineman of last resort. If he blew it, Joe got nailed with all sorts of unpleasant consequences: lost yardage, an interception, a fumble, or, worst of all, bodily harm.

Traditionally, a blind-side pass rusher—the outside linebacker—would be defused, blocked, or delayed by a running back or tight end. However, this was made more challenging as linebackers became bigger and quicker. But "bigger and quicker" doesn't describe a man who arrived in the NFL in my third season: New York Giants outside linebacker Lawrence Taylor—"L.T."—a player who appeared to have more of what it took to put an end to my increasingly successful passing offense.

As an outside linebacker—the blind-side attacker—Taylor was one of those players who changed the game forever because of his ferocious aggressiveness coupled with phenomenal physical gifts, all part of an astoundingly well-honed physique: 6 feet 3 inches, 237 pounds—most of it angry muscle.

He was a paradox: a massive human wrecking ball who was lightning quick and seemingly unstoppable because he could virtually flick a backfield blocker out of his way to execute an unimpeded assault on an often unsuspecting and defenseless quarterback. In 1985 Taylor executed a blind-side tackle that mangled the bones in the right leg of Super Bowl quarterback Joe Theismann. His career was over before the gurney arrived to transport him off the field to the emergency room. Everyone who saw it happen on *Monday Night Football*—the leg bones visible through the skin, blood spurting—remembers the nausea they experienced. And plenty of quarterbacks and coaches saw it.

It was a manifestation of the violence that Taylor created and the fear he instilled in a quarterback's mind. He wasn't bashful about furthering his malevolent image as a mindless brute who sought to mug the quarterback. He publicly bragged about his attack on Philadelphia Eagles quarterback Ron Jaworski: "I hit Jaworski . . . with an over-the-head ax job. I thought his dick was going to drop in the dirt."

Among other things, Taylor was trying to instill fear in the minds of opposing quarterbacks even before kickoff—to get each one looking over his shoulder for Lawrence Taylor rather than for receivers. A quarterback who gets skittish or gun-shy is finished. It takes a lot to get into a great quarterback's mind, to really scare him. Most are not afraid to take a hit. But that changes completely when you get hit by a truck.

When Lawrence Taylor joined the New York Giants under head coach Bill Parcells, I perceived the threat to our organization's system very quickly. Taylor had the potential to shut down my pass-based offense. It was evident that its viability was directly linked to our ability to stop Lawrence Taylor from getting to Joe Montana's body or into his mind.

Hoping that one of our running backs or a tight end weighing fifty pounds less than the Giants' blind-side backer could stop him was unrealistic. Additionally, my system used the tight end and running backs as receivers. Tying them down to block would greatly diminish the potential of our pass-based offense.

A solution was imperative but not evident. The most likely candidate to take on the burden was our left tackle, Dan Audick, who was closest to the area Taylor would come stampeding through on his way to Montana. Unfortunately, Dan was no match for Taylor—he was shorter, not as strong or quick, and unlikely to do much damage. I decided to make a bold move—in reality, a countermove to L.T. and the damage he could inflict.

I decided to make our left guard, John Ayers, playing next to the *center*, the designated defensive player who would stop Lawrence Taylor. Immediately after the snap he would check to see if anyone was attacking over center and then step back and to his left in preparation for a serious collision.

John Ayers was bigger and stronger (6 feet 5 inches, 270 pounds) but not quicker than Taylor. Importantly, John seemed to have a low center of gravity, which made it very difficult to knock him off his feet or push him around. He was a formidable presence.

I put John under the tutelage of Bobb McKittrick, our extremely talented offensive line coach, who reconfigured our assignments in preparation for an NFC play-off game at Candlestick Park against the New York Giants and Lawrence Taylor. It would be a sumo wrestler (John Ayers) trying to stop the rampage of a Brahma bull (Lawrence Taylor).

And it worked.

At first, Lawrence didn't even know what had hit him. Boom! When he realized that he couldn't move John Ayers around at will, he even tried attacking from the other side to avoid our creatively utilized left guard. But now Joe Montana could see him coming and react accordingly. The blind-side threat was neutralized.

Regardless of context, competitive endeavors at the highest level are fluid and ever-changing and constantly present new challenges requiring novel solutions. The advent of a Lawrence Taylor in the NFL and its existential threat to my offensive philosophy is no different from the kind of challenges a company faces regularly from competitors. When a threat like this occurs, we cannot allow ourselves to hope for the best or wait to see how bad the damage might be. A leader must be perceptive and respond swiftly.

When Lawrence Taylor entered the NFL, not everyone understood how much his presence changed things. I did. In fact, because our system relied so heavily on the pass, more so than any other team in NFL, Taylor posed the greatest threat to the San Francisco 49ers.

I created a countermove within our organization that blocked the threat. At least momentarily. But all solutions are only temporary. They last until your competitor makes a meaningful countermove to your own countermove. At which time it's your turn again. They key is to quickly recognize the nature of the threat and then to creatively and expeditiously respond to it. Otherwise, the game will be over before it begins.

The Archaeology of Leadership: Seek Reward in the Ruins

"Roaring back!" would have been a perfect slogan for my third season as head coach of the 49ers: After a torturous and losing second season, the San Francisco 49ers responded in year three by winning the Super Bowl for the first time in their history.

Unfortunately, "Roaring Back!" was the official team motto, one I approved and liked, for the *second* season—a year in which we were outscored by almost one hundred points, suffered through that excruciating eight-game losing streak, lost key players to major injuries, and ended up in next-to-last place in the NFC West division with a 6–10 record.

One unhappy fan sent a special delivery letter to 49er headquarters suggesting that instead of "Roaring Back!" a more appropriate slogan for our second season would be "Don't Get Your Hopes Up!" Nevertheless, my hopes were up at the conclusion of our second year. Here's why and how it led to a Super Bowl championship thirteen months later.

Progress, or lack thereof, in sports and business can be measured in a variety of ways, some much more subtle than others. Often it takes a keen eye and a strong stomach to dig through the "ruins" of your results for meaningful facts. A season's won-lost record (or your market share, sales figures, stock price) may not—will not—tell you what you need to know to be fully informed about the strength of your organization. Thus, I looked for clues that might indicate whether we were moving in the right direction at the right speed and, if not, what we needed to do to address the problems. In this instance, I wanted to determine what our second season's 6–10 record really meant—good, bad, or otherwise.

I also knew from experience that it is often difficult to assess these interior, or buried, signs of progress or dysfunction, strength or weakness, because we become transfixed by the big prize—winning a championship, getting a promotion, achieving a yearly quota, and all the rest. When that goal is attained, a common mistake is to assume things are fine. Conversely, when you or the organization fall short of the goal, the letdown can be so severe you're blinded to substantive information indicating that success may be closer than you would imagine.

Either way—delight or despair amid the accompanying din of fans (or shareholders)—you prevent yourself from searching for the truth hidden within the numbers. I could easily have done that myself, because the second season became absolute hell at times. You'll recall that I decided to hand in my resignation on the flight back from Miami. Instead, I waited until the season ended to conduct a comprehensive evaluation that would give me an accurate perspective—a sort of "state of the union" report on my second year as head coach of the San Francisco 49ers.

I stuck my nose into the task of analyzing year-end statistics along with empirical evidence as it applied to my Standard of Performance. What I found, both encouraging and discouraging, set the stage for winning Super Bowl XVI thirteen months later.

Overall, we had won only six games during my second season, and even those wins had been overshadowed by our free fall during the eight-game losing streak. If those six victories had come at the end of the season, fans would have been eagerly anticipating the future. However, the wins had been split in two by the eight consecutive defeats. All that fans and many others saw was the long losing streak and the two losses that closed out our season.

What generally got overlooked was the fact that we had won more games—six—than in the previous two seasons combined (four). Furthermore, before disaster struck—eight straight losses—we had beaten New Orleans, St. Louis, and the New York Jets. Then Atlanta had taken us down, then the Rams, Cowboys, Rams (again), Tampa Bay, Detroit, Green Bay, and the painful loss to Miami.

But two particular things stood out about the eight losses: We had eventually broken out of the losing streak with our spirits intact, and five of our defeats during the bad stretch had been by five points or less. (Winning those close games would have given the 49ers one of the best records in NFL that year.)

The 49ers went on to win three of our final five games, which was promising because in that late-season "nothing-to-gain" circumstance it would have been easy for players to throttle down their efforts. In spite of our miserable situation, the team did not quit. This was an important fact to assess in evaluating the emerging prospects and character of the players individually and as a unit. They seemed to have something special inside. Perhaps it was heart; perhaps it was my Standard of Performance. In fact it was both.

In continuing my year-end review it became apparent that our offense had started to jell—tied for eleventh overall in the NFL for points scored; up from sixteenth the year before; up from twenty-eighth (dead last in the NFL) the year prior to my arrival—a positive trend line.

The statistics also showed that quarterback Steve DeBerg, although intelligent and able, had a tendency to throw interceptions at crucial moments. This was a fatal flaw on his résumé; controlling the ball—i.e., few interceptions overall and none at critical moments—was central to my offensive philosophy of controlling the ball with the pass.

Conversely, the numbers indicated that as Joe Montana was gradually worked in as our starting quarterback he was 60 percent less likely to be intercepted. (DeBerg was intercepted 5.3 percent of the time when he passed; Montana, 3.3 percent.) Additionally, Montana had established himself as our acknowledged on-field leader when he led the extraordinary comeback against New Orleans. I had identified my quarterback of the future. This was meaningful: One of the most valuable components of our future success was now in place.

Another fact that was overshadowed by our 6–10 season was the loss of Paul Hofer, one of our primary offensive threats because of his great ability to both run and catch the ball. Paul had been injured in an early-season 59–14 loss to the Dallas Cowboys and was out for the year.

I knew that he would return fully recovered for the upcoming third season and greatly complement our emerging offensive stars: Earl Cooper, a rookie running back/receiver, was second in the NFL with eighty-three catches; Dwight Clark was third with eighty-two receptions. (This explains, in part, why Joe Montana led *all* NFL quarterbacks with a .645 completion percentage.) You can understand why I was delighted by those important statistics found in the ruins of our "bad" second season.

The defense was a different story. It had gotten worse since I had taken over and was one of the most porous defensive units in the NFL—only two teams had given up more points during the season than the 49ers—but here again I took a long and hard look at all the evidence and information.

Early in the season we had lost one of the best athletes on our team, defensive end Dwaine Board, in a victory against the New York Jets—he was out for the year. But I knew he, like Hofer, would return in the third season and dramatically improve our defense.

Nevertheless, my search through the ruins showed that unless we added major weapons to the defensive secondary, we would never be contenders, regardless of how many points we scored. Thus, I needed to bring in talented players to dramatically improve the defensive situation. I found this talent largely in three very special individuals—one rookie and two experienced pros.

The primary advantage to a lousy season is that you get to draft early. That's one of the reasons a highly regarded player like USC's Ronnie Lott was available to us. Because of his great speed, power, and intelligence Lott would be able to transform our weakest position—left cornerback—into one of our strengths. He also inspired those around him with his incendiary competitiveness.

In a sense, he was an "old pro" in a rookie's body. (Additionally, we drafted Eric Wright and Carlton Williamson, tremendous defensive players who, along with Lott, brought a new spirit—almost collegiate—to the defensive side of our team.)

Another major addition, one that gave us a seasoned player who provided leadership, was Jack Reynolds; his nickname was "Hacksaw." You could say that Ronnie Lott *had* character and "Hacksaw" Reynolds *was* a character. Thirty-four years old when he joined us as a free agent from the Rams, Hacksaw was an All-Pro who had earned his nickname honestly.

In Jack's senior year at the University of Tennessee, the Vols clinched the Southeastern Conference title but then lost a chance to play in the Sugar Bowl by losing to Mississippi State 38–0. Jack was so furious about the loss that he went to Kmart and bought a hacksaw and twenty blades. He then proceeded to saw his '53 Chevy completely in half. It took a couple of days, but when he finished, Jack Reynolds had a new name. "Hacksaw" Reynolds had an insanely competitive spirit and work ethic. He became a tutor for our younger players, positioning them perfectly during games against a wide assortment of offensive alignments.

These two guys, one a top draft pick, the other a free-spirited free agent, brought quantifiable talent to weak areas of our defense as the third season of my head coaching got under way. (Six of our first seven draft picks were defensive players. You can see I was addressing what my search through the ruins had revealed.)

One other immeasurable addition early in the season turned out to be the final piece of the puzzle: Fred Dean, a terrorizing pass rush specialist, was acquired from San Diego during the fourth week of our third season because of a contract fight with Chargers owner Gene Klein. With Dean sacking quarterbacks and our greatly strengthened defensive secondary, San Francisco became a contender. (Dallas quarterback Danny White was sacked two times and "disrupted" seven times by Fred in his first game as a 49er—a 45–14 victory. Fred Dean was our sack leader for three consecutive seasons.)

And so, as I looked ahead to my third year as head coach—the year that really should have been called "Roaring Back!"—I felt the pieces were in place for a significant improvement in our 6–10 record. The Joe Montana–led offense seemed to be on the verge of breaking through to big-time performance—a maturing quarterback, top receivers, a strong line, and a returning running back, Paul Hofer, who was a reliable producer.

The defense, with the youth and extraordinary talent of Ronnie Lott (plus Carlton Williamson and Eric Wright) and the experienced leadership and ferocious competitiveness of Jack Reynolds (plus formidable 49er veterans such as Randy Cross, Lawrence Pillers, Jim Stuckey, and Dan Bunz), looked like it might be only a couple of years away from matching the level of our offense.

All of this could have been overlooked or misinterpreted had I been distracted by the enormity of the eight-game losing streak and 6–10 record, had I not been a good organizational archaeologist.

Every leader does year-end reviews and comes to conclusions of one sort or another. My observation is that two leaders—coaches—looking at the same information will not see the same thing. The one who's a more skilled analyst, who digs deeper and wider, will benefit more. It is an endeavor to which I allocated as much energy as my preparation for every game and opponent.

Following my review of that second season—and the steps I subsequently put in play—I believed the San Francisco 49ers might be contenders for a championship in two or three years. What nobody, including me, could have predicted was the rate at which the talent of our squad would come together in the environment created by my Standard of Performance.

As we headed to training camp, I had no way of knowing that in my third season as head coach of the San Francisco 49ers the pieces were in place and that we would win a Super Bowl several months later. It happened in large part because of the importance I placed on archaeology as applied to our football team. (Much was made of the great San Francisco offense. However, the 49er defense was spectacular and came "roaring back" from near worst in the NFL to second best.)

In planning for a successful future, the past can show you how to get there. Too often we avert our gaze when that past is unpleasant. We don't want to go there again, even though it contains the road map to a bright future. How good are you at looking through the evidence from the past—especially the recent past? There's a certain knack to it, but basically it requires a keen eye for analysis, a commonsense mind for parsing evidence that offers clues to why things went as they did—both good and bad. And, of course, it often requires a strong stomach, because what you're rummaging through may include not only achievements but the remains of a very painful professional fiasco.

The Problem Solver

Mike White, Assistant Coach, San Francisco 49ers

What Bill Walsh did is easy to describe: (1) He could identify problems that needed to be solved; and (2) He could solve them.

Pretty straightforward, right? But the magnitude and range of his problem-solving ability was pretty spectacular, especially when coupled with an amazing capacity to understand all aspects of a football organization—what people were supposed to do individually and as part of a team and how to integrate those two components so that the whole was more than the sum of its parts.

For example, he knew that organizations have leaders within, not just one leader, the CEO or head coach, but interior leaders who make possible *or* prevent what the guy in charge is trying to accomplish. In football they're called locker-room leaders, and ultimately they play a major role in creating the culture of the team—instilling either a positive or negative mindset. Every organization has them, influential people who've got your back—or are putting a knife in it.

Bill understood that at one end of the scale there were locker-room leaders who were positive and supportive and at the other end influential players who were very negative. Most important, he understood that all the guys in the middle could go one way or the other; they were up for grabs.

He began addressing the issue immediately when he arrived through simple math: addition and subtraction—retaining and adding talented personnel who were ready and willing to get on board with his program, "subtracting" (i.e., firing) those who were negative. But here was the tough part: Some of his most talented players were among the dissenters; on paper, at least, their talent held the key to our future.

Bill was smart enough, strong-willed enough, to get rid of talented people if they were contributors to a negative organizational culture—not team players. Those he allowed to remain he allowed to thrive—letting guys like Joe Montana and Ronnie Lott influence others in their own positive and individual ways without Bill telling them how they should do it.

He understood the power of the culture—the mindset of people in an organization—and recognized that changing the San Francisco 49er culture was paramount because it was so toxic. Here's how crazy and chaotic things were the year prior to his arrival.

One head coach (briefly), Pete McCulley, was from the East Coast, and when he came to San Francisco to take over the 49ers he *stayed* on East Coast time—didn't change his watch. When he told us to be at work at 7 A.M., he was talking about 7 A.M. on the East Coast! That's 4 A.M. in California. It was unbelievable. I started living in a motel near our offices so I didn't have to get up at 3 A.M. for the drive across San Francisco Bay to work. (McCulley got fired after we lost seven out of the first eight games—didn't even have to change his watch when he went back to the East Coast.)

During one game, our linebacker coach, Dan Radakovich, a talented guy who had worked with Chuck Noll's great Pittsburgh Steelers teams, got so upset with how San Francisco was playing that he went up into the stands and sat with his wife. He couldn't stomach being on the sidelines with us for the rest of the game.

Our management didn't trust anybody, locked everything up. To get to your office you needed four sets of keys—a key to get into the building, a key to go down the hall, a key to get to your office, a key to get into the bathroom. It was crazy because there was nothing to steal—the headquarters were barren.

We were a classic example of a football franchise going nowhere—no rudder, no captain, no nothing, dysfunctional top to bottom. Enter Bill Walsh, the problem solver.

Now, Bill and I had been buddies since we worked together as defensive assistants many years earlier under Marv Levy at Cal (University of

California–Berkeley). Bill really had no experience at that time, and so to impress Levy he walked in and handed him his master's thesis on defensive football that he had written at San Jose State. He was very proud of it. Marv just tossed it over on a shelf, didn't even look at it, and told Bill to go out and start recruiting with this guy White—me. That's how we got to know each other.

What I noticed first about Bill was not what he knew about football, but how hard he was willing to work. We put everything we had into selling Cal, which was a tough sale in those days because the students were revolting against everything and the campus looked like a war zone at times. Those were the days of the free speech movement, sex, drugs, and riots on campus.

Can you imagine trying to sell a parent on letting their talented kid come to Cal to play football when that's what they saw in the papers? It was a tough sell, but Bill and I had some success in spite of the university's public image that we had to overcome.

Gradually I saw his football mind appear, because he was always drawing on napkins—plays, diagrams, routes. It just came out of him naturally, spontaneously, even during meetings. When Marv was standing at the chalkboard diagramming some X's and O's, Bill would get up and say, "Have you thought about doing it this way?" And he'd start drawing out some complicated play he'd thought up.

Of course, this really rankled Levy, in part because Bill was supposed to be working the defensive side of things. It got to be funny because Marv was right-handed and Bill was left-handed. I remember watching them up at the blackboard together—Bill writing and Marv erasing. As fast as Bill could write something with his left hand Marv would follow next to him erasing it with his right hand. Levy wanted no help from Bill on plays. Marv Levy was not the only guy—just the first guy—along the way who failed to see the brilliance in what Bill was coming up with. Throughout his career, Bill Walsh was constantly underestimated.

Accordingly, when Bill arrived at San Francisco 49er headquarters, I didn't see a messiah walk through the door; I didn't see a golden touch. We were so deep in the hole, trying desperately to survive, that you could hardly look up. However, I soon began to understand his instincts and his approach.

What was so striking, especially in retrospect, was how he imagined, planned, and prepared everything. *Everything.* He had given every aspect of everything so much deep thought and careful planning. He had most of the answers, and what he didn't know he quickly figured out.

This was apparent, for example, with assistant coaches like me. Talent wasn't enough. Knowing what you needed to know was only part of his job description. Bill prized communication and understood that all the knowledge in the world meant little if you couldn't communicate effectively. So, and this may be hard to believe, he had his coaches *practice* our coaching on one another. He knew you might be able to bullshit a player by blowing your whistle loudly, but you couldn't bullshit another coach.

He would ask me to get up and "teach" my offensive techniques to a defensive coach, who would play the part of a student—a player. Bill would critique us, teach *us* how to communicate better and better so that the players would be more fully informed. No other coach in the NFL was coaching his coaches like this. And it was serious business with him.

By his sheer will, he got us analyzing what we did and how to express what we wanted to convey. You couldn't fake it with him. There was no going through the motions of blow the whistle, run, tackle, now do it again. It had to be very well thought out, totally defined in our minds. To that end, he encouraged us to go out and give speeches to local groups like Rotary or Kiwanis, knowing it would make us think even harder about what we were saying and how we were saying it. He also knew it was good public relations.

He brought in very good coaches and taught us how to be great coaches. Maybe that explains why so many of his assistants eventually became head coaches in their own right. In the history of coaching, nobody's had more of his assistant coaches—first- and second-generation—go on to head coaching positions.

Bill forced us to think at a higher level, which was the starting point for getting players to play at a higher level and the organization to operate at a higher level. That was his total focus, like an obsession. All he talked about was improvement. And he knew how to teach improvement.

Maybe you can't ultimately explain greatness—the kind Bill Walsh had—but let me offer this observation. He had a brilliant mind for football, and from the start back at Washington High School, where he was a head coach, Bill had been studiously preparing himself for the opportunity he was finally given at San Francisco—learning and *thinking* at every single step. When Eddie DeBartolo called him with the offer to become head coach of an NFL franchise, Bill knew he was ready and believed his system would work.

Because of that belief, he had the discipline to stay with it even when things were bad. That's not to say he didn't have his rough patches, because he was very insecure and took some knocks that shook his belief in himself. Listen to this: After his seventh or eighth year—I had moved on to a head coaching position by then—he got so down and depressed he called me up to see if I had any interest in taking over as head coach of the 49ers so he could concentrate on executive duties. And he meant it; he was ready to go to DeBartolo and talk him into letting me take over as head coach. I declined, and soon after that, Bill was back on his horse and into the fray.

On the field he was advanced. He conducted practice at a fast tempo, full-throttle delivery of information with extraordinary demands for precision in execution. If you were supposed to go twelve yards and you added an extra half yard, it was a big deal. You heard about it in no uncertain terms. Accuracy, accuracy, precision in execution of everything at all levels. No sloppiness. *Game*-level focus was the price of admission.

Obviously, the physical component is huge in football, but what Bill did was make the mental component even bigger. He taught what he wanted done, and he was a great teacher. He taught players, he taught coaches, he taught staff, he taught, taught, taught. And in that teaching he created belief in ourselves as a team, an organization, because it was apparent that what he was teaching was not only absolutely right, it was advanced. He cleared the deadwood dissenters out and taught the rest of us what it took to get the job done at the highest level.

I would tell you this: Bill's gift for teaching created belief in him, conviction in us. Bill Walsh was the consummate teacher. With the naysayers gone, he had a team of talented people who were ready and willing to be led to the promised land.

PART III

Fundamentals of Leadership: Concepts, Conceits, and Conclusions

"I Am the Leader!"

Someone will declare, "I am the leader!" and expect everyone to get in line and follow him or her to the gates of heaven or hell. My experience is that it doesn't happen that way. Unless you're a guard on a chain gang, others follow you based on the quality of your actions rather than the magnitude of your declarations. It's like announcing, "I am rich!" when you're broke. After your announcement, you're still broke, and everybody knows it. In a sense, Barry Switzer found this out in Dallas with the Cowboys when he took over.

As head coach at the University of Oklahoma, he had achieved tremendous results, including three national championships and one of the highest winning percentages of any college coach in history. Some consider him one of the best college football coaches ever.

When Switzer moved to the NFL and took over for Jimmy Johnson as head coach of the Dallas Cowboys (Johnson "retired" as head coach because of ongoing struggles over control and credit issues with owner Jerry Jones), he inherited a terrific football team that had won the previous two Super Bowls by a combined score of 82–30 (the Buffalo Bills were the opponent in both games).

Initially, Coach Switzer got results from the Cowboys on the momentum of what Johnson and Jones had built. However, in my opinion, Switzer's continuing freewheeling lifestyle, habits, and behavior—he was generally viewed as a "good ol' boy"—did not command the respect necessary to keep superstar quarterback Troy Aikman, Hall of Fame running back Emmett Smith, and other outstanding Dallas performers functioning as a cohesive, dedicated, and overpowering football team. Things gradually began to erode.

Barry Switzer's off-field conduct (e.g., being detained while carrying a gun in his briefcase at the Dallas airport, reports of carousing, and other distracting activities) continually got him the wrong kind of publicity. Plus, he favored the "buddy system" approach to coaching; he had favorites among the players, and everybody knew it. Of course, those who weren't "buddies" inevitably began to feel like second-class citizens, which usually leads to the creation of a second-class organization.

Additionally, his organizational abilities and attention to detail—painstaking attention to perfecting small but important issues—were relatively laid-back. This last item is important because if the person in charge is casual in these areas, others will follow suit.

The Dallas Cowboys' intense focus, commitment, and consequent extraordinary performance results went down during Switzer's four seasons there. His leadership skills at the NFL level may not have commanded the respect or generated the loyalty necessary for ongoing dominance from that extremely talented Dallas organization.

All of this contributed to the decline of the Cowboys—which had long-lasting effects: The Cowboys did not repeat as Super Bowl champions in his first season; during Switzer's second season, Dallas won Super Bowl XXX, but two years later he was out following a 6–10 season and a fourth-place finish in the NFC East. He never coached again in the NFL, and during the five years following his departure, the Dallas Cowboys lost 60 percent of their games. Would this have occurred had Jimmy Johnson remained as head coach? I doubt it.

Declaring, "I am the leader!" has no value unless you also have the command skills necessary to be the leader. This is true anywhere. Barry Switzer had skills that made him a top college football coach. His skills and style were less effective in leadership at the highest levels in the NFL. It took a while, but ultimately what he did and how he did it caught up with him and the Dallas Cowboys.

The Common Denominator of Leadership: Strength of Will

There is no one perfect or even preferable style of leadership, just as there is no perfect politician or parent. Bill Gates is different from Steve Jobs; Vince Lombardi was different from me.

We have, however, seen a move away from the dictatorial type of leadership, an approach that didn't fit me and that I do not think is conducive to long-term success, especially in a corporate setting. You may get results for a week or a few months, but the cumulative effects of bullying people, creating an environment of ongoing fear, panic, and intimidation, are a situation where employees become increasingly tuned out and immune to all of your noise. And, of course, the talented ones look for a job with a better outfit.

The tyrant still exists in leadership, in both sports and business, but is in retreat. The strong-willed personality, however, is not disappearing anywhere anytime soon, whether in sports, nonprofits, or corporate America.

The leader who will not be denied, who has expertise coupled with strength of will, is going to prevail. Here are three people, head coaches I know personally and whose abilities I respect, who are dissimilar in many ways but exactly the same in one area—strength of will. They *will* not be denied:

Mike Holmgren's Green Bay Packers won Super Bowl XXXI, and he's been very successful as head coach of the Seattle Seahawks; before that he was one of my assistant coaches at San Francisco, so I know him pretty well. Here's my capsule description of Mike: He is thoughtful, intelligent, and assertive—an excellent teacher who, beneath his surface appearance of being amenable and open to everything, absolutely knows what he wants and gets it; and everybody in his organization understands that.

Mike is unswerving in moving toward his goal.

Tom Landry won Super Bowl VI and Super Bowl XII as head coach of the Dallas Cowboys. Almost as impressive is his streak of twenty consecutive winning seasons. Here's my description of Landry: Tom had a tremendous mind for technical football and was inordinately well organized and very strong mentally—a no-nonsense guy greatly respected for the exemplary standards he demanded of himself and those who worked with him. Tom didn't like to show emotion. (Walt Garrison, a former running back for Dallas, was asked if he'd ever seen Landry smile. He replied, "No, but I was only on his team for nine years.")

And, like Holmgren, Tom Landry was unswerving in moving toward his goal.

Jimmy Johnson won a national championship as head coach of the University of Miami Hurricanes and two consecutive Super Bowl championships at Dallas. Here's my description of Jimmy: a smart guy with an exuberant personality who brought in outstanding people and delegated well. He was not the technical football expert that Landry was, but a better salesman. (Landry was a good salesman unintentionally. Jimmy *intended* to be good at selling himself and his system, and he was.)

And, like Holmgren and Landry, Jimmy Johnson was unswerving in moving toward his goal.

I pick these three because they've all enjoyed the ultimate success in football—a Super Bowl championship (or two)—and because they are so different in many ways, Holmgren seemingly amenable and flexible, Landry stoic and stern, Johnson like Robert Preston in *The Music Man*— exuberant and lively.

What they share beyond expertise and great success, however, was their indomitable will. They simply would not quit in their effort to install their own system, to push forward with their plan, not someone else's or a committee's. Keep in mind that all three of them were handed tough jobs, teams in trouble (e.g., Dallas was an expansion franchise and went 0–11–1 in their first season under Landry).

Some leaders are volatile, some voluble; some stoic, others exuberant; but all successful leaders know where we want to go, figure out a way we believe will get the organization there (after careful consideration of relevant available information), and then move forward with absolute determination. We may falter from time to time, but ultimately we are unswerving in moving toward our goal; we will not quit. There is an inner compulsion—obsession—to get it done the way you want it done even if the personal cost is high.

It is good to remind yourself that this quality—strength of will—is essential to your survival and success. Often you are urged to "go along to get along," solemnly advised that "your plan should've worked by now," or told other variations that amount to backing away from a course you believe in your heart and know in your head is correct.

You look around the room and find yourself with only a few supporters. Or perhaps not even a few. Heads are bowed, everybody's eyes are lowered, looking down at their hands, embarrassed to look at you. You may be standing alone. This is when you find out if you're a leader.

In my years as a head coach, I wanted a democratic-style organization with input and communication and freedom of expression, even opinions that were at great variance with my ideas. But only up to a point. When it was time for a decision, that decision would be made by me according to dictates having to do with one thing only, namely, making the team better.

And once the decision was made, the discussion was over. My ultimate job, and yours, is not to give an opinion. Everybody's got an opinion. Leaders are paid to make a decision. The difference between offering an opinion and making a decision is the difference between working for the leader and being the leader.

I was never a screamer, but everyone knew not to buck me when I'd decided what we were going to do. Just like Mike Holmgren, Tom Landry, Jimmy Johnson, and many others, I was unswerving in moving toward my goal. Once I had accumulated and evaluated the available information, I did it my way. And so should you.

Now, let me address a problem this prerequisite leadership trait— strength of will—can pose, namely, the problem of determining when "my way" is the wrong way.

Be Wrong for the Right Reasons

Coaches, like leaders anywhere, often try to force a plan past the point of reality. In football we may want to establish a passing game and persist too long because we're preoccupied with it, determined by our own will to make it happen even when it's ill conceived or ill timed. This is no different from a corporate leader who imposes a plan of action beyond the point of no return, the point where continuing makes no sense and becomes destructive.

It's a delicate balance: You must persevere to achieve anything of import, but at what stage does perseverance become pigheadedness? When does your unswerving determination to do it your way—what you deem the "right way"—take you and your organization over the cliff?

Years ago, when I was head coach at Stanford University, we played Tulane University in the second game of our season. In my pregame preparation, while watching hours of game film, I had determined that we could—and would—rely on our running game against a mediocre Tulane defense. The previous week in the season opener we had lost by only six points to number one–ranked Colorado and had run the ball successfully.

Now we were in New Orleans for the Tulane game, and I announced in the middle of a press conference that I *challenged* Tulane to deal with Stanford's ground game, dared them to try and stop us. Well, they did.

It took me into the middle of the third quarter to realize I was a victim of my own mistaken assessment, rhetoric, and subsequent stubbornness: We were behind 17–6 and on the verge of losing because I was determined to show that our "unstoppable" running game couldn't be stopped.

Somehow it dawned on me: I was staying with a bad plan because my ego was committed to the stupid challenge I had made while boasting about our running game to the media. Tulane's defense was stronger than I had concluded after watching their game films. However, I didn't want to be proved wrong in front of sixty-five thousand spectators in the Super-dome who had read my boast in the sports section of the *New Orleans Times-Picayune* or heard it on radio or television.

When I recognized the mental trap I had set and stepped into, I abandoned our ground game and allowed quarterback Guy Benjamin's passing skills to get us going. The results were immediate, and Stanford won 21–17. However, I had jeopardized the game by locking my ego into a strategy that was failing. I did not allow logic or the reality of the game to pierce my veil of pride. It was my ego and strength of will that had almost killed us.

I had all but lost that game for our young team because I didn't want to back off something I'd bragged about. I was caught up in my own rhetoric about Stanford's running game when I had a quarterback who was one of the finest passers in college football. Even now I'm a little embarrassed to think about the level of immaturity I demonstrated during an important game. Obviously, this was not my best moment as a leader.

Here's a similar example, away from the game of football, that you may recall. Years ago, the executives at Coca-Cola decided to replace classic Coke with a new version of it. Tests seemed to suggest that the new flavor was favored by potential buyers over the time-tested Coke that had become a worldwide brand and a proven phenomenon. Coca-Cola went ahead and replaced it—took the classic Coke off shelves worldwide—amid great fanfare. The sales results were not good. In fact, it was a fiasco. But those same executives, committed as they were to the new product and having spent tens of millions of dollars on it, recognized "their way" was the wrong way. New Coke was introduced in April and taken off the shelves in July.

So the question is this: How do you know when it's time to quit, to try another approach, to move in a different direction, regardless of whether it's a commitment to a football team's running game, a company's marketing plan, or a new hire? When is it time to say, "I'm wrong"? Here's the answer: There is no answer; there is no cut-and-dried formula.

We all have in our mind inspiring examples of individuals who persevered beyond the point of reason and common sense and prevailed. We tend to ignore the more numerous examples of individuals who persisted and persisted and finally *failed* and took everybody down with them because they would not change course or quit. We ignore them because we never heard about them. Failure rarely garners the amount of attention that victory does.

Thus, the epic journey of Arctic explorer Ernest Shackleton is worth noting because we've heard about him. Shackleton took the crew of the HMS *Endurance* on a monumental and courageous expedition aimed at crossing the Antarctic on foot. Many have been inspired by his exploits; even the name of his ship—*Endurance*—is used for motivation.

I also greatly admire his courage, loyalty, and dedication, but in case you forgot, his expedition was doomed; it ended in failure: The HMS *Endurance* was trapped in ice and crushed. Shackleton's incredible commitment to his men ultimately saved them from death, although three of the rescuers died in the process. The magnitude of his ultimately success-ful rescue effort—rather than the failure to reach his primary goal—is what we remember. I, too, am inspired by his raw drive to save his men. I also keep in mind the loss of his ship and the failure of his expedition.

In every leader's work there are times when you must coldly evaluate the path down which you are taking your organization. In my own work, the Tulane experience was valuable because it was an example of persisting for the wrong reason.

The lesson I took from it was this: A leader must be keen and alert to what drives a decision, a plan of action. If it was based on good logic, sound principles, and strong belief, I felt comfortable in being unswerv-ing in moving toward my goal. Any other reason (or reasons) for persist-ing were examined carefully. Among the most common faulty reasons are (1) trying to prove you are right and (2) trying to prove someone else is wrong. Of course, they amount to about the same thing and often lead to the same place: defeat.

Losing—failure—is part of the package for a leader in a competitive career. I was always reluctant to change a course of action that I had com-mitted to in pursuit of a goal, but after my pigheaded persistence against Tulane University, I became scrupulous in analyzing when a change of course was appropriate, when "my way" was the wrong way.

A leader must have a vision, which is simply an elevated word for "goal." Significant time and resources will be applied to achieving that goal. Therefore, it is of paramount importance that you proceed and per-sist for the correct reasons; your tactics must be sound and based on logic seasoned with instinct. If I led our team down the road to failure, I wanted to make sure the quality of my reasoning was very solid. If we went down, I wanted to go down for the right reasons. That's tough enough to take, but what is toughest of all—what is inexcusable—is to fail because you are unwilling to admit that your way was the wrong way and that a change of course is your only path to victory.

Few things are more painful for a leader than losing because your rea-soning is faulty, your conclusions flawed, your logic skewed by emotions, pride, or arrogance. One of the great leadership challenges is to recognize when hubris has you in its grip before it is too late to change. Here's a short checklist worth keeping in mind when it comes to persevering, to doing it "your way" at all costs:

1. A leader must never quit.
2. A leader must know *when* to quit.
3. Proving that you are right or proving that someone is wrong are bad reasons for persisting.
4. Good logic, sound principles, and strong belief are the purest and most productive reasons for pushing forward when things get rough.

Protect Your Turf

The head of the 49er scouts, Howard White, was incensed when I was named general manager; he wanted the job and felt he deserved it. During a tense meeting in which I told him he wasn't going to be general manager, White announced that not only was he resigning but *all* of our scouts were quitting out of loyalty to him.

His threat carried tremendous weight, since the scouts happened to be in town for a predraft conference, a series of meetings that would chart our future talent acquisitions and, in effect, my future. My authority—my leadership—was being challenged at a critical moment. Howard knew it and was more than pleased to put a gun to my head.

I felt, however, that I had no option but to call Howard out and call him on his threat. I knew more about judging talent for my system than anyone, including Howard. I therefore accepted his "resignation" and then asked John Ralston, a member of our staff, to immediately inform all of the other scouts that we accepted their resignations as tendered by their boss. That was a bombshell.

The scouts' response was swift and unequivocal: "We want to stay; we're not unhappy that Howard White is leaving; we didn't offer to follow him out the door," or words to that effect. My problem was over, but only because I had stood my ground and protected my turf when my position and authority were challenged. Leaders who don't understand what their territory is and how to protect it will soon find themselves with no turf to protect.

Be a Leader—Twelve Habits Plus One

A defining characteristic of a good leader is the conviction that he or she can make a positive difference—can prevail even when the odds are stacked against him or her. A successful leader is not easily swayed from this self-belief. But it happens.

When you fall prey to the naysayers who eagerly provide you with all the reasons why you won't succeed, why you can't win, and why you should quit, you have lost the winner's edge. When that happens, the game is over, regardless of your profession.

In addition to expertise and knowledge of the specific competitive environment, I believe a leader must also have certain habits (to use a word popularized by Dr. Stephen Covey) that contribute to his or her effectiveness, that create and cement his or her winner's edge. In my view a truly effective leader must *be* certain things. Here are twelve habits I have identified over the years that will make you *be* a better leader:

1. **Be yourself.** I am not Vince Lombardi; Vince Lombardi was not Bill Walsh. My style was my style, and it worked for me. Your style will work for you when you take advantage of your strengths and strive to overcome your weaknesses. You must be the best version of yourself that you can be; stay within the framework of your own personality and be authentic. If you're faking it, you'll be found out.

2. **Be committed to excellence.** I developed my Standard of Performance over three decades in the business of football. It could just as accurately (although more awkwardly) been called "Bill's Prerequisites for Doing Your Job at the Highest Level of Excellence Vis-à-Vis Your Actions and Attitude on Our Team." My commitment to this "product"— excellence—preceded my commitment to winning football

games. At all times, in all ways, your focus must be on doing things at the highest possible level.

3. **Be positive.** I spent far more time teaching what to do than what not to do; far more time teaching and encouraging individuals than criticizing them; more time building up than tearing down. There is a constructive place for censure and highlighting negative aspects of a situation, but too often it is done simply to vent and creates a barrier between you and others. Maintain an affirmative, constructive, positive environment.

4. **Be prepared. (Good luck is a product of good planning.)** Work hard to get ready for expected situations—events you know will happen. Equally important, plan and prepare for the unexpected. "What happens when what's supposed to happen doesn't happen?" is the question that you must always be asking and solving. No leader can control the outcome of the contest or competition, but you *can* control how you prepare for it.

5. **Be detail-oriented.** Organizational excellence evolves from the perfection of details relevant to performance and production. What are they for you? High performance is achieved small step by small step through painstaking dedication to pertinent details. (Caution: Do not make the mistake of burying yourself alive in those details.) Address all aspects of your team's efforts to prepare mentally, physically, fundamentally, and strategically in as thorough a manner as is humanly possible.

6. **Be organized.** A symphony will sound like a mess without a musical score that organizes each and every note so that the musicians know precisely what to play and when to play it. Great *organization* is the trademark of a great organization. You must think clearly with a disciplined mind, especially in regard to the most efficient and productive use of time and resources.

7. **Be accountable.** Excuse making is contagious. Answerability

starts with you. If you make excuses—which is first cousin to "alibiing"—so will those around you. Your organization will soon be filled with finger-pointing individuals whose battle cry is, "It's his fault, not mine!"

8. **Be near-sighted and far-sighted.** Keep *everything* in perspective while simultaneously concentrating fully on the task at hand. All decisions should be made with an eye toward how they affect the organization's performance—not how they affect you or your feelings. All efforts and plans should be considered not only in terms of short-run effect, but also in terms of how they impact the organization long term. This is very difficult.

9. **Be fair.** The 49ers treated people right. I believe your value system is as important to success as your expertise. Ethically sound values engender respect from those you lead and give your team strength and resilience. Be clear in your own mind as to what you stand for. And then stand up for it.

10. **Be firm.** I would not budge one inch on my core values, standards, and principles.

11. **Be flexible.** I was agile in adapting to changing circumstances. Consistency is crucial, but you must be quick to adjust to new challenges that defy the old solutions.

12. **Believe in yourself.** To a large degree, a leader must "sell" himself to the team. This is impossible unless you exhibit self-confidence. While I was rarely accused of cockiness, it was apparent to most observers that I had significant belief—self-confidence—in what I was doing. Of course, belief derives from expertise.

13. **Be a leader.** Whether you are a head coach, CEO, or sales manager, you must know where you're going and how you intend to get there, keeping in mind that it may be necessary to modify your tactics as circumstances dictate. You must be able to inspire and motivate through teaching people how to execute their jobs at the highest level. You must care about people and help those people care about one another and the team's goals. And you must never second-guess yourself

on decisions you make with integrity, intelligence, and a team-first attitude.

Sweat the Right Small Stuff: Sharp Pencils Do Not Translate into Sharp Performance

Coach George Allen was a demon on details. As head coach of the Washington Redskins, he was preparing to face the Miami Dolphins in Super Bowl VII at the Los Angeles Memorial Coliseum. A few days before the game, he sent a staff member out to the Coliseum for an entire afternoon to chart the movement of the sun during the hours when the game would be played. George wanted to know exactly where it would be so he could calculate the "sun advantage" if the Redskins won the coin toss. This is an example of sweating the right small stuff.

Later, in a turbulent and brief tenure as head coach of the Los Angeles Rams, George supposedly took time off from his coaching responsibilities to design a more efficient system of serving food, a way of reducing the amount of time players spent in the lunch line. He took time out of his jam-packed schedule to personally draw up a schematic for those players wanting soup with their meals: One line was designated for those wanting crackers with their soup; the other for those who didn't want any crackers. This is an example of sweating the wrong small stuff. Owner Carroll Rosenbloom fired him before the regular season even began. (I should note that while George wasn't fired for designing a "crackerless" line, it may have been symptomatic of what he was doing—sweating the wrong details.)

While it is critically important to concentrate on the smallest relevant aspects of your job without losing sight of the big picture, it is easy to become so completely overwhelmed by ongoing setbacks that you start focusing on issues completely extraneous to improvement in an attempt to keep from having to look at intractable problems.

Seeing it in others, I watched for it in my own behavior—as you should in yours—knowing that it would significantly reduce my ability to be effective, that it was dodge, a way of diverting my attention. A coach who becomes afflicted with the malady of "trivialities" might suddenly and compulsively worry about whether all of the practice uniforms have been laundered correctly ("Can't you get *all* of those grass stains out?"); obsess over luncheons with local fan clubs; and take inordinate pride in various award ceremonies or alumni gatherings.

All of this is an escape mechanism—a method of distracting yourself from the tough work ahead. George Allen isn't the only NFL coach who became immersed in the meaningless at the expense of the meaningful. A Seattle head coach once diverted himself from the hardships of fixing a dismal team and organization by focusing more on how the Seahawks performed during the national anthem than on how they performed during a game. Valuable practice time was actually spent rehearsing the national anthem "formation"—lining players up by height and number in a perfectly straight row, feet together, helmets held in the left hand by the face guard, no gum chewing, no movement, shirttails tucked in, and actually singing the words. This was going on at a time when the team was in the tank.

Of course, it's an easy trap to fall into, because the trivialities I noted are typical of what a desperate leader can grab onto and *control* when everything seems out of control. It creates a false and fatal sense of accomplishment, a trap with serious consequences because it keeps you from addressing the key thoughts and solutions, the tough decisions that are at the core of accomplishing a very difficult task; that is, the task of turning things around.

As a leader, when you find yourself with a host of problems that seemingly defy solution and start dwelling on the least relevant or even irrelevant aspects of your job—constantly sitting on the phone with nonessential conversations, doing endless e-mailing, writing memo after memo, fiddling around getting all your pencils sharpened and lined up perfectly, being excessively concerned about hurting feelings and trying to make sure everyone is comfortable, straightening out your desk drawer, getting wrapped up in the details of the annual Christmas party, and a million other kinds of stupid busywork, tell yourself this: "There'll be plenty of time for pencils, parties, and socializing when I lose my job, because that's what's going to happen if I continue to avoid the hard and harsh realities of doing my job."

And that's exactly what happened to the coach of the Seattle Seahawks. Just like George Allen, he was fired, in spite of the fact that his team could sing the national anthem better than any other outfit in the NFL.

Sharpening pencils in lieu of sharpening your organization's performance is one way to lose your job. Here are ten additional nails you can pound into your professional coffin:

1. Exhibit patience, paralyzing patience.
2. Engage in delegating—massive delegating—or conversely, engage in too little delegating.
3. Act in a tedious, overly cautious manner.
4. Become best buddies with certain employees.
5. Spend excessive amounts of time socializing with superiors or subordinates.
6. Fail to continue hard-nosed performance evaluations of longtime—"tenured"—staff members, the ones most likely to go on cruise control, to relax.
7. Fail to actively participate in efforts to appraise and acquire new hires.
8. Trust others to carry out your *fundamental* duties.
9. Find ways to get out from under the responsibilities of your position, to move accountability from yourself to others— the blame game.
10. Promote an organizational environment that is comfortable and laid-back in the misbelief that the workplace should be fun, lighthearted, and free from appropriate levels of tension and urgency.

For leaders in all professions, including coaches in the NFL, looking for relief from the high anxieties, deep frustrations, and toxic emotions that go with the job can lead you to do everything *but* your job—worrying about issues of lesser and lesser relevance with greater and greater consequences.

The tangential aspects of your job become attractive because they're monumentally easier to control than what you're there to do; specifically, to create high performance; this is the toughest part to live with, concentrate on, and control. You use the peripheral stuff as an escape mechanism, rather than tackling what may appear, and indeed may be, unsolvable problems until finally you're done, finished, sitting there with nothing to show for your leadership efforts but a cup of sharp pencils.

Good Leadership Percolates Down

The trademark of a well-led organization in sports or business is that it's virtually self-sustaining and self-directed—almost autonomous. To put it in a more personal way, if your staff doesn't seem fully mobilized and energized until you enter the room, if they require your presence to carry on at the level of effort and excellence you have tried to install, your leadership has not percolated down.

Ideally, you want your Standard of Performance, your philosophy and methodology, to be so strong and solidly ingrained that in your absence the team performs as if you were present, on site. They've become so proficient, highly mobilized, and well prepared that in a sense you're extraneous; everything you've preached and personified has been integrated and absorbed; roles have been established and people are able to function at a high level because they understand and believe in what you've taught them, that is, the most effective and productive way of doing things accompanied by the most productive attitude while doing them. Fundamentally sound actions and attitudes are the keys.

Consequently, I was very pleased when I began overhearing 49er coaches repeating my ideas to one another and subsequently to our players. Later, when I heard the players using my terms or phrases—my personal dialogue or choice of words that represented concepts and ideas—I knew that I'd made a connection, that my leadership had percolated down. (Of course, seeing it produce an improving won-lost record was better evidence.)

This is extremely important because an organization is crippled if it needs to ask the leader what to do every time a question arises. I didn't want an organizational psyche of leadership dependency, of being semi-dysfunctional without me around making every decision. Here are specific examples in which my leadership philosophy percolated down.

My battle cry was "Beat 'em to the punch!" which I repeated over and over to coaches and players through the years. It meant, "Hurt your opponents before they hurt you. Strike first." It was like a mantra of competition for me. Soon I was hearing it repeated by others. I saw it on the field as the 49ers became known for establishing an early lead, which, of course, changed the dynamics of a game in our favor.

Another was "Commit, explode, recover (if you're wrong)!" which was shorthand for having a plan of attack, executing it suddenly and powerfully, and then reacting quickly and intelligently to the results of what you've done. It was a way of thinking and performing, a philosophy—*my* philosophy, my approach to competing. It, too, was soon part of our organization's vernacular and attitude.

"Four-minute offense" meant we were ahead late in the game and wanted to take time off the clock, avoid penalties, not go out of bounds, control the ball, and more. When that situation arose, I didn't have to say anything. Players would be shouting it to each other: "Four-minute offense! Four-minute offense!" It was satisfying to hear because it meant they had come to understand and embrace what I was teaching.

I instructed our maintenance crew to put up a white five-foot-square grease board with "I WILL NOT BE OUTHIT ANY TIME THIS SEASON!" printed in bold letters across the top. I got out my Magic Marker and signed it—"Bill Walsh." Then everybody on the team signed it. It was a frame of mind, an attitude that I sought to instill.

"I will not be outhit any time this season!" was about the physical aspect of the profession, but also about the mental and emotional—a state of mind. And everybody on the team literally signed up for it—a contract. This, too, was soon in the air, repeated, absorbed, part of our DNA.

My leadership had percolated down and had begun taking on a life of its own. It went beyond my phrases, of course, and included everything from offensive and defensive schemes to the precision and professionalism applied to all matters in training camp and the regular season. And much more.

Ultimately, you hope your ideas and way of doing things become so strongly entrenched that the organization performs as effectively without you as with you. That's the goal and, in fact, it happened to me.

When I retired as head coach of the 49ers following our victory in Super Bowl XXIII, the organization moved forward without a hitch and continued its dominance for years. Why? In part because my leadership philosophy had become ingrained within the San Francisco 49ers.

It takes nothing away from my successor George Seifert's coaching nor the great abilities of his coaching staff to suggest that my Standard of Performance had become so ingrained with the 49ers during my decade of teaching that when I retired they were able to practice, prepare, and perform at the same level of excellence—higher, in fact—as during my final season.

This is a reliable indication of an effective leader, namely, one who creates a self-sustaining organization able to operate at the highest levels even when he or she leaves.

The responsible leader of any company or corporation aggressively seeks to ensure its continued prosperity. It's the mark of a forward-thinking leadership. A strong company that goes south after the CEO retires is a company whose recently departed CEO didn't finish the job. If everything goes great when you're around but slows or stops in its tracks when you're not there, you are not fulfilling your responsibilities. Your leadership has not percolated down.

Nameless, Faceless Objects

Demonizing the competition is a common but contrived method for stirring up emotions. We see it used in sports (most frequently), business, or war to motivate people, to light a fire under them. Coaches will attempt to incite players by reminding them that the upcoming opponent "wants to embarrass us on *Monday Night Football*; wants to make us look like fools in front of the whole goddamn country!" or "is trying to take away your job so you won't be able to send your kids to a good school," or a laundry list of other supposedly incendiary but usually silly declarations. (The "genius" tag the media put on me was used in this way occasionally by coaches to stir up their teams, to demonize me.)

I generally preferred the opposite approach in characterizing the other team and its players. To me they were objects that were both faceless and nameless: Nameless, Faceless Objects.

My logic was that I wanted our focus directed at one thing only: going about our business in an intensely efficient and professional manner—first on the practice field, later on the playing field. I felt that moving attention away from that goal to create artificial and manufactured "demons" was artificial and usually nonproductive, especially when done repeatedly (as is usually the case with those who like the technique).

Whether it's sports, sales, management, or almost any other competitive context, consistent motivation usually comes from a consuming desire to be able to perform at your best under pressure, namely, the pressure produced by tough competition. If a player needed me to light a fire under him by turning the other team into a demon, he was lacking something I couldn't give him. Of course, there are exceptions to every rule.

On some occasions I would resort to the "demonizing" tactic to spark life into a player or group of players who for unknown reasons were flat. Keep in mind, I used this device intermittently and unpredictably, which is exactly why it worked. When I launched into a demonizing speech, the players didn't just roll their eyes and think, "Oh, boy, there goes Walsh again, trying to get us fired up." Here's an example of the way I would use it, although the circumstances were unique.

On the bus ride from our hotel to Giants Stadium for a game against the New York Giants, the energy was flat, the players' voices not just subdued but nearly silent, almost eerily silent. I became increasingly uncomfortable with what I sensed from my seat at the front of the bus. Was it complacency, lack of confidence, or something else? Regardless of the cause, the effect could be a disaster in just a few hours. So I decided it was time to manufacture a demon.

Leaning across the aisle, I instructed the bus driver to pull into an empty parking lot just a few miles from Giants Stadium. The lot was in a desolate part of town—a few deserted buildings were nearby, a liquor store was on the corner, trash blew across the blacktop. It was an unusual place to stop.

The bus driver opened the doors in what looked like the middle of nowhere; I stood up and shouted over the heads of players and coaches, "Everybody out! Right now, let's go. Move it! Move it!"

The team was confused but complied—gathering alongside the bus and studying me as I paced back and forth, fuming, with a rolled-up copy of the *New York Post* in my hands.

I opened the *Post* and looked down at it with an anguished and disgusted expression on my face. Slowly I started shaking my head back and forth and then looked up at the team and launched into an angry tirade.

"Have any of you read this?" I asked with disgust. Of course none of the players knew what "this" was so they remained silent or shook their heads. It was like they had been called into the principal's office for unknown but ominous reasons.

"Goddamn it! I'm sick and tired of what the New York media elite is saying about us!" I yelled, waving the *Post* in their faces. "The papers, television, fans—everybody out there is trying to make us look like some Brie-eating, wine-sipping pushovers; we're back to being called a laughingstock!"

I threw down the paper and stormed away.

The team was stunned. They simply didn't know how to respond. Immediately, I returned and continued the diatribe: "They're ridiculing us and who we are, all that we've accomplished, making jokes about us and the big 'genius' who coaches you, and I'm *sick* of it. I can't take this. I just can't stand this shit any more!"

I walked slowly along the loosely assembled front row of 49ers—studying them like General George Patton inspecting his troops. My anguish burrowed in: "I had to tell you this, fellas; I had to tell you because you've got to put a stop to it; you've got to help me get control of this thing. A team like ours has so much tradition; it's absolutely unforgivable that this organization is being mocked! Will you help me? Can you shut 'em up? Can you stop this kind of crap from continuing any longer? Can you stuff it down their goddamn throats?"

Before I could finish that last sentence, the team roared back their support, shouting some expletives Patton might have smiled at. There was blood in the air. As the players poured back into the bus with a vengeance, I glanced at Bobb McKittrick, one of my assistant coaches, and he gave me a little wink. Bobb knew exactly what I was up to.

My show of contrived anger directed toward the New York "demon"—the media, not the New York team itself—was effective only because it was so atypical of my usual cold-blooded perspective on opponents; namely, that they were "Nameless, Faceless Objects," simply anonymous prey to be dispatched. And the New York Giants were easily dispatched that particular Sunday afternoon.

Bill Parcells, when he was head coach of the New York Jets, once created a "demon" out of his own team. Disgusted with the effort the Jets were displaying in the final practice before a crucial *Monday Night Football* appearance with the New England Patriots, Coach Parcells angrily stormed off the field in a rage and took all of his coaches with him.

Veteran Jets players were forced to lead the team through the final hour of practice. Everyone got the message implicit in Parcell's show of disgust with them. The players picked up the level of performance and intensity which ultimately created a 24-14 victory over the Patriots at Foxboro, Massachusetts

Afterward, Parcells said there was no intent on his part to stir up the emotions of his team, no connection between his actions and the outcome of the game, nothing contrived at all. Of course, the ability to say that with a straight face is proof of Bill's exceptional acting ability.

Leaders who regularly employ this tactic of demonizing opponents destroy its effectiveness because it's soon recognized as a ploy to stir up emotions. As soon as that happens, it's ignored. Nevertheless, it had value in my system because it was used sparingly and performed convincingly.

I often wonder what would have happened if Bob Costas or some other announcer had happened to drive by just as I was delivering my speech in that desolate Meadowlands parking lot.

The Rules May Change, But the Game Goes On: I Strike Out the First Time, Not the Second

A strike in 1987 by the Players Association tested the judgment of everybody in the NFL—owners, players, union officials, management, and, of course, the head coach of each team. This was not the first time I had been called upon to deal with a strike. Earlier, during my disastrous fourth season at San Francisco, the league had faced a players' strike. In addition to our reeling from the aftereffects of winning our first Super Bowl, the suspension of games that year turned everything on its head and created one of the worst seasons I ever had in football. I simply was unprepared for events.

My own choices through that strike-shortened season had not been good. This time around—'87—I wanted to make decisions that would benefit the organization in what was going to be a tumultuous time. It was particularly challenging because nobody really knew for certain what was going to happen.

Owners had decided to continue playing—no suspension of games or the season—with teams consisting mostly of replacement players. Many in the league assumed that games played during the strike wouldn't actually count; many considered them virtually exhibition games. I didn't make that mistake. This time around, I intended to use whatever logic and resources were available so that when the strike ended, the San Francisco 49ers would be standing tall amid whatever wreckage ensued.

We all knew going into the season that a strike was imminent. It was only a question of when. Consequently, in training camp we invited a disproportionate number of players to join us, knowing that many of them wouldn't make the regular "prestrike" team. What we were interested in, however, was scouting individuals as potential replacement players. I also recognized that having them with us in camp would familiarize them with the 49er system in the event that they were called back during the upcoming strike.

By the end of training camp, we had a virtual replacement roster in order. Assistant coaches had spent lots of time with them, teaching them the 49er way of doing things. When the strike was called by the players' union, we were as ready for it as an organization could be. Most other teams couldn't make that claim. In fact, in our first "strike" game—the one in which I "demonized" the New York media on the way to Giants Stadium—we faced a New York organization coached by Bill Parcells, who had made assumptions completely the opposite of mine. His organization apparently didn't believe the strike games would count and didn't make contingency plans in case the games mattered. It was a big mistake. We won that game—beat the Giants handily on the way to a 13–2 regular season record. (We later lost in the NFC play-offs to the Minnesota Vikings.)

The lesson I had learned in fumbling through the earlier strike was useful this time around; namely, don't assume because of odd circumstances that everything will somehow sort itself out. Rather, play for keeps all the time. The clock never stops running; there is never a "time-out" when what you do is somehow less meaningful.

Leading into and during the 1987 strike, I made a conscious decision that the NFL season was going to be played in a different and complicated new way—that a new set of rules and assumptions was going to be utilized—and I did my best to figure out those rules and assumptions to the advantage of our organization. The season was extremely trying, but the results were excellent. I had learned my lesson the first time around.

You Must Have a Hard Edge

From a very early stage in my development as a leader, I found myself at odds with the common practice of abusing individuals emotionally, physically, or psychologically. When I came into the NFL as a very low-level assistant with the Oakland Raiders, I was deeply affected in a negative way by how roughly people were treated. Oakland was not the only team with a heavy-handed approach. A boot-camp mentality was the prevailing paradigm for NFL coaches. For reasons I can't clearly define, it struck me as Neanderthal, clumsy, and a counterproductive way to achieve maximum productivity.

Having said that, I also recognized that a leader needs a very hard edge inside; it has to lurk in there somewhere and come out on occasion. You must be able to make and carry out harsh and, at times, ruthless decisions in a manner that is *fast, firm, and fair*. Applied correctly, this hard edge will not only solve the immediate difficulty, but also prevent future problems by sending out this important message: Cross my line and you can expect severe consequences. This will have ongoing benefits for your organization.

In my second year as 49er head coach, I was presented with a difficult situation that required action but could easily have been put off because of the situation. One of our top players, left tackle Ron Singleton, had decided during the off-season that he deserved not only more publicity and attention, but also much more money—almost twice as much as he was being paid on his contract. He had a good point: At 6 feet 6 inches and 287 pounds, he was responsible for protecting the blind side—the back—of our right-handed quarterbacks—Steve DeBerg and Joe Montana. It was a crucial position, and Ron was doing a good job. And he knew it.

To further his cause, Singleton hired an agent, somewhat unusual at the time but fine with me, and began trying to renegotiate his contract with the team.

I felt that his demands were out of line with the relatively frugal salary schedule of our team (the lowest in the NFL) but nevertheless found myself in a tough situation, because he was an outstanding member of an offensive line that was exhibiting real potential.

However, the problem wasn't the attempt to increase his income. The fatal flaw in behavior was the unfortunate tendency he and his agent had of playing the race card. They argued that racism was built into the 49er organization, that we were unwilling to negotiate seriously and give him more money because he was an African American. This was absolutely false. Everyone was treated the same, especially when it came to money; specifically, *nobody* got paid very much, including me (my first-year salary as head coach and general manager in the National Football League was $160,000, probably the lowest in the league—and I had to fight for that).

Additionally, Ron was verbally abusive to certain staff members, a very serious breach of my Standard of Performance, which demanded respectful behavior toward all others on the 49er payroll.

Things came to a head after an unproductive contract session, when Ron left my office and proceeded to walk through our locker room making disparaging remarks about me and the 49ers, throwing in several racially charged comments for good measure, right in front of our equipment manager, Chico Norton, to whom he also made dismissive remarks. A few minutes later, news of what was going on filtered back to my office.

Immediately, I called in R. C. Owens, a former 49er player and cocreator of the "alley-oop pass," who worked in public relations for us, and asked him to go to Mr. Singleton's locker and clear it out: "Shoes, shirts, socks, everything. Put it all in a box and deliver it to his house." In less than an hour, R.C. had placed the cardboard box and its contents on the front steps of now ex-49er Ron Singleton.

Word of my decision circulated fast. Everybody knew what had happened and why. It sent out a vitally important message: There are consequences—at times harsh consequences—for ignoring the spoken and unspoken code of conduct that was part of the standards I had established. Ron Singleton was not exempt from my code of behavior just because he was an important component of our future. People got the message: If a top player such as Ron Singleton could be fired for breaking some fundamentally important element of my Standard of Performance, so could anyone.

The "cardboard box" incident became a focal point, a reminder throughout the 49er organization of the hard edge, the severe action I was willing to take if circumstances dictated, if I was pushed too far. It served me well over the years.

From time to time, leaders must show this hard edge. They must make those around them somewhat uneasy, even ill at ease, in not knowing what to expect from you, the leader. The knowledge that there is this hardness inside you can have a very sobering effect on those who might otherwise be sloppy—those who occasionally need to be reminded of your policies and practices.

Members of your organization should be empowered by the expertise and motivation you offer—the Standard of Performance you have defined—but also by their very clear understanding of the consequences of taking you too far.

There's a positive aesthetic to my persona; it's an image that can be misleading because it suggests a professorial—soft—attitude; a reluctance to bring down the hammer. But inside I have a hard edge, a willingness to mete out punishment and take action that may hurt individuals. It doesn't reveal itself often, but it's there. And those within our organization learned to respect it. You will benefit if that same understanding exists within your team.

The Inner Voice vs. the Outer Voice

Leadership is expertise. It is not rhetoric or cheerleading speeches. People will follow a person who organizes and manages others, because he or she has credibility and expertise—a knowledge of the profession—and demonstrates an understanding of human nature.

With rare exceptions, San Francisco 49er football players did not attain some new level of performance because of my pregame or halftime talks (although I felt pleased with myself and it satisfied me to give those inspirational speeches, especially if someone said afterward, "Great job, Bill.").

After years of coaching, I knew that by the time our players went through the tunnel and under the goalposts onto the field, my inspirational words were history—forgotten.

On the field, the 49ers depended totally on the regimen and skills they had learned. My teaching and the great teaching of the 49er assistant coaches was the decisive factor in competition, not halftime speeches or homilies delivered standing on a chair in the locker room.

Furthermore, once the game started, the players responded to me not on the basis of my sideline shouting (seldom done), but because I could function under stress. I was clearheaded and made sound decisions. They saw it and knew it and responded like professionals.

The same is true elsewhere. Whatever great excitement you may stir up in your employees with a rousing speech about a big quarter or blowing away a sales quota starts to evaporate the minute they exit the conference room.

The true inspiration, expertise, and ability to execute that employees take with them into their work is most often the result of their inner voice talking, not some outer voice shouting, and not some leader giving a pep talk.

For members of your team, *you* determine what their inner voice says. The leader, at least a good one, teaches the team how to talk to themselves. An effective leader has a profound influence on what that inner voice will say.

The great leaders in sports, business, and life always have the most powerful and positive inner voice talking to them, which they, in turn, share with and teach to their organization. The specifics of that inner voice varies from leader to leader, but I believe all have these four messages in common:

1. We can win if we work smart enough and hard enough.
2. We can win if we put the good of the group ahead of our own personal interests.

3. We can win if we improve. And there is *always* room for improvement.
4. I know what is required for us to win. I will show you what it is.

Montana's Leadership by Example: Cool, Calm, and Collected

Quarterback Joe Montana's historic career included four Super Bowl championships (three Super Bowl MVP awards) and was due in large part to the fact that in addition to having talent he was a natural-born leader. The manner in which he accomplished all of this is worthy of examination as it offers invaluable insights on the essence of leadership.

At first I was puzzled by Montana's effectiveness as a leader, because he didn't have the swagger of a Joe Namath or the rough-and-tough attitude of a Dan Marino. He didn't stand out as what sociologists call the alpha male—a man whose aggressive competitive instincts are readily apparent, like his great teammate in later years, Steve Young.

If you watched Joe Montana interact with a group of athletes, he wasn't the guy you'd pick out as "the Man" around whom everything focused and everyone congregated. He didn't appear to need attention or acclaim and was good at sharing credit. Others sought and fed off attention, but not Joe. This is a little unusual among superstars in sports (or business).

Nevertheless, this superb player (by way of Pennsylvania's Ringgold High School and the University of Notre Dame), a guy who never saw a professional football game in person until he played in one, was a leader of the highest caliber who led with one fundamental and powerful leadership technique: his own example.

There were several reasons for his effectiveness that became apparent as I watched him over the early years. Of course, Joe had the talent, but talent alone won't make you a leader (as we see each year with various NFL teams and assorted CEOs). He had courage, but the ability to risk physical injury from human wrecking machines like the New York Giants' great cornerback Lawrence Taylor did not in itself instill loyalty in his teammates.

Beyond his rare talent, there was something else working for Joe that had a profound effect on others and created a willingness to accept him as the on-field leader—the kind of leader you would put your faith in and follow into battle. And it was something that is especially applicable in a corporate setting.

Joe Montana's leadership was grounded in this key characteristic: Despite the fact that he was the starting quarterback, with all of the trappings that come with that position, he never played favorites or believed that a person's reputation, status, or credentials entitled him to special treatment. When you worked with Joe, you were treated as an equal. There were no stars in the Montana system, *including* Joe Montana. That corny old cliché, "One for all and all for one," could have been written with him in mind.

His leadership skills were demonstrated more by behavior on the field or in the locker room than by what he might say just before or during the game. Joe's interaction with other players and coaches was democratic, sincere, and understated. He led with his own talent, quiet confidence, and unassuming demeanor.

Joe never stood up and gave a rah-rah speech to our team at halftime, but as the gravity of a situation increased, so did his own intensity. He could become almost trancelike at times of heightened pressure. This accounted for the amazing thirty-one fourth-quarter comebacks he engineered during his NFL career. Equally impressive—perhaps more so—is the fact that in four Super Bowl games he never threw a single interception.

Joe didn't have to talk the talk because he walked the walk. And without really working at it, he found that everyone else was walking the walk right behind him.

What he did and the way in which he did it offers a great model that is applicable in any setting. Joe Montana is one of the best examples I have ever seen that proved you don't need to shout, stomp, or strut to be a great leader—just do the job and treat people right. Isn't that an essential element in getting people to trust and follow you?

Incredibly, his personality and style didn't change when Joe began to emerge as maybe the best quarterback in history and the center of attention for every football writer and television reporter in America. He remained conscientious about sharing credit. Consequently, nobody resented, was jealous of, or envied all the adulation and publicity he received.

These traits, which I'm sure were instilled by his parents, Theresa and Joe Sr., were a perfect match for the Standard of Performance I had established within the 49er organization. A fundamental component of my system was the recognition that everyone in our organization—regardless of his or her responsibilities, reputation, or paycheck—was a respected member of the group. Others had to be taught this, but Joe understood it before he ever put on a 49er jersey.

I was lucky to have a quarterback in my years at San Francisco who exhibited this important leadership quality right from the start. His leadership example of doing your job, treating others with respect, expecting people to do their jobs, and holding them accountable is a formula for success that will work in any good organization.

Montana's kind of leadership is a great starting point, in my view, for what any good leader strives to do, namely, bring out the best in people. In order to manage people effectively, you must act responsibly and professionally in your capacity as leader. In this regard, you should employ an approach that is based on the following principles:

1. **Treat people like people.** Every player on our team wore a number; no player on our team was "just a number." Treat each member of your organization as a unique person. I was never pals with players, but I never viewed any of them as an anonymous member of an organizational herd.
2. **Seek positive relationships through encouragement, support, and critical evaluation.** Maintain an uplifting atmosphere at work with your ongoing positive, enthusiastic, energizing behavior.
3. **Afford everyone equal dignity, respect, and treatment.**
4. **Blend honesty and "diplomacy."** At times, it is both humane and practical to soften the heavy blow of a demotion or termination with compassion and empathy. It will also help prevent or reduce a toxic response that can ripple

through the organization when word spreads that someone feels he or she has been treated roughly without cause. Nevertheless, "rough treatment" serves a purpose occasionally.

5. **Allow for a wide range of moods, from serious to very relaxed, in the workplace depending on the circumstances.** Set the acceptable tone by your own demeanor, and develop the fine art of knowing when to crack the whip or crack a joke. In the middle of our second Super Bowl season, Joe Montana threw three interceptions against Cincinnati in the first half. We were getting beaten decisively. What was the correct response from me? Bark at him to bear down and try harder, scold him, or what? As he came off the field following his third interception, I pulled him over and asked him innocently, "How's it going out there, Joe?" He got my joke, and I think it took off some of the pressure and anger he had at himself. Things improved, he got going in the second half, and we won. Maybe in another situation my approach would have been more critical. You have to have a feel for it.

6. **Avoid pleading with players to "get going" or trying to relate to them by adopting their vernacular.** Strong leaders don't plead with individuals to perform.

7. **Make each person in your employ very aware that his or her well-being has a high priority with the organization** and that the well-being of the organization must be his or her highest professional priority.

8. **Give no VIP treatment.** Except on a very short-term "reward" basis that is understood as such—for example, a special parking spot for the employee of the month.

9. **Speak in positive terms about former members of your organization.** This creates a very positive impression and signals that respect and loyalty extend beyond an individual's time on your payroll.

10. **Demonstrate interest in and support for the extended families of members of the organization.**

11. **Communicate on a first-name basis without allowing relationships to become buddy-buddy.** Deep resentments

can develop when others see you playing favorites by exhibiting a special bond with select members of the group.

12. **Don't let differences or animosity linger.** Cleanse the wound before it gets infected.

One of the great strengths of General George S. Patton, perhaps one of the best general officers in the history of the U.S. military, was his ability to work with and lead those individuals under his command. The manner in which he did this is applicable beyond the military to sports, business, and leadership in a broad range of areas.

In his "Letter of Instruction Number 1" (from *War As I Knew It*), which was written for officers under his command in the U.S. Third Army, Patton offered six key dictates. You should evaluate each one and determine whether you can utilize it in your own "command."

1. **Remember that praise is more valuable than blame.** Remember, too, that your primary mission as a leader is to see with your own eyes and be seen by your own troops while engaged in personal reconnaissance.

2. **Use every means before and after combat to tell troops what they are going to do and what they have done.**

3. **Discipline is based on pride in the *profession* [my italics] of arms, on meticulous attention to details, and on mutual respect and confidence.** Discipline must be a habit so ingrained that it is stronger than the excitement of battle or the fear of death.

4. **Officers must assert themselves by example and by voice.** They must be preeminent in courage, deportment and dress.

5. **General officers must be seen in the front line during action.**

6. **There is a tendency for the chain of command to overload junior officers by excessive requirements in the way of training and reports.** You will alleviate this burden by eliminating non-essential demands.

There is much in Patton's letter to think about. Obviously, some of it pertains only to war, but almost all of it has relevance to what you do if you adopt and adapt it appropriately: praising rather than blaming; getting out and working amid your "troops"; precisely describing what you want done; taking pride in the profession; paying attention to details; creating habits that hold up under pressure; and removing nonessentials in the workload. It's all great stuff from a great leader.

Don't Let Anybody Call You a Genius

Nobody, including me, expected the 49ers to win the Super Bowl so soon after I was hired as head coach—going from a 2–14 record my first year to world champions twenty-four months later. (To put it another way, we lost twenty-six of the first thirty-five games I coached; then sixteen games later we won Super Bowl XVI.) Consequently, and in part because of the complexities of our pass-based offense, the media began referring to me as "the Genius."

When the name was first attached to me, I was naive enough to be flattered and did nothing to discourage writers from using it. I may have even been thinking, "Hey, maybe there's something to it." I hope not, but everybody likes to read and hear good things about themselves. Besides, what possible downside could there be?

I learned soon enough that an inflated label like "Genius," or any other form of hyperbole, comes with a big downside—that buying into what people say about you can create both external and internal problems, making your life and job a lot tougher than they already are. It happened very soon for me.

Following our first Super Bowl victory, the San Francisco 49ers *lost* twelve of our next twenty-two games—just over 50 percent. (In fact, our record was 3–6 in the strike-shortened season immediately following that Super Bowl championship.)

Soon some writers, coaches, and fans began using the nickname "Genius" dismissively, even derisively. When a play backfired, somebody in the stands would inevitably shout, "There goes the Genius again," or "Hey, Genius, back to the laboratory."

I learned that opposing coaches would incite players by talking sarcastically about the big "Genius" who was sitting calmly at his desk in San

Francisco thinking up new ways to embarrass them on Sunday. Reporters wrote columns analyzing whether I was a "Genius" or a flash in the pan; whether the West Coast Offense was real or a house of cards.

I must admit, all of this was painful for both me and my family. Believe me, my wife, Geri, never operated under the illusion that she was married to a genius. In fact, at one point, after a hard-fought but narrow loss to the New Orleans Saints at Candlestick Park, she and I were leaving the stadium when an older woman wearing a 49ers scarf noticed us and eagerly rolled down the window of her car and waved in our direction. "Bill, Bill Walsh? May I ask you a question?" she inquired. We walked over to within a few feet of her car, and I leaned toward her open window with a smile on my face.

Suddenly she erupted: "You stupid son of a bitch! That was the worst job of coaching I've ever seen. You owe me a refund." She rolled up her window and drove away. Geri and I stood there stunned, embarrassed. Then we started chuckling. "She shouldn't talk to a genius like that," my wife said with a smile. "By the way, don't forget to clean out the garage when we get home. We need to make room for all of your trophies."

The incident only reminded me of what I already knew; namely, that the title I really wanted—the title that indicated the highest praise—was "teacher" or "coach"; combined, they make you a leader. The "Genius" label was an albatross around my neck.

Nevertheless, it's easy to get caught up in or enamored of lofty titles, praise, and flattery as you subconsciously attempt to become the character others have created out of who you are. That character isn't you, but it's an addictive attraction if the plaques, awards, and commendations start rolling in. Believing your own press clippings—good or bad—is self-defeating. You are allowing others, oftentimes uninformed others, to tell you who you are.

The real damage occurs when you start to believe that future success will come your way automatically because of the great ability of this caricature you have suddenly become, that the hard work and applied intelligence you utilized initially are not as crucial as they once were. That's when you get lazy; that's when you let your guard down. When that happens, you're not a genius—you're a genuine fool.

When the "Genius" title turned on me, I backed away from it as far as I could get. A story got going among fans that the sign on my parking space at 49ers headquarters said "The Professor." It wasn't true, but it would have been an improvement over "The Genius."

The Leverage of Language

You demonstrate a lack of assuredness when you talk constantly in negatives. When attempting to help someone attain that next level of performance, a supportive approach works better than a constantly negative or downside-focused approach.

I could be very cutting, very sharp in criticizing a player or coach, but I always made an effort to counter it by following up the barbs with more upbeat input immediately afterward. I avoided creating a chain of negatives. Here's an example.

One Tuesday morning during a preseason workout at our training facility in Santa Clara, California, future Hall of Fame quarterback Steve Young was practicing a crossing pass route with Brent Jones. Steve threw a bad ball. His mechanics weren't right—in fact, they were sloppy, especially for someone at his high skill level. Young wasn't focused on what he was doing; instead, he was just going through the motions. This may not sound serious—one pass among many at practice—but it is a cardinal sin in my philosophy.

I was standing directly behind him with my arms across my chest and said sternly, "Lousy! That was laughable, Steve. Damn it, do it again, and this time do it right." I was very stern, trying to jack up his intensity and get him focused on what he was doing.

The squad reset, and Steve took the snap, dropped back three steps, and threw a second pass—this time with a beautiful and perfect motion, physical artistry that made it a little work of art. I said, "That was good. Stay with that," and walked away rubbing my hands together. He looked over at me and gave me a thumbs-up. Steve had gotten my message (and the message wasn't so much about his throwing motion as it was about his concentration). My praise was sparse, but meaningful because it was rarely effusive.

When I criticized or gave feedback to someone, it wasn't defeatist. It was always focused on the here and now and never conjured up images or incidents of poor play over the previous days or weeks (for example, "Your motion was lousy. That's why you've been throwing interceptions for the last three weeks. How long is it going to take to get it right? I'm getting tired of seeing this over and over.").

It creates a sense of piling on, of browbeating. When that happens, you lose credibility and respect because the subject of your continuous criticism sees it as a personal attack. Others see it and react the same way. (This is *not* to say I never piled on or wasn't occasionally guilty of browbeating.)

If you're growing a garden, you need to pull out the weeds, but flowers will die if *all* you do is pick weeds. They need sunshine and water. People are the same. They need criticism, but they also require positive and substantive language and information and true support to really blossom.

If you're perceived as a negative person—always picking, pulling, criticizing—you will simply get tuned out by those around you. Your influence, ability to teach, and opportunity to make progress will be diminished and eventually lost. When that happens, you become useless, a hindrance to progress. When your feedback is interpreted as a personal attack rather than a critique with positive intentions, you are going backward.

Constructive criticism is a powerful instrument essential for improving performance. Positive support can be equally productive. Used together by a skilled leader they become the key to maximum results. Most of us seem to be more inclined to offer the negative. I don't know why, but it's easier to criticize than to compliment. Find the right mixture for optimum results.

Don't Beat Around the Bush (When Describing a Bush)

Former Cleveland and Cincinnati head coach Paul Brown taught me a lot during the eight years I worked for him as an assistant coach. Among his many talents was direct communication. He was clear, specific, and comprehensive without an ounce of ambiguity. I like his approach and recommend the same for you. Here's an example of how he insured that everyone was on the same page.

On the first day of each season's training camp, Brown would give a lecture to the squad that covered his own Standard of Performance—what he expected (demanded) in all areas. Of course, a leader's personal example is perhaps the most powerful teaching tool, but words have their own power and specificity.

Brown would start each season with the phrase, "Gentlemen, let's set the record straight," and then proceed to do exactly that. Step by step by step, specific after specific, he would cover every aspect of being on the Cincinnati Bengals football team.

He discussed how to wear the uniform, how to dress for meals, how each player was expected to keep his locker in order. He told players how he wanted them to respond to coaching, how to take notes during lectures, how teaching would be done, and what to expect from each assistant coach.

Brown covered such specifics as punctuality, the training-room rules, what would happen when players were waived (this always sent a chill through the group), and the overall environment he intended to create. Furthermore, he shared his policy of treating each player—stars, backups, veterans, rookies, free agents—equally, with the same high level of respect and dignity.

Each year his lecture, and this was only a sampling of topics, lasted about four hours (and voluminous printed material supplemented the lecture). Paul Brown was thorough enough that when the Bengals personnel left the meeting room they knew precisely what they were supposed to do in the coming weeks and that their head coach expected them to enthusiastically adhere to every procedure, policy, and timetable he had specified.

Needless to say, he continued with this kind of direct and clear communication in the months that followed—in practice, during games, and elsewhere.

What he laid out was measurable. And he measured it on a regular basis—his version of your company's year-end review. (You will note that I included some of Brown's material in my own Standard of Performance and expanded greatly on it. Like Paul Brown, I attempted to be clear, specific, and direct in putting forth my own requirements concerning actions and attitude.)

Vince Lombardi had a similar appreciation for the benefits of direct—specific—communication. Supposedly, he started each season's training camp by assembling the team and announcing, as he held it over his head, "Gentlemen, *this* is a football." That's how Vince began his introduction of the fundamentals of his particular system, with clear communication. Both Brown and Lombardi understood the necessity of spelling out in detail what you expect from employees and doing it in a manner that is unambiguous and comprehensive.

It is an important element in why these great coaches succeeded. Employees can thrive in an environment where they know *exactly* what is expected of them—even when those expectations are very high.

When it comes to telling people what you expect from them, don't be subtle, don't be coy, don't be vague. What is your version of, "Gentlemen, *this* is a football"?

Don't Mistake Grabbin' for Tackling

There's another story about Vince Lombardi worth mentioning because it points out a high-priority responsibility of any leader. During a game in which his Green Bay Packers were giving up one gain after another, as the opponent marched down the field, he screamed out at his defensive players, "Grabbin', grabbin', grabbin'! Nobody's tackling!!! What the hell is going on out there?"

Lombardi could see that his defensive players were not getting it done, were not really doing the hard job of *tackling* runners. He let them know that "grabbin'" was not their job description and simply going through the motions was going to get them beat.

A leader must know when his team is making a lot of noise signifying nothing. UCLA's coach John Wooden summed it up like this: "Don't mistake activity for achievement." (John Wooden, *Wooden on Leadership*.) Lombardi was more graphic in his language but was addressing the same issue.

Communication Creates Collaboration: Big Ears Are Better Than Big Egos

In an earlier time, leadership—most visibly in sports, but also commonly in business—required no greater people skills than those of a blunt-force object. Ohio State's Woody Hayes, Alabama's Bear Bryant, and Green Bay's Vince Lombardi all enjoyed their image as hard taskmasters whose primary people skills appeared to be intimidation and humiliation.

Henry Jordan, one of Vince's top players, reportedly said, only partially in jest, "When Coach Lombardi says, 'Sit down,' I don't look for a chair." (When asked if Lombardi gave his stars special treatment, Jordan replied, "No. He treats us all the same—like dogs.") Leadership in sports and business has generally moved away from this forceful, heavy-handed approach, although there are still plenty of examples of it—some very successful, in fact.

While leadership still involves occasionally using a heavy-handed approach—"my way or the highway"—collaboration is required more than ever these days to obtain optimal results. These results only occur when you are able to bring out the full potential of your personnel. Quality collaboration is only possible in the presence of quality communication; that is, the free-flowing and robust exchange of information, ideas, and opinions. And "having big ears"—the skill of being a great listener— is the first law of good communication. (The second law is "When you're not listening, ask good questions.")

For me it meant I had to set aside certain aspects of my own ego— e.g., talking too much—and really listen to what talented individuals in the organization had to say. I had to learn that communication is not a one-way street; it's a two-way, three-way, every-way street. This is a challenge for some of us to put into practice, because it's usually a hell of a lot easier to tell somebody what to do than to listen to his or her suggestions and ideas (especially when you think that you have all the answers on a wide range of subjects).

As a group, I wanted each of us to be as interested in finding out what others thought as in telling others what *we* thought. (Of course, I also didn't want a staff made up of talented people who just sat there *listening* all the time.)

At 49er staff meetings everyone understood they were expected to participate, communicate, and collaborate, to be part of the discussion regardless of the topic being addressed. I would go around the conference table seeking input from each coach, scout, and executive. If someone said, "That's not something I'm familiar with, Bill," I told them firmly, "Talk to somebody who can get you familiar with it." (Among other things, this had the added advantage of keeping everyone on their toes and tuned in. They never knew when I would solicit their opinion on something.)

An individual doesn't need to be an expert to ask an intelligent question or offer useful insights. A sentence beginning with the words "This may sound dumb, but . . ." can be the start of a fruitful discussion if you've hired talented and intelligent people. The person most familiar with a topic—you, for example—can get myopic, in need of an outside perspective.

I also knew that fear of being shunted aside or told, "That's a stupid question," keeps valid questions from being asked. Rarely was anyone working with me derided for their inquiries or opinions. (Of course, by hiring smart people I eliminated the vast majority of dumb questions.)

Nor did I ever want staff members or others to have cause to say, "Hey, nobody listens to me," just because their idea or suggestion wasn't used. Communication means people will disagree—strongly at times—but they must understand that disagreement should not fester. "Get a cup of coffee, put your arm around the shoulder of the person you're bumping heads with, and say, 'Let's talk about this,'" was my directive. "You're not always right, nor is the other person. Sometimes you're both wrong. Sometimes there are three sides to a coin." I wanted to work with people smart enough to have independent thinking but strong enough to change their opinion when evidence or logic suggested it.

Communication is complex. It's not just the King's English. Body language, gender connection, age connection, role connection, affluence and wealth connection, receiving or taking directions, and the state of mind of one person or another are all elements in communicating with someone.

It's not just being able to talk back and forth. It's recognizing when to say it, how to say it, when to listen, whom you're talking with, how they feel, what you're trying to get down to, how important the circumstance is, what the necessity is timewise, and how rapidly the decision must be made.

These are complex skills you must possess as part of your own basic Standard of Performance that is part of your leadership inventory. While a healthy ego is crucial in leadership, it turns unhealthy when self-confidence becomes arrogance, assertiveness becomes obstinacy, and self-assurance becomes reckless abandon. This is manifested when communication from leadership amounts to "Shut up and listen"—when your ego gets bigger than your ears.

Ironically, a big display of ego is sometimes hiding insecurity or lack of confidence. That kind of individual is overly protective of his or her turf or attempting to establish position in the pecking order by making others conform to his or her wishes. This, of course, reduces or removes creative vitality and collaboration.

If you are uncomfortable walking around your team's workplace, awkward and out of place, you are a disconnected leader—not really part of the team. Sitting in your office with the door closed and issuing edicts from on high is not communication, and is certainly not collaborative leadership.

You should be willing to go to someone's office or desk and help him or her do his or her job. You want to be able to facilitate what people are doing when necessary. The 49ers coaching staff—including me—was not hidden away like a secret cabal that was seen only occasionally. Among many other things, at least once a week each coach spent his lunch hour in the locker room with the team. Eating a tuna fish sandwich and drinking a Pepsi next to players was an unassuming way to break down barriers and facilitate organizational familiarity, which facilitates better interaction. Your can also learn a lot while eating your sandwich.

(Obviously, there was also constant interaction every minute during practice and at other times during the day, but often it was in the context of preparation or planning. Not informal, casual "How's the family?"-style interaction.)

This was similar in a way to the approach of Dave Packard and Bill Hewlett, founders of Hewlett-Packard and charter members of Silicon Valley. They called it "management by walking around." Both men were constantly circulating and talking with their employees in the labs, production areas, and research facilities, recognizing that personal communication was often necessary to back up written instructions.

Dave and Bill were not alone in this approach. Silicon Valley has many billion-dollar companies whose CEO will work directly with a maintenance person when it's important, or sit down momentarily with middle managers and help them do their job. There is no stratification or pecking order where they try to figure out where everybody fits socially. There just isn't room for a hierarchy.

Jack Welch, former CEO of General Electric, called it "boundaryless" communication and worked hard to remove barriers to the flow of information within the corporation. Everybody is in the loop and expected to participate.

As a former boxer, I'd suggest that if your left hand doesn't know what your right hand is doing, you'll get knocked out. Your right hook must be in sync with your left jab. For this to occur, your brain must communicate so your hands can collaborate. The same principle applies in business and in sports.

Be a King Without a Crown

Even though I had virtually complete autonomy through most of my ten years as head coach of the 49ers, I was never called *Coach* Walsh. In fact, everyone in the organization was addressed by their first name, including me. I wanted no barriers such as rank or title to clog up productive interaction, no chain of command to produce a sense that instead of a real team we were just a collection of isolated individuals on a totem pole of power belonging to small independent units.

Rank, titles, or inferred status can impede open communication in an environment where people thrive on helping one another. Here's just one small instance that demonstrates how the absence of such barriers manifested itself in our organization.

At halftime during a midseason game with the New Orleans Saints, I told our offensive team that if we got near the Saints' thirty-yard line I was going to call a specific pass play that I'd been saving for the situation. Sure enough, early in the third quarter we got to the Saints' twenty-seven-yard line, but in the heat of the moment I forgot about the play I'd promised in the locker room to use.

Steve Young, our backup quarterback, who was standing close by, immediately leaned over and reminded me of what I had said earlier. I listened; we scored. (This example demonstrates two important points: (1) Young understood and practiced communication and collaboration. He felt free to speak up even though it might be embarrassing to me since in the heat of the moment I had completely forgotten what I said earlier, and (2) Steve was selfless, team first, in bringing forth information that his "rival" quarterback, Joe Montana, would use successfully.)

I wanted no separate divisions where people felt that the only thing that mattered was their specific area of responsibility, that somehow their welfare was separate from that of the rest of us. Steve was like that—a team player.

Thus, the defensive coordinator understood that doing his job was not all that mattered—that the welfare of the offense was not somehow another island of no concern to him. Everyone understood the only welfare that mattered was the organization's. If our ship sank, we all drowned.

For that to happen—for individuals to merge their own interests with those of the team—good communication must exist in an open atmosphere where intellectual interaction is a given.

Former UCLA basketball coach John Wooden has always urged, "Be more concerned with finding the right way than in having it your way." When you reach the point where someone in your organization comes up with an idea better than the one you've been extolling for weeks or months and it makes you happy, you're an authentic communicator and collaborator.

A leader who just wants to hear "yes" is like a child who only wants to eat candy. Soon the youngster's teeth are gone. Likewise, a leader who wants people standing in line to agree with him or her will soon be history, having sailed into the sunset as captain of the ship of fools.

This involves setting aside your ego, resisting the temptation to let the world know how smart you are or *think* you are. If you're doing your job, the team will recognize your abilities. In turn, you must recognize their talent and bring forth their potential in a collaborative way.

A sales manager who resists input from his or her sales team automatically limits its potential; a manager who holds forth at the conference table might as well be sitting there alone; a football coach with small ears and a big ego will soon be watching the game on television at home instead of from the sidelines.

"Listen and learn" isn't a bad motto; neither is "Listen and lead." In most organizations the leader's example sets the tone for everyone else. One of the greatest and most neglected skills in leadership is the ability to listen. If someone told me that leadership is as easy as one, two, three, I'd reply, "Only if the one, two, and three are as follows:

1. Listen
2. Learn
3. Lead"

Fourteen of the assistant coaches who worked with me at San Francisco went on to head coaching jobs in the NFL or at the college level. I believe a big part of the reason for this extraordinary upward mobility was that they were fully included in the communication and collaborative decision-making process during their tenures with me. They were also good listeners.

They did well because our organization valued communication and collaboration; I did well for the same reason. Everybody can be a winner when "Be a Good Listener" is at the top of your leadership mission statement. Good collaboration begins with big ears.

Create Uncertainty

Great leaders are not necessarily predictable people. One of the best I've ever known is Pete Newell, who for many years was head basketball coach at the University of California–Berkeley. Among other things, his team won the national championship—March Madness—in 1959, and he was later voted Coach of the Year. His teams were consistently competitive, well taught, and among the nation's best.

Coach Newell did lots of things right, but I was particularly intrigued by his ability to keep individuals sharp and on their toes—to keep them from falling into a mental comfort zone, which can occur when the person in charge becomes too predictable. This comfort zone is dangerous because it creates an often almost imperceptible lowering of intensity, focus, and energy, which leads directly to reduced effort, additional mistakes, and diminished performance.

Watching Pete's Golden Bears during practices at their gym in Berkeley, I saw that he could suddenly become very worked up, severe, and critical—lashing out without warning or apparent cause. He would spot some minor miscue, and suddenly *everything* would change. It was something to witness—out of the blue, lightning and thunder from Newell over seemingly nothing situations.

And then just as quickly—usually, but not always—his verbal and emotional squall would pass. When he had addressed the little "issue" that had set him off, Pete would become lighthearted and even engage in humor as the practice resumed. But it was evident the players were now on edge and would subsequently ebb and flow with his demeanor, attitude, and emotions—looking to him for a response and reacting to his behavior. *He* was the focal point the others responded to.

Of course, the little "issue" that had set him off—for example, a pass that he declared not crisp—was often an excuse to fix the larger concern, which was usually the level, or lack thereof, of intensity, energy, and attention.

Players were kept on their toes because Pete Newell was somewhat unpredictable. They knew that a toughness lurked within and that he was willing and able to bring it forth if he felt it necessary. It kept them on their toes.

Effective leaders often have this quality. They understand that if you're *predictably* difficult or *predictably* easygoing, others become *predictably* comfortable. In a highly competitive environment, feeling comfortable is first cousin to being complacent.

Personally, when I sensed from time to time that our team or staff was getting comfortable, I wasn't afraid to exercise whatever acting skills I could summon. During a practice that was lacking high energy and laser-like focus, I might suddenly just let my emotions boil over, throw down my clipboard, chew out an assistant coach (they knew what I was up to), and exhibit the emotions and language I'd seen Pete Newell display so effectively: "I can't take this anymore! We've got to pick it up or I'm gonna make some changes here, because *this* has got to stop!" The players didn't even know what "this" was. It didn't matter.

What I was doing in that instance was for effect, something to shatter their comfort zones. Having jarred their attention, given them a jolt, I'd get right back to business. Rarely would I get personal or do any damage. It was a somewhat contrived outburst that served like the snarl of a tiger when you get too close to its cage. Used sparingly, it is an effective leadership tool.

The people around you must feel somewhat on edge with you at times because they know there's another side of your personality—ill at ease because they don't always know what to expect and have come to understand there's a toughness within you. Ideally, those you lead are driven to excel by the expertise, example, inspiration, and motivation you offer— the Standard of Performance you define and personify—but sometimes you have to snarl to remind them of the consequences of straying from your standards.

This is part of the tough (at times severe) side of leadership necessary to eliminate a comfort zone, which can creep into an organization and keep it from pushing on to higher and higher levels. One of the tools I used to accomplish this was to emulate Pete Newell—to shake things up with a somewhat contrived show of temper that comes from nowhere and disappears just as quickly.

There are times, of course, when a snarl must be replaced with a bite, when you are not acting, but instead taking serious action. One year during practice at our training camp in Rocklin, California, a rookie lineman, a muscular and swaggering guy trying out for the squad, broke through the offensive line and got to Joe Montana. At that point, he knew what to do, namely, nothing. You do not make contact with our quarterback during practice drills or plays.

This fellow didn't follow the rule. Apparently to show us what a great tackler he was—or maybe he was just stupid—he proceeded to deck Joe with a vicious hit. It's not overstating it to say this guy put our whole season on the line for an instant. I fired him right there, before Joe even got back up on his feet. "Get that son of a bitch out of here," I yelled at an assistant coach. "Right now. Don't even let that son of a bitch take a shower!"

Sometimes you snarl; sometimes you bite; sometimes you smile and give a thumbs-up. There's a little bit of the actor in all good leaders.

Play with Poise

Leadership requires poise under pressure. An organization that witnesses its leader at loose ends when troubles arise will look elsewhere for strength and direction. Knowing in advance what I would do in various situations—for example, scripting a game—was insurance that I could stay poised when it counted. Here's a good example of how it stabilized my thinking and behavior in a high-pressure, pivotal game that was played under arctic conditions and afforded the winner a trip to the Super Bowl.

The 49ers had arrived in Chicago during an arctic cold-snap to face the Bears at Soldier Field in a game that would decide the NFC championship. Local fans and media had started proclaiming the Bears "the Team of Destiny" because, after preseason media reports suggesting the team was fading, they had gone 12–4 during the regular season.

Having won Super Bowl XX three years earlier, they were now a game away from a return trip, and Chicago had begun to celebrate early. Why? Because their opponents were coming in from the West Coast, meaning they were "wine-sipping, Brie-eating, effete athletes," as one popular Midwest image of the 49ers had it. Adding substance to that characterization was our tough 10–9 midseason loss to the Bears in a game at Chicago.

During the warm-up in freezing conditions, Chicago's big and seemingly less intelligent linemen were parading around in short shirtsleeves and strutting their stuff like tough guys. Some of the 49ers looked over and wondered, "What's wrong with them? They're gonna freeze to death." But the posturing continued, a little psychology to intimidate or embarrass us. (The previous season, in San Francisco, the Bears had lost to the 49ers 41–0. Immediately after the final gun, Mike Ditka, a tempestuous, in-your-face coach, had reacted to our cheering fans by hurling his gum into the stands on his way to the locker room. Of course, he got three hundred pieces of gum thrown right back at him. Somebody even filed assault charges for being hit by Ditka's wad of gum. The Chicago media, of course, played this up in the days before our NFC championship game.)

Now I was in Chicago with their screaming fans, the wind howling with a twenty-six-below-zero windchill and the entire season at stake. In addition to all the play-off pressure and other distractions, there was this: Right behind our bench was a Cyclone fence holding spectators back. Standing at the fence was an inebriated Bears fan with a big megaphone that could have called across the Great Lakes. The guy had picked his spot carefully, because his plan was to ride me mercilessly during the game.

Before it even started, he was shouting through his megaphone, with the volume turned up, about my anatomy, which he decided was not adequate for most males. He questioned my sexual preferences, with accompanying speculation. This went on and on—really crude stuff, but as the game progressed and it got colder and colder, his mouth began to freeze up. He'd try to say, "Walsh, you've got a big fat a-a-a-a-a-sssssss," until finally he couldn't even talk any more. You would think I could tune out somebody like that, but it's tough. It was just another factor that could easily have interfered with my focus and decision-making abilities. It didn't.

We had a well-designed game plan with thorough contingency options that were right in front of me on my clipboard. We stuck to the plans, because there was no way I could consistently make intelligent and rational decisions with the freezing wind, the noise, the cold, the megaphone man, the Bears' great team, and sixty-seven thousand fans bearing down on us.

We won 28–3, and I defy anyone to think they're so strong, so able, so gifted they can make clear-cut *good* decisions in the middle of that kind of pandemonium under that kind of stress.

The San Francisco 49ers had talent and were well schooled. Neither matters if the person in charge falters or fails when it matters most. Having a clear idea of what your options are—situational planning—helps you be a leader when leadership is required.

Two weeks later, we won Super Bowl XXIII.

Teaching Defines Your Leadership

People say there are winners and losers in life. But typically, it's more like this: There are winners, and there are people who would *like* to be winners but just don't know how to do it. Intelligent and talented people who are motivated can learn how to become winners if they have someone who will teach them.

Leadership, at its best, is exactly that: teaching skills, attitudes, and goals (yes, goals are both defined and taught) to individuals who are part of your organization. Most things in life require good teaching—raising a family and educating children, running a company or sales team, or coaching athletes—so it's unfortunate that more people don't spend the time and thought required to do it effectively.

I was fortunate in this area, because I learned through the observation and study of tremendous teachers. Consequently, when I look back on my years as an assistant coach and head coach, what gives me great satisfaction is not necessarily a Super Bowl championship or an award, but the experience of recognizing ability in a person and then teaching that individual how to reach his potential in ways that helped our team.

That process—seeing someone I had evaluated, selected, and taught break out and do great things—is what it's really all about for me, the source of my greatest pleasure in leadership. In my experience, this is what it takes to be a good teacher: passion, expertise, communication, and persistence.

1. Passion is not just having a desire to do the job of teaching.

Passion is a love for the act of teaching itself—believing in your heart that it is not a means to an end, but an end in itself. In order to have passion, you must love the topic you teach. My love of football and teaching it is so strong that when I was a coach it became hard to shut my mind off and think about something else.

I might be half asleep or dreaming, or talking to someone, and my mind would drift away from the conversation and a play would take shape in my mind. I could see all twenty-two players moving in response to what I had drawn up.

Diagrams of plays kept flowing through my head—the *X*'s and *O*'s, the lines and arrows going through my mind constantly, like a computer's screen saver where the objects keep changing shape and moving around.

Once during a get-together with friends, I was sitting on a couch in front of the fireplace with my arm around my wife, Geri. Unconsciously I began diagramming a passing play on her shoulder with my index finger while carrying on a conversation with someone across the room.

After a while, Geri looked at me and asked, "Honey, did it score a touchdown?" I didn't know what she was talking about until she told me; I didn't know I had been drawing a play on her arm with my finger. That's how much I love it; that's how much you need to love teaching your team. It is not a duty or burden that you get out of the way so you can move on to "important" things. It *is* the important thing.

For me it was a fundamental source of personal joy. I was consumed by the process of developing the abilities of others. You do it because you really care for it; you do it because you have to.

2. Expertise is the inventory of knowledge and experience you possess on a particular subject.

You're not necessarily born with it; you develop it, research it, thrive on learning as much about your subject as you possibly can.

The greater your expertise, the greater your potential to teach, the stronger and more productive you can be as a leader. Without it you are disabled and will garner less and less respect from your team because they will sense that you're not on top of things, let alone able to teach them something meaningful. People know when you don't have the answers.

Here's a good rule of thumb: "The more you know, the higher you go." To advance in any profession, I believe it is imperative to understand all aspects of that profession, not just one particular area: Only *expertise* makes you an expert.

When assistant coaches approach me and ask, "Bill, what is the best route to getting a head coaching position?" I tell them they must expand their base of knowledge and develop their inventory of skills and proficiencies in all phases of the job: "You may be an offensive coordinator and making more money than your offensive line coach who's reporting to you, but unless *you* know offensive line coaching, he's the de facto offensive coordinator. He determines your fate, because he knows more than you do."

Your team will sense it, that you are not as knowledgeable in what you do as you should be. They will sense that you don't have the answers, that you lack a strong understanding of the "how" of doing things. When this occurs, they will not follow you.

A teacher gains expertise by seeking out great teachers, mentors, and other sources of information and wisdom in a relentless effort to add to his or her own knowledge. My teachers—outstanding in their own particular ways—included John Ralston at Stanford; Al Davis at Oakland (and by default, the great Sid Gillman under whom Al had served in San Diego with the Chargers); the Bengals' Paul Brown; Tommy Prothro of the San Diego Chargers; Bob Bronzan, my coach at San Jose State, where I was a wide receiver; and others who showed me the value of teaching and how to do it. (In business this means *actively* seeking the counsel of those you respect in your profession, as well as studying printed material and publications that you determine will provide pertinent input.)

3. Communication is the ability to organize and then successfully convey your informed thoughts.

Many mistakenly believe that just presenting facts—information—is teaching. Successful teaching is a two-way process. Just as a pass is not successful until the receiver catches it, successful teaching requires reception, retention, and comprehension of your message. Some teach by word, others by deed—their example is the teacher. The best teaching uses both forms of communication, word and deed. And in all situations, enthusiasm for the subject matter is what powers the communication connection to those you teach.

I have spent literally thousands of hours in front of an overhead projector diagramming and explaining plays to a bunch of easily bored athletes sitting on hard metal chairs and taking notes in a dimly lit room with bad ventilation. This can get dull fast, even if you're the player in the diagram who's going to be carrying the ball for a touchdown.

To me, the intricacies and potential of each individual play were exciting; each one was like a ten-thousand-dollar Rolex watch with unique, highly crafted, and precision-made features that I cherished. I wanted to convey my sincere enthusiasm and real excitement to the players.

I did it with facial and body language—moving assuredly and with energy, rubbing my hands together as if I were savoring a fine meal. And I did it with an enthusiastic tone of voice and positive words. The goal was to get the team as enthusiastic and excited as I was about the play's potential. I couldn't do it by reciting information as if I were reading from a phone book.

Here is a list of descriptions I used to set up and create excitement for seven different plays during a presentation in preparation for a game with the Dallas Cowboys:

- "Guys, this one should knock 'em on their asses!"
- "Now, here's one I think is almost *perfect* for us."
- "I think we're gonna have some *fun* with this one. It's a beauty!"
- "Fellas, this next one should *score*. No question about it."
- "Here's one play that is really just *excellent*. Forget excellent. It's *better* than excellent."
- "*This* one will work just great. You'll see why right now."
- "Oh, *boy*, this is terrific. Just look at what this one does!"

Bang! Bang! Bang! Bang! Each one was something special, with its own special introduction and personality. Other teams might use just a number to identify a play. My plays were never just numbers to me, and I didn't want them to be just numbers to our team. They were distinct entities with personality, character, and potential of their own. Never a number. They were my children, and I bragged about them like a proud parent.

After presenting the details of a specific play, I'd repeat a variation of my opening observation: "I'm telling you, we could have a five-hundred-yard day!" or, "Wait'll they see this one coming. They won't know what hit 'em!" I started and finished my description with nothing but optimism, *enthusiasm*, and belief. Never a caveat, no "ifs," no hesitancy.

My body language and positive words were never contrived, phony, or overdone. I genuinely had great affection—love, in fact—for what I was teaching. But *X*'s and *O*'s, squiggly lines, and squares and circles with arrows pointing in various directions can be boring, even deadening when presented without energy and enthusiasm. I wanted to convey to the team that what I was offering them was alive, that it had magic in it. I made sure my demeanor conveyed that; I showed them I really cared. You must do the same if you want to light a fire in those you lead.

Your enthusiasm becomes their enthusiasm; your lukewarm presentation becomes their lukewarm interest in what you're offering.

I came to understand over my years as an assistant coach that when the audience is bored, it's not their fault. And when they're plugged in and excited, it's because of you, the person in charge.

4. Persistence is essential because knowledge is rarely imparted on the first attempt.

One of the keys to successfully executing the complexities of the West Coast Offense was my devotion to the principle of persistence.

We did the same drills over and over again; I said essentially the same thing over and over, discussed the same information, concepts, and principles over and over. Gradually, my teaching stuck. Eventually, successful execution became almost automatic, even under extreme duress, because like air, my teaching was everywhere.

While passion, expertise, communication, and persistence are the four essentials of good teaching and learning, I would also add these nuts-and-bolts practices to facilitate what you do as a leader who is a great teacher:

1. **Use straightforward language.** No need to get fancy.
2. **Be concise.** For many leaders it's harder to be brief than to be long-winded. We love to hear ourselves talk.

3. **Account for a wide range of difference in knowledge, experience, and comprehension among members of your organization.** For me it could be seen in the way I communicated one on one with an experienced superstar such as Jerry Rice or a first-year offensive guard who was learning the ropes of our system. This difference in content depending on whom I was talking to and in what circumstance was always factored in to my teaching.

4. **Account for some members of the group being more receptive and ready to learn than others** (for reasons out of your control).

5. **Be observant during your comments.** Know if you're connecting.

6. **Strongly encourage note taking.**

7. **Employ a somewhat unpredictable presentation style.** "Droning on" is the most common style, and you may have to work on stepping it up so that you don't fall into the "drone trap."

8. **Organize with logical, sequential building blocks in your communication.**

9. **Encourage appropriate audience participation.**

10. **Use visual aids.**

11. **Remember Sun-tzu: "With more sophistication comes more control."** The more you work at refining your teaching—increasing its sophistication—the greater your control of the teaching (and learning) process.

The Thrill of Teaching

Now that I've outlined my ideas about teaching, it should not surprise you to know that the most gratifying time of my life as a teacher was probably not with the San Francisco 49ers. It was much earlier, when I was with the Cincinnati Bengals, when I was personally responsible for teaching a wide assortment of skills and ideas to a diverse group of individuals—quarterbacks, wide receivers, tight ends—and creating and implementing the passing game. And I did this all without the great responsibilities that come with being a head coach, with the "distractions" that took me away from teaching.

During practice at Cincinnati, I would devote a specific amount of time exclusively to the wide receivers, at other times just the quarterbacks, then the entire offense; later I would work alone on offensive schemes and then teach them to others. I was always teaching or thinking about how to be more effective as a teacher.

Today four different coaches would be hired to handle these jobs, but I was lucky in being able to do them all—no administrative duties, no executive responsibilities, no financial issues as I assumed with the 49ers. Just plain, old-fashioned teaching. I was a kid in a candy store and loved it all—every single minute of it.

When my results were productive, it was even more satisfying—Bruce Coslet became an outstanding tight end and later head coach of the Cincinnati Bengals; Bob Trumpy became an All-Pro tight end; Chip Myers, Isaac Curtis, and Charlie Joiner were All-Pro wide receivers; Virgil Carter maximized his quarterbacking skills, Ken Anderson led the NFL in passing and was an MVP. But the deepest satisfaction was in the process of teaching itself. Witnessing the evolution of their abilities and seeing it applied in the context of our organization—and on the field during games—was the source of great gratification.

That Cincinnati experience was as much fun as I've ever had in football, maybe as gratifying as Super Bowl championships or financial rewards, because I had the opportunity to do more hands-on teaching than I did later on. It was just great fun. Although before the pressure and huge expectations got built up, the 49ers' experience in the first few years was thrilling too. Both were so fulfilling for the same reason—teaching, helping people achieve higher and higher levels of performance in the context of competing (and often prevailing) in my profession. I suppose you could conclude that for me the process of getting to the top was much more gratifying in many ways than the process of trying to stay on top.

Interesting enough, many executives have told me they experience the same pleasure in developing and advancing the skills of their own employees. Companies led by good teachers, those with passion, expertise, communication skills, and persistence, do very well.

Looking back, perhaps the lesson I would draw is this: If you don't love it, don't do it. I loved it—teaching people how to reach in deep to fulfill their potential, how to become great. And when you do that with a group, you, as the leader, enjoy the thrill of creating a great team. For me it was like creating a work of art. Only instead of painting on a canvas, I had the great joy of creating in collaboration with others.

The House Cleaner

Bill McPherson, Assistant Coach, San Francisco 49ers

Starting day one as head coach and general manager of the San Francisco 49ers, Bill Walsh came in and started cleaning out the building of people—fired everybody that he could fire, like assistant coaches, staff, and office personnel. He couldn't fire the players all at once, but he was quick to start getting rid of them, too, the ones who didn't meet his performance or attitude standards.

Within two years, much of the team he had inherited was gone. The Super Bowl champions his third year only had a few of the original holdovers. He had cleaned house.

One coach he kept on from the prior administration, Mike White, he knew from when they had been assistant coaches together, and Bill liked his expertise and attitude. But there weren't many, hardly any at all. He wanted people in his new organization who did it his way, and believe me, he had a crystal clear concept of what "his way" was.

I knew Bill going back further than anybody in the organization when he hired me that first year—back to his days coaching football at Washington High School, and before that when I had seen him as a boxer.

Later, I was an assistant coach at Santa Clara College and he was coaching a semipro team called the San Jose Apaches. They were such a low-budget operation they didn't even have their own football field to practice on—they worked out at nearby Wilcox High School. In fact, they didn't even have their own projector to watch game film on. Bill would come over to Santa Clara College and use ours and while he was there basically give us his "chalk talks," just casually explain his philosophy when it came to football. It was evident that his mind was extraordinary. He was a mismatch for the ragtag team he was in charge of—like a Formula 1 race car on a dirt track.

Nevertheless, I was surprised years later, when we began to work together at San Francisco, to see how comprehensive his knowledge was. He just had the whole thing thought out in his mind. Those staff meetings were really something, because it was apparent he knew exactly, precisely, what he wanted to do, which included exactly what he wanted *us* to do. And to make sure we did it, he gave us his big red binder playbook with all of his complex formations in it.

But it wasn't like any regular playbook I'd ever seen. He had gone out and had it printed up almost like a textbook; routes and *X*'s and *O*'s were neat and clean—*professional*, not hand drawn and messy. Nobody had done it like that before. That's what characterized everything Bill Walsh did: professionalism, first class.

Bill liked order. If he walked into an office and saw a picture hanging crooked, he'd go over and straighten it. That sounds silly, but it goes to his desire for precision in how things looked and were done—a picture on the wall had to be exactly right, and a play on the field had to be exactly right.

That same attitude applied to media relations and the message the media got from the 49ers organization. One man gave the media the message: Bill Walsh. The coaches who worked with him were not supposed to talk to reporters about the team. Bill did that; Bill controlled the output of information to the media.

He was a master at making us feel that we were persecuted by the outside world—discounted or ridiculed. Bill had a hundred different ways to get the team cranked up about having to *prove* to the media or other teams that they were wrong to dismiss us.

He didn't like showboating or anything that suggested somebody was better than anybody else in his organization. Mutual respect among all employees was big for him, and boy, if he saw evidence to the contrary, he'd go off. One of his assistant coaches owned a Corvette with a personalized license plate that drew attention to himself—that this guy was a coach with the 49ers, which suggested, "I'm a big shot."

Right away Bill spotted it in our parking lot, and that night during our coaches' meeting, he lit into it: "Somebody in this room has a red Corvette with a stupid license plate on it. I want the #@*!*% license plate off that car before you come in here to work tomorrow." He was livid. "Whoa," I thought to myself, "this guy is tough." Of course, that's what Bill wanted me and the other coaches to think.

He was a great motivator because he had such a grasp of all the techniques to keep individuals plugged in and paying attention. He could really read a room—he'd love you up, but then, if you screwed up, watch out. You were always on a short string, on the edge of your chair, because he kept you guessing. He could turn it on and turn it off at exactly the right times. We were nervous about getting too happy and even more nervous about getting down in the dumps, because we knew Bill would tolerate neither.

He'd say to us coaches, "I'm going to yell at you in front of the players once in awhile. When that happens, don't get upset with me. Your players will work even harder for you because they'll feel sorry for you." Bill used that one in training camp. However, most of the time he wasn't doing it for effect.

I remember him spotting an assistant coach allowing a slant pattern to be run just a little bit off the exact route Bill had designed. It was just a few inches off, but from the other side of the field he saw it and started running all the way across the practice field, shouting to do it right.

Bill would get incensed if you messed with his plays. He knew they would work, but only if they were done exactly right. That's why it was so important to him when he began hiring his assistant coaches at San Francisco that we be good teachers. He wanted things taught properly—his offense, of course, but then the defense, the special teams, the staff responsibilities. I think he felt those plays he was designing were very special, like a new invention that was guaranteed to work, but they wouldn't work unless the coaches were good teachers.

He didn't want puppets, however, guys just taking orders. He would even throw out some radical schemes on plays for us to consider, just to shake up our thinking. He wanted input, but once the decision was made, he wanted it carried out precisely.

Bill would be there at practice with three-by-five cards and one of those little golf pencils in his back pocket. If he pulled out a three-by-five card and starting writing, you just hoped it wasn't about something you'd done wrong, because he'd let you know about it that night.

Bill raised the self-image of the organization. Players, for example, eventually had lockers with their pictures and names on them and plaques under their names listing any awards they had won—MVP, Pro Bowl, and others.

He had a brilliant mind coupled with a steel will. When it came to leadership, running the whole show, Bill was very strong—no question about who was in charge of things. But he had another side to him that was harder to understand. Several times during his ten years with the 49ers, he got so discouraged, depressed maybe, that he was on the verge of calling it quits, giving up.

After his fourth season, which was miserable, he instructed John McVay, vice president for football administration, to tell all of us coaches to go to the East-West Game and look for jobs. [Editor's note: The East-West Game was an all-star game with top college players that drew a large group of coaches from NFL teams.] Why? Bill was intent on quitting, and that meant we'd probably get fired by his replacement. He changed his mind, but a lot of us were asking around about jobs at that game.

Bill put so much into his coaching and leadership that he became drained emotionally over time. He never let down, even for a second, but I think the fun kind of went out of it for him after the second Super Bowl championship.

But through it all, you really wanted to fight for him. And we did.

PART IV

Essentials of a Winning Team: People, Priorities, and Performance

Money Talks. Treating People Right Talks Louder.

The most important attribute of any organization is the way it treats its people, its commitment to the individuals on the team. San Francisco owner Eddie DeBartolo insisted on a first-class operation—travel, accommodations, and more. He was willing to spend money and spent lots of it over the years. But money alone doesn't determine whether an organization is first class.

We had no money initially. What we had was an organizational philosophy, the internal culture I installed, which was first-class in its treatment and respect for people. From the first day I took over, we treated people right. More than money, that's what made the San Francisco 49ers a first-class organization internally. I had extremely high expectations—the Standard of Performance—of everyone on our payroll, but in return they could expect fair and decent treatment from me. And they got it.

Some critics claimed the 49ers won Super Bowl championships by spending exorbitantly on salaries and perks. Those critics ignore the fact that we won our first Super Bowl championship with the lowest salaries of any team in the entire NFL. As mentioned, my own pay as head coach and general manager—typically two separate jobs—was $160,000, and I had to fight to get that, even though it was at the bottom end of the salary scale for head coaches in the league.

In those earliest days, when I was building a team that would become highly competitive in just three years, it wasn't money talking; it was dedication, expertise, and intelligently applied effort. It was sacrifice and commitment to our people. In turn, I got the best those people had to give our organization.

Additionally, Eddie had a gift for connecting with players and staff and showed his appreciation and friendship in small ways that made a big impression—a birthday card to a player (or a player's child); a note of condolence when something bad happened to an employee; social events such as special dinners for staff members and their wives, who became football widows during the season because their husbands worked such ridiculous hours; personal contact with and a true interest in the lives of the people on his payroll.

Eddie spent big money along the way, but these smaller expressions told people in the organization, "You're part of a family here," and they responded. He was really good at that because he meant it. Money may buy you the best car in racing, but it won't go very far (or fast) unless you treat it right. The same goes for the individuals on your team. The highest-paid, most talented people that you can go out and hire will not perform to their potential unless they feel as if they are part of something special—a family that treats them right.

You're as Good as Your Good People

The bus carrying head coach Paul Brown and most of the team from the hotel to the stadium took a wrong turn and got lost. It became apparent that the guy behind the steering wheel didn't know what he was doing and was going around in circles. Brown was livid. He stormed up to the driver and barked: "Fella, I'm not mad at *you*. I'm mad at the SOB who hired you."

Brown understood organizational accountability—where the buck stops. He knew that an organization is only as good as the people who work there and that the leader determines who works there.

I came to appreciate and utilize this fact after an unusual situation developed soon after I joined San Francisco as head coach. Within hours, we began diligently looking for a new general manager—the guy largely responsible for determining "who works there." Unfortunately, nobody we wanted wanted us. Miami's George Young, Seattle's Dick Mansberger, and Baltimore's Ernie Accorsi were among those who perfunctorily turned me down when offered the job as 49er GM.

It dawned on me that San Francisco was Siberia in the eyes of knowledgeable executives and managers in the NFL. They viewed our dire situation as hopeless, worse than a new expansion team starting from scratch, simply unfixable in the foreseeable future. (I even offered George Young more money than he was making in Miami to come out west and run things for the 49ers.) We were getting nowhere.

Things took a new direction during a breakfast meeting with Eddie DeBartolo and his trusted aide, Carmen Policy. Out of the blue, Eddie suggested that since the turndowns were piling up we stop looking and that *I* take the job—be head coach as well as general manager. It was a somewhat unwelcome suggestion, because I felt my hands were full already. But it very quickly made sense: I'd be the one hiring *my* staff—the people who would decide *my* future and the future of *my* organization. I was disappointed that I hadn't come up with the idea myself.

I proceeded expeditiously to sign up proven talent—coaches and administrators, my staff—who were both attuned to my philosophy and compatible with my personality. After being turned down by everyone, I was suddenly hearing yes, yes, yes. Why? Simple. I offered jobs to outstanding people I had previously worked with or worked for or knew very well—the cream of the crop from a list of former associates in my contact book going back all the way, in one case, to my days as an amateur boxer. They knew and believed in me as much as I knew and believed in them. A general manager from the outside would not have been able to do this—more likely, he would have been hiring people from his own contact book, imposing his associates on me. It might have worked, but it would have been a long shot.

Each of these talented men accepted my job offer and came to San Francisco as a known and compatible quantity. There was mutual respect and understanding, and often a proven record of being able to work together. They hit the ground running, and two of them, Denny Green and Norb Hecker, didn't have far to run. Both were just a few miles down the freeway from the 49ers headquarters at 711 Nevada Street in Redwood City,

California. They began work immediately. (Another, George Seifert, an outstanding defensive coordinator when we worked together at Stanford, joined us in my second season with the 49ers.)

Thus, from early in my tenure at San Francisco, I was surrounded and supported by staff who didn't have to learn about me or my system. And vice versa.

It was a transforming experience; in the course of a few weeks I'd gone from casting about for a general manager who would come in with a steep learning curve about me—how and why I did things—to putting together a really excellent staff that was soon in sync.

As a result, there were no bad mis-hires and we were able to proceed right from the start almost as if we'd been working together successfully for years. And in a way, there was some truth to it. This, in large part, explains what some viewed as an inexplicable turnaround by San Francisco—from NFL doormats to the NFL's dominant team, champions—in so short a time. We had a first-rate, compatible staff in sync right from the start.

Nevertheless, even in a situation as ideal as this, you must expect differences in performance levels among staff members and recognize the necessity of getting and keeping them on the same page—*your* page—in their new environment.

Here are two short lists I created that address what I deem as essential traits in a staff member and the way I went about keeping them on the same page of their new book—the book called "The San Francisco 49ers: Bill Walsh, Head Coach, General Manager, Boss."

My checklist of personal qualities—assets—in potential staff members:

1. **A fundamental knowledge of the area he or she has been hired to manage.** You may think this is so self-evident it's insulting to include. However, often we are tempted to hire simply on the basis of friendship or other user-friendly characteristics. They can be important. Expertise is more important.

2. **A relatively high—but not manic—level of energy and enthusiasm and a personality that is upbeat, motivated, and animated.** Groups will often collectively take on the personality of their department head (e.g., in football, their

position coach). A negative, complaining staff member will be emulated by those he or she is in charge of. So will a positive go-getter.

3. **The ability to discern talent in potential employees** whom he or she will recommend to you.

4. **An ability to communicate** in a relaxed yet authoritative—but not authoritarian—manner.

5. **Unconditional loyalty to both you *and* other staff members.** If your staff members are chipping away at one another, the organization is weakened from within—like a tree full of termites. There is, in my view, no offense more serious than disloyalty.

My checklist for keeping good staff members on the same page:

1. **You must establish clear parameters for your staff regarding the overall method by which you expect things to be done.** They must be reminded—instructed, when necessary—of your Standard of Performance: philosophy, style and substance, strategies and tactics.

2. **Any philosophical differences that crop up must be identified and addressed by you in private meetings with the individual(s).** Sweeping them under the rug is misdirected management.

3. **You must recognize that staff members may work in different ways, using approaches that are at variance with yours.** This can be relatively inconsequential as long as you and the staff member are philosophically compatible on the key issues (e.g., attention to detail, exhibiting respect to all members of the organization). Insisting on a totalitarian, lockstep mentality removes creativity from within.

4. **To ensure unanimity throughout the staff, make unannounced visits to various department meetings.** You can lose elements of your team to a maverick staff member if you're invisible long enough.

5. **Don't cede inordinate power or control to a staff member**

simply because you are relieved to have an experienced and proven performer come on board. Assigning complete control without any monitoring of methods or means can allow a separate kingdom to develop, which will split your organization into factions.

6. **Sometimes a staff member may intentionally teach a philosophy that is at odds with your code of conduct, in the belief that it conforms to your philosophy.** He or she may also, on occasion, *unconsciously* revert to his or her own techniques or philosophy. This does not constitute insubordination until you have firmly pointed out the issue and the staff member continues to put forth ideas that are counter to what you want done. Then you must take corrective action that goes beyond a "reminder."

7. **Be alert for those staff members who seek to use their position to teach and express their *personal* beliefs.** Politics and religion are the two most common areas.

8. **Remember Mike Ditka's comment on leadership after his Bears won a Super Bowl championship:** "Personal contact is part of hands-on management. Go to the other guy's office; tell him what you have in mind so there is no misunderstanding."

The Over and Under: The Art of Managing Confidence

More people are more familiar with losing than with winning. Consequently, losing is not that difficult to deal with, in the sense that we've all faced it, lived it, and are familiar with the fallout it can produce. We have seen people lose heart, self-destruct, turn on one another, and become disloyal. We know the whole syndrome of losing, but leaders often don't think very much about the other side of the coin—winning; especially winning big.

As with losing, there is fallout from success, and many of the symptoms are the same. The only difference is that you go down with a smile on your face instead of a frown.

Our first Super Bowl championship team had forty-five dedicated and disciplined players on the roster. Soon afterward, and to varying degrees, eight of them self-destructed and ended their careers too early by mishandling their lives through drugs and alcohol, stupid lifestyles, and becoming consumed with themselves. A couple of them still can't cope with life. Many other good players and people on that team were also thrown off stride to varying degrees. Why? Because they *won* the Super Bowl; we were the world champions of football.

This response—being knocked off balance emotionally and mentally—is one of the fundamental reasons it is so difficult to continue winning; it's true in business as in sports. Repeat winners at the high end of competition are rare, because when success of any magnitude occurs, there is a disorienting change that we are unprepared for. I, too, was somewhat thrown off by our first Super Bowl victory. Having navigated through long losing streaks and losing seasons, having climbed to the top and led a team at the bottom of the barrel to a world championship, I had little knowledge of the new terrain.

How else can you explain that in the season immediately following that championship—Super Bowl XVI— and with virtually the same personnel, we lost twice as many games as we won in that strike-shortened season? The explanation is, in part, quite simple: Success Disease.

The second-richest man in America, Warren Buffett, says one of his biggest challenges is to help his top people—all wealthy beyond belief—stay interested enough to jump out of bed in the morning and work with all the enthusiasm they did when they were poor and just getting started.

Buffett is addressing that difficult situation of trying to motivate yourself or your team when you've become a winner. Success Disease—overconfidence is a major symptom—can happen in any profession and can be as difficult to remedy as underconfidence. Over- and underconfidence are an ongoing challenge in leadership.

When you reach a large goal or finally get to the top, the distractions and new assumptions can be dizzying. First comes heightened confidence, followed quickly by overconfidence, arrogance, and a sense that "we've mastered it; we've figured it out; we're golden." But the gold can tarnish quickly. Mastery requires *endless* remastery. In fact, I don't believe there is ever true mastery. It is a process, not a destination. That's what few winners realize and explains to some degree why repeating is so difficult. Having triumphed, winners come to believe that the process of mastery is concluded and that they are its proud new owners.

Success Disease makes people begin to forego to different degrees the effort, focus, discipline, teaching, teamwork, learning, and attention to detail that brought "mastery" and its progeny, success. The hunger is diminished, even removed in some people.

"Complacency" may be too strong a word to describe it, maybe not. Perhaps "contentment" describes it. You feel content after navigating up the hard and treacherous road to victory. This is understandable; you should feel satisfaction and contentment. But when it lingers—sets in— you and your team are suffering from Success Disease. It can create a lack of respect for the competition, a feeling of superiority, and an assumption that you can win at will, turn it on when it counts. The time to turn it on (and leave it on) is before it counts. In fact, my belief is that it counts *all* the time.

And, of course, when you couple contentment with underestimating the competition, you—all by yourself—have set yourself up for defeat. Imagine that.

There are specific actions I took based on the lessons learned after the 49ers' experience with Success Disease following our first Super Bowl championship. They are very effective, although there is no guarantee that in following them you will fend off the fallout from achievement; specifically, Success Disease:

1. **Formally celebrate and observe the momentous achievement—the victory—and make sure that everyone feels ownership in it.** Praise, bonuses, and other rewards can make it special. This is a unique opportunity to strengthen the bond everyone feels to your organization, especially the special role players who get less attention.
2. **Allow pats on the back for a limited time.** Then *formally* return to business as usual by letting everyone know the party

is over. Nevertheless, don't tighten down too far. Victory can produce enormous energy—so powerful and overwhelming that in sports grown men will burst out in tears and run around like little children at Christmas. You must channel that powerful force and enthusiasm into the work ahead to solidify and build on the gains made by your team in achieving their recent success. Make sure the power of your victory propels you forward in a controlled manner.

3. **Be apprehensive about applause.** Instruct your team on the pitfalls of listening to accolades from those outside (and even inside) the organization. The praise can become a hindrance to buckling down to the hard sacrifice that will be required ahead. Ongoing applause can turn the head of the most disciplined and determined member of your team. Watch that it doesn't turn your own head.

4. **Develop a plan for your staff that gets them back into the mode of operation that produced success in the first place.** Don't assume it will happen. Hold meetings to explain what steps must be taken to sustain momentum; refocus personnel by covering in detail why success was achieved; review with them *why* they prevailed.

5. **Address specific situations that need shoring up; focus on the mistakes that were made and things that were not up to snuff in the success.** Point out deficiencies and the need to find remedies for them.

6. **Be demanding.** *Do not relax.* Hold everyone to even higher expectations. Don't relax your Standard of Performance. The Standard of Performance is always in a state of refinement to raise performance. That's your gold standard, the point of reference above everything else, including the won-lost record, Super Bowl titles, shareholder value, quotas, sales, or praise from people who don't have to get down in the trenches with you and do the real work.

7. **Don't fall prey to overconfidence so that you feel you can or should make change for the sake of change.** Change is inevitable, but change is not a casual consideration. When

you're flush with victory, you can take on a mind-set that says, "Hey, let's try this!" Only in the most desperate situation is change made simply for the sake of change.

8. **Use the time immediately following success as an opportunity to make hard decisions,** including elevation or demotion of individuals who contributed—or didn't—to the victory. This window is brief. Use it.

9. **Never fall prey to the belief that getting to the top makes everything easy.** In fact, what it makes easier is the job of motivating those who want your spot at the top. Achievement, great success, puts a big bull's-eye on your back. You are now *the* target—clearly identified—for all your competitors to aim at.

10. **Recognize that mastery is a *process*, not a destination.**

When your organization achieves a significant goal, you must demonstrate the strongest and most demanding adherence to your own established ideals and principles—the Standard of Performance you abide by. This is essential, because if you fall prey to the consequences of winning, you will soon be dealing with the consequences of losing.

This, in my experience, is the reason it's tough to repeat, whether it's a regional or national sales contest or a number one position in a high-tech industry. It's one of the reasons only six teams in the history of the NFL have won the Super Bowl and then repeated by winning it again the next year. The San Francisco 49ers are among that small group of organizations that fought off Success Disease—if only for two years. That may not sound like much, but in the history of the Super Bowl, no team has been able to win three in a row. Success Disease is one of the reasons why.

When things are going best is when you have the opportunity to be the strongest, most demanding, and most effective in your leadership. A strong wind is at your back, but it requires an understanding of the perils produced by victory to prevent that wind from blowing you over.

The Under: Strive to Be a One-Point Underdog

It is extremely difficult to resist the debilitating temptations of Success Disease—to work even harder and smarter than before, to fend off over-confidence. Of course, you should allow for elation and celebration without letting it contaminate the future, but it takes some creativity and mental agility to *keep* your team focused when they are on top—when they are feeling full of themselves and invincible. Thus, when we faced an opponent the 49ers were expected to easily beat, I had to come up with some innovative reasoning as to why we could just as easily lose, why we should consider ourselves the underdog—ideally a one-point underdog.

For example, we faced Kansas City during a season in which the 49ers were defending Super Bowl champions, while the Chiefs had *lost* five consecutive games and were just getting worse and worse.

As we prepared for the mid-November game at Candlestick Park, I earnestly told our team, "Fellas, I'm afraid of these guys; I really am. The Chiefs are angry because they've been humiliated publicly and privately for over a month. Honestly, this is a very dangerous situation for us. They can put it all behind them by knocking us off. They can come out and just explode on us." I continued with this line of reasoning for many minutes.

Of course, everybody on the outside was telling our players the opposite—that Kansas City would just lie down. Having won Super Bowl XIX several months earlier, and in spite of a regular season that was far from stellar, some 49ers might have been inclined to listen and take a little breather and let up. That's when Success Disease insinuates itself into the organization. (In fact, it seemed to have already begun. After that 18–1 Super Bowl season, we were 5–5 going into the Kansas City game—perhaps the best 5–5 team in NFL history.)

It was always my goal to create and maintain a working environment both on and off the field that had a sense of urgency and intensity but did not feel like we were in constant crisis mode. Ideally, I wanted to instill in each member of our group the belief that, regardless of the opponent, we were a *one-point underdog,* that the upcoming team was just a little better than we were or had motivation enough to really raise their level of play—the Kansas City Chiefs, for example. I wanted our team to believe that we could win, but only if we worked hard. This was challenging when they were surrounded by evidence of how "great" they were—public adulation, acclaim, and Super Bowl rings and a trophy that were still fresh in their minds.

When you can instill the one-point-underdog attitude in both yourself and your organization, complacency and overconfidence are kept at bay. My ability to do that was one of the primary reasons San Francisco was focused during the week's preparation for Kansas City. We won 31–3, in part because I had temporarily immunized our team against Success Disease.

(My comments for that game, in fact, addressed two different attitudes that may have existed within the team. Some players were victims of Success Disease—overconfidence—because of the Super Bowl championship. Others may have started cashing out on the season because of our 5–5 won-lost record. Either way, cocky or cashing out, I needed to create a positive attitude adjustment and the one-point-underdog mentality was part of the solution.)

Nevertheless, the ongoing and ultimate safeguard against attitudes that are detrimental to the team is your dedication and monumental adherence to the Standard of Performance you have created. This is always the way to win, the road to a goal even more elusive than success; namely, *consistent* success.

Seek Character. Beware Characters.

Cedrick Hardman, an extremely talented defensive end, found himself increasingly unhappy when I took over the 49ers, because he had just gone through two losing seasons, including a 2–14 year just prior to my arrival. His discontent grew greater during my first year as head coach, which produced another 2–14 won-lost record. Four victories over two entire seasons can cause despair in some.

Nevertheless, he had been an outstanding player with the organization for several seasons (the leader in sacks for eight straight years), and

I strongly believed he was going to be a key performer, a leader, on our emerging team. Unfortunately, he proved me wrong.

Cedrick was basically a good guy who was just unable to cope with his perception that things would not get better. As a result, his attitude worsened and his performance on the field suffered. Because of his disappointment, perhaps despair, and the fact that he wasn't getting what he wanted out of the game—namely, victory—he began sniping at and belittling teammates for their efforts as we continued to lose nearly 90 percent of our games that first season. Then he began disparaging the assistant coaches, the owners, the staff, and eventually me. I tolerated it longer than I should have because of his talent, even though in his state of mind his play was far below what he was capable of had he gotten his act together.

Under more favorable circumstances, Cedrick might have been a positive force. However, given the situation as he viewed it, he became a negative and disruptive force—howling at everything, wounded and frustrated. While he was capable of being a leader under positive circumstances, he was not capable of doing it under losing circumstances. It takes extraordinary fortitude to stay with it when times are bad. Cedrick didn't have it.

I determined that it was impossible to resurrect his enthusiasm for being a 49er and knew that every minute he continued to be with us he did damage to those who hadn't given up. I called Al Davis across the Bay in Oakland and arranged a trade with the Raiders for our disgruntled defensive end.

Hardman had given up on the San Francisco 49ers too soon. Twenty-four months after the trade, we won Super Bowl XVI. In some small way, the championship came about because I had been willing to remove players—even those with great talent—whose actions or attitude didn't conform to the Standard of Performance, who didn't get with the program.

It's worth remembering that some individuals have "situational character"—their attitude (and subsequent performance) are linked to results. Good results? Great attitude. Bad results? Bad attitude. Cedric was like that by the time I took over at San Francisco. He was a negative presence in our midst—a malignant force within the organization.

A leader must be able to identify these types of situations and not shy away from removing malcontents from the organization. It takes true character to stay with an organization when things seem to be at their bleakest.

It is also my opinion that lack of the "stick-with-it" attitude is accompanied by a certain lack of intelligence; not always, not with Cedrick, but often. The thick-witted person can't deal with the hard knocks after a while, and that's when the complaining begins.

Some define character as simply aspiring to high ideals and standards. I disagree. Many people have lofty aspirations. Unfortunately, aspiring isn't enough. You must also have the strength of commitment and sacrifice to adhere to those standards and ideals in both good times *and* bad.

Ronnie Lott, a 49er defensive back who had been an All-American at USC, was a model player who had no trouble adhering to high standards, regardless of the circumstances. In doing so, he brought others on our team up to his level. This quality of character was equal in its own way and importance to us to his Hall of Fame talent. (Lott was one of the hardest-hitting defensive backs in the history of the NFL. An opposing player described being tackled by Ronnie as equivalent to having someone hit you on the head with a baseball bat.)

Commitment and sacrifice are among the personal characteristics I value most highly in people. Ronnie had both. One example may shock you.

During the final game of the '85 regular season, against Dallas, he crushed the tip of his little finger—the pinky—tackling the Cowboys' running back Tim Newsome. The finger failed to heal properly during the off-season, and bone-graft surgery was scheduled. However, because of the long recovery time necessary for the graft to "take," Ronnie wouldn't be ready to play at the start of the season, including our season opener against Tampa Bay.

During a consultation with his doctor, Ronnie asked if there were any alternatives to the bone-graft operation that might speed things along. His surgeon replied, "I don't recommend it, but we could amputate your finger, put the whole hand in a cast, and you'd be okay to play that first game."

I wish I could have seen the look on his surgeon's face when Ronnie said, "Well, that's what we'll do. Take it off, doctor." Ronnie Lott was in the starting lineup a few weeks later against Tampa Bay, wearing a big cast and minus part of the pinky on his left hand.

While he was highly volatile—very overt—he had no grand plan to bring people along, but did it with his own drive, personality, and determination. He provides a good example of how good character is contagious.

Ronnie drove others to sacrifice at his level by setting extreme personal standards of physical intensity and concentration for himself in practice (*especially* in practice, where it can be tempting to coast) and games that exceeded even my own expectations.

He simply demanded maximum effort and effective execution from himself at all times and refused to quit until it was achieved. Since he never felt it was totally and completely achieved, he never quit.

His will to improve created a very real sense that if you wanted to associate with him professionally—to be on a "Ronnie Lott" team—you were expected to sacrifice to the same extreme degree he did. When a grueling set of push-ups was concluded by the coaching staff, Ronnie would often call for more; *he* would be the one setting the standard higher and higher. This was true during the season he joined us and San Francisco won a Super Bowl; it was equally true the following season when our won-lost record went in the tank: 3–6. He never quit.

"Ronnie Lott" character reveals itself most starkly in two completely different circumstances: when victory or success is almost a given, and conversely, when there is little or no likelihood of victory. The former tempts an individual to become complacent, to ease up; the latter tempts an individual to start bellyaching and quit. Ronnie never gave up or let down. Consistent commitment and sacrifice in all situations was his trademark.

He did what individuals with this kind of character do when facing either circumstance: Lott was constant in his drive to excel. This is very hard for an individual to do, but imagine how it transforms those within the organization. And imagine the pleasure it brings to the life of a leader.

Human nature is such that we are drawn to those with fortitude—whether it's in the military (General Dwight Eisenhower), exploration (Sir Edmund Hillary), religion (Martin Luther King Jr.), or anywhere else. Ronnie Lott had that same stuff. His character transformed those around him in a positive, even profound way.

In his own personal example, he became a de facto coach, one whose specialty was teaching others what it meant to give it everything you've got. When evaluating our people, this was a key characteristic that I valued highly. I understood the impact it has on others in the organization; I recognized that it made my job much easier.

In building and maintaining your organization, place a premium on those who exhibit great desire to keep pushing themselves to higher and higher performance and production levels, who seek to go beyond the highest standards that you, the leader, set. The employee who gets to work early, stays late, fights through illness and personal problems is the one to keep your eye on for greater responsibilities.

When you bring a "Ronnie Lott" into your organization, you are actually bringing several "Ronnie Lotts" aboard, because they create others in their own image. His teammate and fellow Hall of Fame player, running back Roger Craig, shared that same work ethic, intensity, and enthusiasm. Here's an example: Roger would often race all the way to the goal line when he carried the ball—in *practice*. I didn't ask him to do that; he had that drive within. Push. Push. Push. Lott and Craig were two different personalities that exuded their formidable character in different but equally effective ways.

I've seen athletes have great performances right after a personal tragedy occurred in their life. I've also seen the opposite—individuals who are unable to compete because of something that happened in their life that they allowed to cripple them.

Otto Graham, a member of the Pro Football Hall of Fame, demonstrated tremendous strength of character when he forced himself to compete in the NFL Pro Bowl Game just weeks after the tragic death of his son. Somehow he was able to summon the fortitude not only to perform, but to perform at a level that resulted in being selected as MVP. Otto just felt he had to continue with his life, to go on. Ultimately, he simply would not allow himself to opt out, even after such a catastrophic personal tragedy.

On the other hand, I've known people who played poorly or not at all because some distant relative they hardly knew had died months earlier and it was still on their mind; they couldn't get over it, couldn't perform. They allowed themselves an excuse for poor performance. Character was at the core of both kinds of responses.

My point is that the Otto Grahams of this world are hard to find. The other kind are all over the place. Guys like Ronnie and Roger aren't found all over the place. Both exemplify the message of UCLA's coach John Wooden: "I wanted players who *had* character, not players who *were* characters."

Of course, sometimes you get both. Jack "Hacksaw" Reynolds, who played such an important role in our first Super Bowl year, was a tremendous competitor with character. He also *was* a character. On many occasions, before games, he would put on his San Francisco 49ers uniform at his house, smear the eye black under his eyes, and call a cab to take him to the game. He would arrive at Candlestick Park ready to go, in full uniform, including cleats! And then Jack Reynolds would deliver the goods out on the field.

You go nowhere without character. Character is essential to individuals, and their cumulative character is the backbone of your winning team.

A Big Cheer for a Big Ego

Don't let anybody tell you that a big ego is a bad thing. Tiger Woods, Bill Gates, Warren Buffett, and Cal Ripken Jr. have lots of ego, and so does anyone anywhere who is dedicated to taking his or her talent as far as it will go. I've got a big ego too.

Here's what a big ego is: pride, self-confidence, self-esteem, self-assurance. Ego is a powerful and productive engine. In fact, without a healthy ego you've got a big problem.

Egotism is something else entirely. It's an ego that's been inflated like a hot-air balloon—arrogance that results from your own perceived skill, power, or position. You become increasingly self-important, self-centered, and selfish, just as a hot-air balloon gets pumped with lots of hot air until it turns into some big, ponderous entity that's slow, vulnerable, and easily destroyed.

Unfortunately, a strong, healthy ego often becomes egotism. When Jerry Jones, owner of the Dallas Cowboys, fired his head coach Jimmy Johnson immediately following the team's second consecutive Super Bowl victory, ego may have been replaced by egotism in one or both men. The consequences were ultimately devastating for the Cowboys and took years to repair.

In evaluating people, I prize ego. It often translates into a fierce desire to do their best and an inner confidence that stands them in good stead when things really get rough. Psychologists suggest that there is a strong link between ego and competitiveness. All the great performers I've ever coached had ego to spare.

However, when I sense ego turning into egotism, I sit down and talk with the individual to help him understand his problem, to recognize why he's on the team, to see if we can't get his perspective back in balance and minimize his inflated sense of value to the organization. Either the egotism goes away or the individual flaunting it does, because the damage a swaggering egotist can do to the organization always outweighs the good.

Have there been times when your own ego has turned unhealthy, been pumped up for various reasons into egotism? Have there been instances where you hurt yourself because you got caught up in your self-importance? Be careful. People can sense it, they can see it. When they do, your effectiveness is dramatically reduced. At times it can even be fatal. That's why it's worth monitoring in yourself and your staff.

While the dynamics within a professional football team are unique in many ways, the element of dealing with egotism, arrogance, and the self-styled big shots is perhaps similar profession to profession.

In football, if your team's any good, what you have in the locker room is a superstar or two, along with a few people who have immense egos but aren't superstars, perhaps are not even very good, just adequate. Peer pressure is one way for dealing with the egotists—maybe the best way—but the leader ultimately is the one who has to control the situation. If I talked enough about "professionalism," how we carried ourselves and performed, how we *interacted* and respected one another, the huge egos were sometimes embarrassed out of their behavior because they understood that they were out of whack with the rest of the team.

Most of those who strutted around were the less intelligent players. And being less intelligent, they couldn't understand my message and ended up being isolated by their teammates—ostracized to one degree or another. That's the single best way, the most effective corrective method, because almost everyone seeks some peer approval or acceptance. One way or another, however you do it, you as a leader must recognize and remedy the egotists within your organization before they can damage what you've built.

The Bottom 20 Percent May Determine Your Success

At the beginning of each year's training camp, I made the following promise to our team: "Every single one of you guys will have at least one chance to win a game for us. I ask you to prepare for that opportunity with the attitude that it's a certainty, not a possibility. Prepare and be ready when your time comes, because it *will* come. Can you do that for me?"

When Joe Montana first heard me say this, he may have thought, "Is Bill crazy? That's what I'm here for, to win games." But of course, my statement wasn't directed at Joe.

Those comments were aimed specifically at the so-called bottom 20 percent of our team—the backups, "benchwarmers," and special role players, those who didn't see much action during the regular season. In a sports organization this is the group that often determines your fate—they make the difference between whether you win or lose. In business it may be a customer-service representative or another less prominent "player" who fails to address a problem due to lack of readiness or a feeling that his or her particular job doesn't really mean that much in the big picture.

Future Hall of Fame players such as Steve Young, Jerry Rice, Roger Craig, and others with plenty of playing time didn't need me to remind them to get physically, mentally, and emotionally ready for action. Rather, it was the bottom 20 percent who were more likely to feel overlooked, unimportant, and unattached to our organization.

Additionally, when they did play it was often in a physically dangerous situation such as a kickoff return, the football version of being a kamikaze pilot, where your career can end suddenly with an injury. They risk life and limb and yet can often feel unappreciated.

While these employees may have a limited role, in just one play they can destroy the efforts of everyone else; their impact, though limited, can be calamitous. Or they can save the game.

Members of this group can become a serious distraction and liability, because as their attitude worsens, their commitment wavers and their carping increases. When the bottom 20 percent is dissatisfied—doesn't feel they're a real part of your team, that is, appreciated—their comments, perspective, and reactions—their "bitching"—is seen, heard, and absorbed by those who are positive and productive.

For reasons I've never quite figured out, the bitching of the bottom 20 percent often overshadows the positive enthusiasm of the other 80 percent. I always thought it should be the other way around, but it isn't. The whiners seem to have a disproportionate impact. Thus the need for my "be ready to win a game for us" speech at the start of each training camp, which attempted to give those who might come to feel disenfranchised a reason to stay plugged in, positive, and ready to perform. And this was only the start.

I was conscientious in repeating that message privately through the season and acknowledging them publicly; talking about their roles and their potential impact in the future; working to keep them feeling that their contribution to the team was important (because it was very important); working hard to ensure that they were integrated and assimilated into everything we did so they didn't feel left out or part of a second tier on the team. If I noticed the same groups always sitting together at lunch or dinner, I would have the assistant coaches start mixing them around so that people got more familiar with one another. This also meant there was less likelihood of the same little group of complainers sitting together and adding members.

During team meetings I would often give a one-hundred-dollar bill as a reward to a role player who had made a big contribution in the previous game. It was another chance for them to be recognized by me in front of the whole squad, for me to give them ownership in the organization's results. While coaching at Stanford University, I instituted a "12th Man Award," which, of course, didn't involve money, but did acknowledge publicly the effort being made by those who were less visible. I wanted them to know they were an essential part of the success of the team and, as such, should focus and train for the moment they would have a chance to make a big play. I strove to avoid having a "second tier" of lower-class players or staff members.

A leader who ignores this element of the organization—the "bottom 20 percent," those who play subsidiary or special roles—is asking for trouble. When these individuals begin to feel extraneous, their discontent can spread through your entire organization just like a cancer spreads through a body.

Be conscientious in evaluating the effectiveness of the steps you take in connecting the role players on your team to the team itself. Helping them understand that they make a difference can be the difference in making it to the top.

Avoid the Dance of the Doomed

On the steppes of Africa, a "dance of death" occurs when a wildebeest is run into exhaustion by a lion. Waiting to be killed as the lion circles, the wildebeest meekly submits to its fate—head drooping, shoulders slumped, eyes glazed over. It is the posture of the doomed, the same look you often see in competitors in sports and business who have given up after deciding that failure is inevitable, their competitor unbeatable.

During my ten years as head coach of the 49ers, we won more than our share of division, conference, and Super Bowl games; we also *lost* sixty-three games. During some of those defeats, the dance of the doomed could be clearly seen on the faces of some 49er players, even by fans in the upper decks of a stadium. And certainly by our opponent right across from us on the field.

On those occasions I would say to the team in various ways, "Fellas, I guess we're gonna lose today. How do you want to do it?" They knew what I meant. I was asking them to stand up and fight and if they lost, at least to lose with dignity.

The impact this can have was demonstrated in an amazing comeback against New Orleans when we trailed at the half, 35–7. It came during that stretch in our second season when we had just lost seven out of nine games and were trying to pull out of the death spiral our season had become. As we ran off the field at the half, 49er fans let us know how disgusted they were with us, booing disdainfully and hurling paper cups and debris down on our heads.

In the locker room my comments were honest in describing what was at stake, and it wasn't the final score: "Some of you may think we have already lost this game," I began. "You might be right. We may lose this afternoon, and if we do, I can live with it. This is only a football game. However, if we go down, you must decide how you want it to happen. How do you want to go down? Nobody would blame you for coasting the rest of this game, for throwing in the towel. And in fact, when you come back here in sixty minutes, only you will know if you did; only you will know if you let New Orleans continue this assault or if you stood your ground and fought back. Frankly, I care a lot more about *how* we lose than *if* we lose. Gentlemen, in the second half you're going to find out something important; you're about to find out who you are. And you may not like what you find."

That's all I said. No rah-rah speech along the lines of "It's never over 'til it's over!" No angry shouting about lack of effort or stupid mistakes; no threats. I simply pointed out that we had arrived at an important threshold of discovery—that moment when you find out what you're made of.

When I finished my brief comments, there was complete silence. We looked at one another—Dwight Clark, Freddie Solomon, Lenvil Elliott, Earl Cooper, Randy Cross, Keena Turner, Joe Montana, Dan Bunz, and all the others—in a way that probably happens in the military before the battle; you're looking into one another's competitive souls.

I turned and left the room while our assistant coaches gathered with their own units to go over changes to be made in the second half. Those tactical changes were not significant. The big change had to be in their attitude.

What I had attempted to do was remind our guys of the Standard of Performance that I had been teaching from the day I arrived. Among the multitude of rules, concepts, and prescribed attitudes it embraced was the matter of poise: Even in the worst circumstance (and this was pretty close to being the worst), do not unravel mentally or emotionally; continue to fight and execute well, even if the cause appears to be lost; act like professionals.

"Who are you?" I asked them. I wanted to know; in the second half I found out. The 49ers outscored the Saints 28–0 and won the game in overtime on Ray Wersching's field goal, 38–35. At the time, it was considered the greatest comeback in the history of NFL football. And it was not a fluke. Our team had resisted the temptation to perform the dance of the doomed.

The second half of the game demonstrated to me that the values, rules, and ideals I had been inculcating for the previous eighteen months—the Standard of Performance—were beginning to sink into the consciousness of the team, defining us to the core.

Among other things, I had taught players—those who needed to be taught—to comport themselves in a manner that demonstrated pride, poise, and a determination to never, ever quit, even if we trailed by a hundred points.

Your competitor must never look at you across the field, conference table, or anywhere else and conclude, "I not only beat you, I broke your spirit." The dance of the doomed tells them they've broken your spirit. That message can hurt you the next time around.

And almost always there is a next time around.

Use the Four Most Powerful Words

You need to stretch people to help them achieve their full potential. Joe Montana and Steve Young are quarterbacks who came to the 49ers with the highest personal expectations of themselves; neither lacked in confidence, and both believed they could do just about anything. I let them know I thought they could do even *more* than anything. You can do the same with your own talented staff and personnel.

The most powerful way to do this is by having the courage to say, "I believe in you," in whatever words and way are comfortable for you. These four words—or their equivalents—constitute the most inspirational message a leader can convey. There are many different ways to do it, but the fundamental and underlying message must always be the same: "I believe in you. I know you can do the job."

Few things embolden and create self-confidence in a person like hearing those words from an individual whose judgment he or she respects, especially if that person is you, his or her boss.

Joe Montana—perhaps the greatest quarterback in the history of professional football—was not highly sought after by NFL teams when he graduated from Notre Dame. While he personally had a strong assessment of his own talents, most scouts didn't share his opinion. When they saw him play, they did not see a future NFL superstar.

His performance in college, while brilliant at times, was inconsistent. He did not have a strong arm and was rather slight by NFL quarterback standards (at 6 feet 2 inches and 185 pounds, he looked like a Swedish placekicker). Additionally, Joe didn't exude the "presence" usually associated with dominating team leaders; he was almost shy.

Consequently, when it came to quarterbacks that year, Phil Simms was the guy everybody wanted, and Joe was still available in the third round of the draft when the 49ers picked him up. (Prior to my drafting Joe, my friend and fellow coach Sam Wyche tracked him down in southern California for a workout. We flew to Los Angeles International Airport and took a cab to a little public playground nearby. When Joe started throwing the ball, I knew immediately that he was very special—poise, nimble feet that reminded me of Joe Namath's exquisite footwork, and a "look" I liked when he threw the football, even though his strength was not the long pass.)

While he came to us with great confidence and competitive instincts, Joe Montana didn't envision four Super Bowl rings in his future, nor that he would become a shoo-in for the NFL Hall of Fame. Regardless of the opinion Joe Montana had about his future when it came to Super Bowl rings, I let him know in word and deed that I *believed* in him, his potential, and his value to our team. Our relationship focused relentlessly on improving and perfecting his physical and mental skills, pushing to a higher level and nourishing his self-confidence so he could realize his optimum potential. I want to be clear that Joe believed in himself—very much. My role was to reinforce and *expand* that confidence and teach him how to translate it into performance at the highest level.

Joe absorbed this ongoing support and teaching and saw that I was ready and willing to work hard with him in bringing forth his best effort. For this same reason, most quarterbacks I've worked with have also done very well, often becoming ranked as some of the best performers in their league. My first QB was Greg Cook with the Cincinnati Bengals, who soon led the league in passing efficiency. Next came Virgil Carter and Ken Anderson, who became rated at or near the top of the league in this same important category. Later, Hall of Famer Dan Fouts of the San Diego Chargers made huge improvements in his skills as a passer under my direction. When I coached at Stanford University, Guy Benjamin and Steve Dils led the NCAA and Steve Stenstrom broke all Pac-10 Conference records for passing efficiency.

Of course, the great Steve Young, who followed Joe Montana as the 49ers' starting quarterback, went from languishing in Tampa Bay to setting NFL records that put him in the Hall of Fame.

This pattern of significant improvement in quarterbacks—and I could give multiple examples at other positions and among our staff—was not an accident. Even though each man had different strengths and weaknesses (and all of them had problems that needed fixing), even though each had a different mixture of confidence and uncertainty, they all got one fundamental message from me: "I believe in you." I said it, meant it, and had the expertise to teach them how to get better and better.

It's true with starting quarterbacks and backup quarterbacks; it's true with salespeople, department heads, staff members, and virtually everyone else we work with. As a leader you must have the strength to let talented members of your organization know you believe in them—nurture their belief in themselves, teach them what they need to know, and then watch what happens. It's amazing and one of the things I love most about leadership—teaching a person how to reach higher and higher, to achieve great things with his or her talent.

And always keep this in mind: Nobody will ever come back to you later and say "thank you" for expecting too little of them.

Extreme Effort Requires Extreme Prudence

Aggressive leaders—effective ones—push individuals hard, and then we push harder, knowing that one of our responsibilities is to get that extra effort necessary for an organization to achieve top results. A good leader believes that he or she knows the secret (or secrets) for bringing a group up to maximum productivity, and in fact, if you don't know how to do it you'll soon be gone.

However, it's just as important to understand that "extra effort," in whatever form it takes (mental, physical, emotional), cannot be sustained without eventual damage and diminishing returns. There has to be a very acute awareness on your part as to the level of exertion and the toll it's taking on those you lead. A head coach is no different from a CEO or department head in needing to know when it's time to let up a bit, allow for recharging of the internal batteries of those on your team.

One of your great challenges is finding the middle ground between the well-being of the people who work with you and the achievement of your goals. My observation is that many leaders have risen to the top in part because we work "too hard." That's one of the reasons we got to the top in the first place. It's only natural that we think everybody should follow our extreme example. Most, however, do not desire to become consumed by work, to let it virtually take over their lives. That's just a fact.

The art of leadership requires knowing when it makes sense to take people over the top, to push them to their highest level of effort, and when to take your foot off the accelerator a little. If your team is constantly working on adrenaline, in a crisis mode, running as hard as they can, they become vulnerable. When an emergency arises, when the competition suddenly presents an unexpected threat, your team has no next level to step up to, no reserves to draw on. The best leaders are those who understand the levels of energy and focus available within their team. They also recognize which situations require extreme effort and which do not. Knowing the difference ensures that your organization is fresh and fully able to perform at its uppermost levels when it's necessary.

In my own estimation, I was extremely good in this area, adept at knowing when to push very hard and for how long and in what manner. The one time I really missed the boat on it probably cost us a Super Bowl and almost got me fired.

During my ninth year as head coach of the 49ers, NFL players went on strike after the second game of the season. It was not unexpected by our organization, and we did an excellent job getting ready for the consequences of having the regulars walk out. However, when the strike ended and they returned, there was a lot of pent-up anger and emotion that came out; some were extremely upset with me for decisions I had made; others were angry at the NFL and/or their teammates. It was an emotionally bruising return to action, but somehow we came through it in great shape and won nine of the next ten regular-season games—overall the best record in the NFL at 13–2 (the strike caused the cancellation of one regular-season game) and designation by many as the odds-on choice to win Super Bowl XXII. And now it was time for me to prepare our team for the play-offs leading to the championship game.

For the first time in my career, I did something I had never done before; namely, during practices I ran our team into the ground. I'm still not sure what I was thinking when I pushed the team to their limits in those days prior to our NFC play-off game against the Minnesota Vikings, but it was fatal.

We had lost in the first round the two previous years, and that had been very hard to take. Perhaps I decided subconsciously that this time around I was just going to have to push them harder in areas I felt needed improvement—deep passes, for example. But there were always components of our game that I felt could be improved. That was nothing new. In this instance, however, I began driving the team harder and harder, offensive players especially, until ultimately they were essentially exhausted at the worst possible time: They were about to face a very strong Minnesota Vikings team with a defensive line that had come into its own during the season; the Vikings meant business.

This game, obviously, was a situation that called for stepping it up, extra effort, extreme exertion. Unfortunately, our guys, Jerry Rice, for example, were still physically and mentally worn down because of the grueling nature of my ongoing pre–play-off workouts. We got beat because we *were* beat. There was very little left in the tank by the opening kickoff. Minnesota won 36–24, but the game may not have been as close as that score suggests.

Eddie DeBartolo was furious and seriously considered firing me. He was correct in the sense that it was *my* poor leadership judgment that had been responsible for our bad performance. It was my fault. I had strayed from my instincts and understanding that when it comes to demanding extreme effort, a good leader must exercise extreme prudence.

This is one of the most difficult areas of leadership. By instinct we—leaders—want to run hard all the time; by intellect we know this is not possible. Reconciling those two positions in the context of leadership is an ongoing challenge. I believe the one time in my career when I didn't successfully reconcile the two, it cost us a championship.

It's an easy trap to fall into—pushing your team to the brink and then over—because there is comfort in knowing that if we are defeated, at least *we* worked—and worked our team—as hard as possible. For a hardworking leader that's easy to do. What's difficult to do is recognize when extra effort, extreme exertion, working "as hard as possible" starts to produce diminishing returns.

The Bubba Diet: You Can't Transplant Willpower

Bubba Paris is a man whose outstanding talent and potential for greatness were exceeded only by his big heart and large appetite. While he had a great college career at Michigan and was a valuable member of the 49ers, I tend to think his craving for food eventually cost him his job in the National Football League.

Ideally, Bubba's best weight was at something less than 300 pounds, but his voracious eating habits skyrocketed him into the vicinity of 350 pounds and beyond, dramatically reducing his quickness and stamina. Adding to the urgency of the issue was the fact that doctors were telling him, "Mr. Paris, you won't live past the age of fifty if you don't lose weight." With 49er training camp workouts being conducted in hundred-degree heat at Sierra College in Rocklin, California, I worried that Bubba might not even reach forty if he didn't get his weight under control.

Consequently, our nutritionist and team trainers worked conscientiously with him during camp and encouraged Bubba to eat fewer fries and more fish, less pie and more pasta, Diet Coke instead of double-thick chocolate shakes.

Bubba was trying to get with the program, but it just didn't seem to be working—the weight wasn't coming off, in spite of the obvious fact that he was also giving it his best effort during practice and at the training table. This became very frustrating for us, and I came to recognize that a metabolic issue was the probable explanation for all the extra weight and his failure to lose any of it by the end of training camp. I was convinced of it. What more could Bubba Paris possibly have done to lose weight? Well, I found out.

On the Saturday morning when we broke camp to head back to San Francisco, the maid's supervisor in charge of the dormitories—a stern woman who reminded me of the head nurse in *One Flew Over the Cuckoo's Nest*—came to my office. "Mr. Walsh, I think you should take a look at how some of your athletes live," she announced. Uh-oh.

Dutifully I followed her to Bubba's room in the dorm—empty now. When I entered, there was a pleasant surprise. "What's the problem here?" I thought to myself. "Nothing's broken. Very clean. No holes in the wall. Looks good." I smiled and nodded politely in her direction. Maybe I'd misunderstood. Perhaps the problem was with some other player's room, one of those who occasionally got overly rambunctious. I was wrong.

Solemnly I watched as she marched over to Bubba's closet and opened the door. She reached inside, flipped the switch, and turned on the light. I took a look.

There, stacked one on top of another in the back of the closet, were scores of grease-stained, extra large, red-striped Kentucky Fried Chicken boxes—the empty remnants of all the terrific meals Bubba had smuggled in during the past few weeks. Crumpled up and scattered around the closet floor were KFC napkins, empty soda cups, straws, even a couple of dried chicken bones that had also been left behind—final evidence of an appetite out of control.

Bubba was eating like a bird at the training table, but the dinner bell didn't really ring until he got back to his dorm room.

All of this was a good lesson for me: Willpower was not a commodity I could simply hand out like a couple of aspirin tablets.

Whether it's a 350-pound tackle, an employee, or a child, we must try our best to encourage, support, and inspire, but eventually—ultimately— people must do it for themselves. No one else can do it for them, including you, regardless of whether you're a head coach, CEO, manager, nutrition- ist, or doctor. A closet floor covered with KFC boxes reminded me of that.

Nevertheless, I'm happy to report that Bubba Paris has gotten a certain amount of control over his weight problem and is leading a much healthier lifestyle—too late to extend his successful football career, but hopefully in time to extend his life.

"Conventional Wisdom" Is an Oxymoron

Coaches and scouts in the National Football League view the raw speed demonstrated in the forty-yard sprint as a litmus test of a receiver's potential, a tried-and-true tool in deciding whether to draft him. Do a good time in the forty and you've probably got a job; less than that and you may have to look for another line of work.

I took a somewhat different view. I valued blazing speed but also prized what I call "functional" speed—how fast a player can move with a ball in his hands *after* he's in stride. To my thinking, that's how it's usually done in a game. Because of my unconventional philosophy, I was able to see the potential in a young man who became the greatest receiver in NFL history.

The night before a 49ers game in Houston during my sixth season as head coach, I was watching a local television station's sports highlights in my hotel room. One of the games it covered involved a tiny college in Itta Bena, Mississippi, called Mississippi Valley State.

The school's top receiver was a kid named Jerry Rice who seemed to find a way to get open, catch the ball, and gain yardage with ease. I think he scored four or five touchdowns in the game, in spite of the fact that he would not have won a medal in the Olympic hundred-yard dash. Once he hit full stride, however, Rice was something truly remarkable. He had functional speed, fantastic moves, and hands that were as sure as a surgeon's. Plus, Jerry Rice had the heart of a warrior.

And I knew I could design plays that got him open and put the ball in his hands. I can still remember the excitement I felt thinking about it as I watched him during that sports highlights show in Texas. Believe it or not, I was in the minority when it came to recognizing Jerry's potential.

He was not considered a top-flight prospect by some prominent scouts around the league, and even in the 49er organization, because he had a "mediocre" forty-yard time—not much better than 4.6 seconds. They considered him a possible fifth- or sixth-round draft pick because he lacked so-called blazing speed off the blocks. I was strongly advised not to waste our number one draft choice to pick him. That was the conventional wisdom.

I knew better, looked beyond his so-so time in the forty, ignored the advice I had been given, and focused on his outstanding speed and moves from fifteen to fifty yards. I was one of only a few who felt this way about the promising receiver, because a trade with New England moved us up enough in the draft to acquire the still-available Jerry Rice with our number one pick. Two other wide receivers were chosen ahead of Jerry by teams that didn't see what I saw in him. And that's how the San Francisco 49ers acquired the services of the greatest receiver, perhaps the greatest player, in NFL history.

Here's my point. Occasionally, when striving to go beyond conventional results, you must go beyond the conventional and against popular opinion. This means trusting your own judgment enough to be resourceful, innovative, and imaginative. It means resisting the herd mentality.

To put it another way: Conventional wisdom often produces conventional results. Conventional thinking didn't produce Jerry Rice.

Make Friends, Not Enemies: Al Davis, Howard Cosell, and *Monday Night Football*

Enemies take up your time, energy, and attention—commodities too valuable to squander frivolously. This is especially true in a profession as public as professional football, because everybody takes potshots at you all the time; it's easy to acquire a long list of individuals with whom you want to even the score.

That's why I instructed everyone in our organization—players, staff, and all others—to do everything possible to get along with people who interacted with us, even when it might appear they were treating us unfairly. We simply couldn't afford to waste resources fighting needless fights, whether with fans, media, vendors, sponsors, other teams, or anyone else, including squabbles among ourselves. You can quickly find yourself doing nothing but chasing so-called enemies.

"Hostile relationships are toxic. Cultivate good relationships," I cautioned. "Be available; avoid making enemies; don't close off communications." I taught those in the organization that it was necessary to initiate communication after a conflict, even if the other person had misunderstood you or wrongfully ridiculed you. And to understand that regardless of the cause of the animosity, negative relationships have *ongoing* negative consequences.

I felt that positive or at least nonadversarial relationships were a tangible and significant organizational asset. I worked hard at following my own advice about having "no enemies," and it paid handsome dividends.

For example, Al Davis, owner of the Oakland Raiders, was a pivotal figure in the evolution of the NFL. He is a man of tremendous ability from whom I learned a great deal when I was one of his assistant coaches. Early in his career he was an outstanding and innovative coach (later general manager); his knowledge, creativity, and charisma made him one of the best. Additionally, Al had tremendous expectations of himself and everyone around him.

Similarly, as an owner he had great results—Oakland Raiders championships in Super Bowl XI, Super Bowl XV, and Super Bowl XVIII.

But Al Davis could be the devil personified if you crossed him or got on his bad side. I did not want his wrath and made very sure that our relationship was very workable. I simply didn't look for a fight, even when Al might test my patience, and he was pretty good at doing that. Among other things, my approach meant that we had a positive and productive connection. I could call Al on the phone and make a deal in a second (as I did in the Cedrick Hardman trade). We got along fine over many years and through a variety of challenges.

Howard Cosell, one of *Monday Night Football*'s biggest stars, was a different story and tested my "no enemies" policy when I met him for the first time.

Months before a chance meeting in New York, I had announced with great irritation during a Tuesday press conference that San Francisco had not been mentioned once on the previous evening's *Monday Night Football* halftime highlights show. The reason? The network, and Howard, didn't want to remind viewers that we had crushed Dallas, 45–14, the day before. And Dallas was playing the Los Angeles Rams in an unusual Sunday-night game on ABC-TV in just six days.

I was offended and told reporters, "The football elitists, jockstrap elitists don't consider us in the comfort zone. There are power sources, influence sources in the National Football League, forty-five-year-old men who are football groupies who prefer that we not exist so they can hold on to their football contracts and associations or power groups. It's a business, and they [ABC] need the Los Angeles–Dallas game to be a big [ratings] game. It's obvious; it's blatant. It's a disservice to the public." I was letting off steam because I viewed the omission as intentional and part of the NFL's view that San Francisco was a backwater of professional football, a team that didn't matter. Nevertheless, once I made my statement, I moved on and thought it was over. But it wasn't over.

Many months later, I was at a cocktail reception in Manhattan and spotted Cosell across the room. I went over to him, assuming he'd want to say hello to me as much as I was looking forward to saying hello to him. I was wrong.

Cosell had not forgotten my "jockstrap elitist" remarks from months earlier and was still incensed: "Who are you, *sir*, to confront someone like me or the people I represent?" he barked in my face as his cigar smoke curled around us. "You are nobody! You are nothing!"

Scores of people witnessed his public browbeating of me. I retreated and disappeared into the crowd (which was buzzing about what it had just witnessed), too astonished and embarrassed by what he had done to utter any defense or apology or mount an attack. Obviously, I was very angry.

But later, after considerable thought, I decided it was appropriate to follow my own "no enemies" policy and write Howard a conciliatory letter explaining that my comments had not been aimed at him, but rather at those at the network who were in management and production. Further, I explained that if he had taken the comments personally I sincerely apologized for any discomfort they might have caused him. Believe me, this was not an easy letter to write.

Howard was appeased. He sent me a friendly note and the following season joined me for dinner in San Francisco before the 49ers' upcoming appearance on *Monday Night Football* while I was head coach. Howard and I cemented our new friendship over martinis at a steak house in downtown San Francisco.

From that point forward, Howard Cosell was a Bill Walsh booster, supporting my cause in all areas, even at times when I was being held up to great public criticism. He had been transformed from an adversary into an advocate.

It was made possible because I was committed to a personal and organizational "no enemies" policy. Everyone on the 49ers payroll knew I expected them to do the same. Over the years, the benefits to us were significant. We simply didn't get bogged down, distracted, or consumed with firefights that amounted to nothing. Or at least we minimized that number.

It's a maxim that one enemy can do more damage than the good of a hundred friends. I believe it's true and worth remembering the next time you get upset with someone and mutter, "I'll fix that so-and-so." While you're getting even, they're getting ahead.

You must be astute enough to avoid becoming the loser in such situations. By being sensitive to the inherent hazards of a hostile relationship, you can give yourself a chance to win the person over to having at least a neutral association with you.

The reality of the situation is that regardless of the reason behind an extremely adversarial relationship, such a relationship can have negative consequences. Conversely, by minimizing the forces working against you, you do away with resultant distractions and free your mind and conserve your energy to focus on your work.

Hold on Until Help Arrives:
Keep Your Boss in the Loop

I was thrust into an organization that was a loser in need of a turnaround. In that situation and under the best conditions—and what I faced was far from the best—you need time to install your ideas and make them work. In one sense, you're trying to keep your superiors from doing anything rash because they want results *now*, while simultaneously working with those under your supervision so they don't give up or mutiny. Here's how I tried to deal with the former, namely, ownership.

Two years before I was hired, Eddie DeBartolo paid $17 million for the San Francisco 49ers. He then turned the organization over to his son, Eddie DeBartolo Jr. Obviously, both men wanted a winner, but it wasn't happening. Over their first two seasons, the team's record was the worst in the league: 7–23.

I came aboard in year three of their ownership and immediately added fourteen additional losses to the books, which meant after three years in the NFL the DeBartolos' football team had a cumulative record of 9–37. The 49ers were bad and appeared to the uninformed to be getting worse. I honestly believe that in those days if we'd given away free tickets to games, we still wouldn't have been able to fill the sixty thousand seats in Candlestick Park.

Obviously, I felt I could turn things around, but I needed to buy time. I did it, in part, by keeping Eddie Jr. in the loop; fully informed—perhaps overly informed—on every single phase of the operation.

This included providing him with a budget manual (thick), an operations manual (thick), a personnel manual (thick), an overall set of job descriptions that included the specific job of each player and my evaluation of that individual (thick), and a detailed listing of my performance goals and expectations (even thicker). On and on and on. Paper. Paper. Paper. The information was not frivolous "filler," but substantive and sizable.

I wanted the owner (and his advisers) to understand that I was applying maximum effort and paying attention to every single solitary detail of the family's massive financial investment. I believe the voluminous detailing of my efforts and plans bought me precious time. The hands-off patience Eddie Jr. afforded me in the beginning contributed greatly to winning our first Super Bowl championship. He was a terrific boss to work for during my early years as head coach and general manager of his team. I believe this was due in some measure to the fact that my ongoing effort to keep him totally informed gave him comfort.

Positive results—winning—count most. But until those results come through your door, a heavy dose of documentation relating to what you've done and what you're doing, planning to do, and hoping to do may buy you just enough extra time to actually *do* it.

Whether they read it or not, flood your superiors with information that is documented—projections, evaluations, reports on progress, status updates. Then ask for periodic meetings. In a very professional way, force them to understand that you're doing everything you possibly can and that it's documented; in fact, they're holding it in that large folder in their hands. Open and honest communication with your superiors, both written and verbal, is a valuable tool in keeping them from coming to the wrong conclusions.

It can be the difference between being stabbed in the back or patted on the back.

Keep Your Eye on the Ball

While mollifying those who may decide your fate during a losing streak or turnaround effort—the boss, board of directors, or shareholders—you also need to be absolutely disciplined in focusing your own attention on what really matters. Here are a dozen daily reminders that will help keep you on the right track:

1. **Concentrate on what will produce results rather than on the results, the process rather than the prize.**
2. **Exhibit an inner toughness emanating from four of the most effective survival tools a leader can possess: expertise, composure, patience, and common sense.**
3. **Maintain your level of professional ethics and all details of your own Standard of Performance.**
4. **Don't isolate yourself.** Keep in mind that as troubles mount, your relationships with personnel become even more critical. They are the key to holding the staff together. (Don't get too friendly, however. Familiarity can be deadly.)
5. **Don't let the magnitude of the challenge take you away from the incremental steps necessary to effect change.** Continue to be detail oriented.
6. **Exude an upbeat and determined attitude.** Never, ever

express doubt, but avoid an inappropriate sunny optimism in dark times.

7. **Hold meetings with staff educating them on what to expect;** teach them that the immediate future may be a rough ride but that things will change under your leadership and with their support.

8. **Don't label some concept or new plan the thing that will "get us back on track."** Keep in mind that simple remedies seldom solve a complex problem.

9. **Ensure that an appropriate level of courtesy and respect is extended to all members of the organization.** When things are tough, civility is a great asset.

10. **Don't plead with employees to "do better."**

11. **Avoid continual threatening or chastising.**

12. **Deal with your immediate superior(s) on a one-to-one, ongoing basis.** Expect betrayal if results are not immediate. (You extend the time before betrayal occurs by keeping your superiors in the loop.)

Make Your Own Mentors: A PhD from the University of Paul Brown, et al.

We learn in many ways from many sources. One of the most powerful is a mentor, usually thought of as an older, wiser person who takes you under his wing—provides ongoing teaching, counsel, direction, experience, and moral support. But being mentored can also be simply a matter of keen observation, analysis, and learning by the "student," whether there is any intent by a "mentor" or not.

I don't think that when I was an assistant in the NFL—first at Oakland, then Cincinnati, then San Diego—any head coach or general manager I worked for thought of himself as my mentor. Nevertheless, they served as such because I consciously assimilated as much of their great know-how as I could—asking questions about the logic supporting their decisions; analyzing their behavior in managing others; drawing my own conclusions about how to incorporate it into my own approach to coaching and leadership.

In this way I cultivated and benefitted from their expertise nearly as much as if they'd taken me "under their wing" as a special friend they were mentoring.

At Oakland, Al Davis introduced me (and anyone else on his staff who cared to pay attention) to an approach to preparation and execution unlike anything I'd ever seen. He was obsessed with achieving superior organizational performance and professionalism. His devotion to quality became Oakland's official team motto: "Commitment to Excellence." And it wasn't just a marketing slogan. Al Davis was deeply dedicated to achieving it; he didn't just mouth the motto, he personified it.

"Ohhhhh, *this* is how you do it," probably summed up my early reaction to seeing him run things.

He loved the pass—the long pass especially—and expanded on the creativity of Sid Gillman's breakthrough approach, which included all sorts of pass patterns to multiple receivers. Consequently, at Oakland I was in a milieu where passes—especially deep passes—were "in the air," the coin of the realm, and I loved it.

Al had a tremendous football background, including being a player personnel assistant, an assistant coach, a head coach, and much more. I saw it manifested in his decisiveness, boldness, and advanced thinking. While he never put his arm around my shoulder and offered tutoring and career counseling as a mentor might, it didn't matter. I was paying close attention; I did lots of learning—the high standards of organization, the embrace of modern passing concepts, and the dedication and loyalty to his players. I learned like a studious apprentice serving a master craftsman.

In a sense, my eight years as Paul Brown's assistant in Cincinnati were like attending a graduate school in leadership and modern football. He taught me so many things, most of them good.

He was by nature extremely meticulous and organized, a severe man whose mind constantly probed for better ways of doing things, whose teams at the high school, college (Ohio State University before Woody Hayes), and NFL (Cleveland Browns and Cincinnati Bengals) levels were all known for their precise execution. In fact, at Ohio State he was dubbed

"Precision Paul." It was an apt nickname; he was precise—punctilious—in every aspect of his leadership.

Here's his own description of what he did and how he did it: "We were painstaking in our preparations and even practiced *how* to practice. I took one complete session to show our players exactly when and where they should go on the practice field and those routines remained the same whether it was a practice day or a game day."

I know this is true because I was there. Brown felt his teaching would be so ingrained that he didn't need to resort to pep talks or phony slogans: "You can't prepare a player that way [i.e., push them to high performance with a pep talk]. The only way to do it is to be so thorough in your work beforehand as to make him totally confident of himself and those around him." I adopted that attitude in my own head coaching at Stanford and San Francisco.

One of the game's great innovators, Paul Brown was the first (or among the first in some cases) to use IQ tests to evaluate players, establish a game film "library" and studiously analyze the footage, teach players in a formal classroom setting, send in plays from the sideline with "messenger" linemen, fit helmets with face masks, expand the network for player recruitment beyond anything that had been seen before, emphasize a wide-open and profuse passing game (especially with the great Otto Graham), and take organizing practice schedules to an almost scientific level, including assigning assistant coaching *detailed* duties—defined areas of responsibility for which they were held accountable. You could say he was one of the men who brought modern management techniques to coaching football.

His approach to quality control, or more accurately, controlling what creates quality, was evident even in his early years. As a high school coach in Ohio (at Massillon's Washington High School), Brown had his football system used by all of Massillon's *junior* high schools so that the youngsters would be familiar with it if they made his high school team—the Tigers.

Paul Brown was one of those pioneers who advanced the way coaches approached doing their job—not as a serious sideline, but as a profession, almost a science. That's the environment—classroom—I was in for eight years. I didn't think of Paul as my mentor, nor did he, but the sheer volume of coaching and leadership expertise I harvested, both consciously and unconsciously, qualified him as such.

San Diego's Tommy Prothro, a fine coach whose greatest achievements were at the college level, where his ability to connect with his players was made into an art form (resulting in a Rose Bowl championship at UCLA and two other Rose Bowl appearances as head coach at Oregon State), demonstrated what it means to truly care about your people.

I believe Tommy's advice when I received an offer from Stanford University—"Take the job, Bill, because a head coaching position in the Pac-10 is significant. For the good of your family and career and peace of mind, go to Stanford."—was perhaps as close to the kind of input a mentor gives as any I've gotten. As noted, this lesson stood me in good stead at San Francisco.

Additionally, I had the good fortune to be a player and assistant for Bob Bronzan, head coach at San Jose State—an astute teacher of football who organized each practice almost to the minute. There was also some traditional mentoring in Bob's relationship with me. I was young, he believed in me, and he told me so in no uncertain terms.

I was also lucky to work as an assistant coach at Stanford for John Ralston—a man with a keen mind for football.

All along the way, I was paying attention to my teachers—unofficial mentors. While I was an assistant coach teaching others how to play football, others were teaching me how to *coach* football. By the time I was named head coach at Stanford University, I had a virtual PhD in coaching and leadership. Stanford football—head coach for two years—was my postdoctorate.

In a sense, the day I arrived at 49ers headquarters as head coach (and soon thereafter, general manager) I could have been wearing a cap and gown and holding a parchment paper that said, "William Ernest Walsh, Doctor of Philosophy, Modern Football, Coaching, and Leadership."

I certainly wasn't the only head coach who had that kind of "academic" credentialing, but I was lucky to be among those who did. My expertise accumulated because I made it my job to study others, to learn along the way.

Some are lucky and find themselves blessed with a mentor who truly makes a difference throughout their life. But you can make the biggest difference of all by yourself. There are mentors in our professions teaching lessons (good and bad) that are free for your inquiring mind. You must be aggressive in acquiring what they teach and adapting it to your own leadership philosophy and playbook.

In my experience, there has never been a leader who arrived fully formed, who figured it out all by him- or herself. Ralph Waldo Emerson described a great and creative person as one who "finds himself in the river of the thoughts and events, forced onward by the ideas and necessities of his contemporaries. Thus all originality is relative. Every thinker is retrospective." We learn from others.

Always there are mentors—some official, some unofficial. We apprentice when we are young, and it should continue even when we are old. A good leader is always learning. The great leaders start learning young and continue until their last breath.

The Fog Cutter

Randy Cross, San Francisco 49er, 1976–88

I witnessed the destruction of a venerable NFL franchise—the San Francisco 49ers—during my first three years with the team before Bill Walsh arrived. This included seeing the headquarters gutted of longtime personnel and the removal of all vestiges of former 49er teams—even pictures of San Francisco legends like John Brodie and Frankie Albert were tossed in the Dumpster by a general manager, Joe Thomas, who wanted to get rid of 49er history.

It culminated in a 2–14 season my third year, when we legitimately could lay claim to being perhaps the worst NFL team in history. It's hard to convey how miserable our situation was as morale plummeted about as low as it could possibly go.

Then we heard this coach from Stanford University was coming in to take over—Bill Walsh. No big deal. He'd be my *fifth* head coach in four years at San Francisco, so I figured he'd last as long as the others; that is, not long. In fact, the whole team was skeptical about his chances. But from day one I could see things were going to be different.

We arrived at training camp and Bill came in and gave a short speech to all of us. He said, "I know what some of you guys sitting there are thinking. You're thinking, 'I was here before Walsh arrived, and I'll be here when Walsh is gone.' Well, you better think about this too: If you can't play for me, and this is the *worst* team in the National Football League, where else are you going to go; who in the hell is gonna hire you?" And many of us sitting there thought to ourselves, "Hmmmm, maybe he's got a point there."

That was my first taste of his ability to kind of twist your mind a little bit. No rah-rah speech, no threats, no promises. Instead Bill came in through the side door. But that's just a tiny example of his comprehensive leadership arsenal.

Of all the coaches and businesspeople I've been around in fifty-four years, I've never known a person who could get a message across, focus that message, and get people ready to perform better than Bill Walsh. He was able to do this, in part, because he was the smartest person I have ever known and the best-organized person I have ever known. And it didn't take weeks to figure that out; it took maybe an hour. Probably less.

I saw immediately that he had a singular focus: on being first class, on being the best, on being the greatest. But lots of guys have that—the desire to be the best. Here's the difference: Bill knew exactly how to do it, the *specifics*, not just for his quarterback but for a receptionist answering the phones; not just for a backup left tackle but for groundskeepers. Somehow he knew what it was, what constituted greatness for every single job in his organization. He had that in his head.

He knew what a spreadsheet looks like, what a marketing presentation should look like, and all the rest. *Detailed* concepts. And he hired the very best people to do the jobs that he needed them to do. And in most cases he had the good sense to get out of the way and let them do their job—a very undervalued management skill.

Bill had a plan for everything, a Standard of Performance for each one of us that was so clear he could spell it out exactly. And he did. If you were a San Francisco 49er, you were not foggy on what his goal was for you specifically—what he wanted you to do—and for the organization too.

Right from the start, he really got out there and coached—rolled up his sleeves and got totally into teaching what he was aiming for. And he did that every day of every year for a decade. Of course, the offense was his baby, his first love, and he was totally involved in coaching the smallest details of its execution. He was not aloof, but right in there with the troops. Sometimes he'd take a break for a few minutes and be over on the side shadowboxing and the next minute be back in the thick of things. (Shadowboxing! That got noticed.)

The year before Bill arrived, we were 2–14 and maybe the worst team in the history of the NFL. The next year, under Bill, we had exactly the same record, 2–14, but we were the *best* 2–14 team in the history of the NFL. We had the germinating seeds of a good offense, and we sensed it. Players are very hard to fool, and we could see things happening because of Bill.

For the first three years, when he was doing this almost miraculous turnaround of the San Francisco 49ers, from the worst in the NFL to champions, we were all like coworkers, so we could really see what he was suffering through; only two wins his first year, followed by a horrible eight-game losing streak in the middle of our second season. That streak just ate his stomach up. It was his team, his deal, and he could not figure out a way to pull us out of it. You saw how it really killed him, because he was in so close with us. We could feel it, what he was going through.

When we'd watch film and see a guard go the wrong way pulling, or a running back hit the wrong hole, or a quarterback ignore the first read, we knew we were screwing up *his* offense. It was ours too, but it was his first. He had created perfection on paper, and we couldn't execute it. But he kept pushing us to get better.

He'd tell us that perfection usually wasn't possible, but that was what he wanted us to aspire to. And the offensive plays he dreamed up needed perfection in order to work. Bill had the same high standard not just for the offense and for the defense and for the special teams, but for everything: the way the office was run, the personnel department, everything and everybody. He had his hands on everything in the organization.

After three or four years, Bill started giving each of us individually the Talk. He called you into his little office in that rat hole of a building we were in on Nevada Street in Redwood City, California, and gave you a synopsis of how he saw your future. You could tell when a guy came down from his office and he'd heard a version of reality from Bill that he didn't like.

He called me in one time after I'd had the best season of my career and said, "Randy, you probably have five to six years left in the NFL. But my guess is that here, with us, you've got three or four years." I gulped: "What?"

I came down from his office with one of those looks on my face I'd seen on others. But he was doing everybody a service, because he was absolutely right. And that's a little piece of why he was ahead of his time. He was looking out for the welfare of organization, but also the players, by helping us deal with that harsh little reality; namely, we weren't playing football forever, and we *certainly* weren't playing for him forever. He didn't lead us down a rosy path. He gave us the truth.

We won a Super Bowl in Bill's third year and the following season basically tanked. After that, he pulled back from us in some ways. Not only did he feel we had forfeited his trust, but also there were veterans on the team and he was going to have to start making some hard decisions about them. So he began separating himself somewhat. From then on, he had a more arm's-length connection emotionally, a more professional relationship than in the early days. He was still hands-on with his coaching, but he pulled back from the personal part of it. It's hard to explain, but there was a change.

Two years later we won another championship, Super Bowl XIX— just tore through people during an 18–1 year, one of the best teams that anybody had ever seen. Once that happened, from that moment on, we had sort of set our own high-water mark. Good luck meeting that one every year. Nevertheless, the pressure on Bill got ratcheted way up by the owner, Eddie DeBartolo. A Super Bowl was the norm; anything less was not acceptable, and the pressure became crushing.

In Bill's final season, his tenth, he really got put through the wringer. We were 6–5 at one point and being written off by everybody. After a one-point loss at Phoenix to the Cardinals, Eddie stormed into our locker room immediately after the game and was livid. He dressed down everybody verbally, I mean really hard. Threatening us. That wasn't such a big deal; we'd been screamed at as a team before, nothing new there. But this time Bill himself was targeted in the threats and dressing-down. He got screamed at along with the rest of us. That was an eye opener right there—a first for us. It had to really hurt him—to be humiliated like that. Looking back, I don't think Eddie would consider it one of his sterling moments.

But that's what that place was about as the years went on. We weren't there to be good, we weren't there to win a lot of games, we were there to win Super Bowls. Otherwise, get out. And personally, I think that level of expectation is productive. It's the only way to go about doing it, even though it cost Bill a couple of years on his career and maybe some more Super Bowls.

Under the pressure he had on him during the last few years, there was no way he could keep going. At the end he would have needed a six-month vacation all by himself on a desert island—making him sleep all the time, making him relax, making him chill out—if he wanted to continue under that load and that pressure.

Throughout the years, Bill's passion was so evident. It became the passion of his team and the staff and everybody in the organization. We stepped up to his level of dedication, his standard, his vision, and his ability to get the job done. And brother, if he detected anything less than an equal kind of passion from any one of us, we'd get the sharp end of the stick.

That's why I chuckle when I see all these pictures of Bill, that image of him being a professor, pensive, the "thinker" with his hand on his chin, contemplating the exact words of his next lecture. Nobody on the outside ever saw the *other* side that he could summon up. Bill Walsh could burn a hole right through you with his eyes. Right through your bones and everything. His eyes could knock you out.

We saw a whole different guy from the professor. He could present a whole different vocabulary when he wanted to—like a longshoreman. But it was part of his passion for greatness.

Bill Walsh had the ability to change the way people thought—not just how we performed a task, but how we thought and *felt* about who we were. In the beginning, when we were as bad as we were, nobody was thinking about a Super Bowl. Our goal in life was just to be pretty good. Bill's goal in life was to convince us that we could be great. And he did; and we were. That's why he was such a great leader.

PART V

Thin Skin, Baloney, and "The Star-Spangled Banner": Looking for Lessons in My Mirror

How You Get Good: No Mystery to Mastery

If you're Jerry Rice, the greatest receiver in NFL history and, according to some, the greatest player, you're practicing a slant pass pattern at 6 A.M. over and over with nobody within a mile of you—no football, no quarterback, nobody but Jerry working to improve, to master his profession.

Why is the NFL's greatest-ever receiver doing this? Jerry Rice understands the connection between preparation and performance; between intelligently applied hard work and results; between mediocrity and mastery of your job. And Jerry has the skill coupled with the will to do it.

Joe Montana, perhaps the greatest quarterback in NFL history, in his last season as a professional, when he was playing for Kansas City, would spend two hours a day every day at the same little practice field at Menlo College near San Francisco. I would work with him on basic fundamentals that would bore a high schooler to death. Joe had four Super Bowl rings. How did he get them? Why was he on that little practice field? Joe Montana understands what mastery means.

You never stop learning, perfecting, refining—molding your skills. You never stop depending on the fundamentals—sustaining, maintaining, and improving. Jerry and Joe, maybe the best ever at their positions, at the last stages of their careers were still working very hard on the fundamental things that high school kids won't do because it's too damn dull.

It wasn't dull to Jerry and Joe, because they understood the absolute and direct connection between intelligently directed hard work and achieving your potential. We all do; you do; I do. Everybody who's a serious player knows what it takes. The difference is how much you're willing to give to get there.

For us, there is no mystery to mastery. And it applies to football players and coaches, general managers and executives in sports or business. It applies to anyone anywhere who wants to get really good—who wants to master his or her profession. It applies to you.

Sine Qua Non: Your Work Ethic—What William Archibald Walsh Taught His Son

For me, the starting point for everything—before strategy, tactics, theories, managing, organizing, philosophy, methodology, talent, or experience—is the work ethic. Without one of significant magnitude you're dead in the water, finished.

Among other things, I knew the example I set as head coach would be what others in the organization would recognize as the standard they needed to match (at least, most of them would recognize it). If there is such a thing as a trickle-down effect, that's it. Your staff sees your devotion to work, their people see them, and on through the organization.

Obviously, it's not enough for you alone to work hard; there must be a similar organizational work ethic for anything of significance to occur. You—the one in charge—are the reference point for what that means.

What does total effort and 100 percent commitment and sacrifice look like? The leader—head coach in my case—is the one who answers that question by example for the entire team; you demonstrate in your behavior what it looks like. Just talking about it, exhorting those in your organization to "give it all you've got" is close to meaningless. It's like telling someone what constitutes a great movie. They've got to see it to know it. Same thing with a voracious appetite for work. Most people don't have it; many people can achieve it; one person is charged with setting the standard and demonstrating what it means: you.

During my years as head coach both at Stanford University and with the San Francisco 49ers, I believe it is safe to say there was no single individual in the organization—player, assistant coach, trainer, staff member, groundskeeper, or anyone else—who could accurately say he or she out-worked me. Not one. I can state that with no fear of contradiction. Some worked as hard—nobody worked harder.

I never asked anyone to do more than I was willing to do, nor what I wasn't willing to do. Nobody could ever—not once—point at me and say, "Walsh sits on his ass in his office all day while we do the work." When that sentiment spreads through an organization, you have signaled that "sitting on your ass all day" is an accepted standard of performance.

I was fortunate in this regard, because when I was growing up my role model was a good one. The guy who set the standard for me was my father. Dad knew what it meant to really work hard. And he did. William Archibald Walsh never went past eighth grade, scrambled around as a young man to make money, and came through tough times, including the Great Depression. He struggled to make a living for his family but showed me what a man does when he has a job to do: He goes out and does it.

During the Depression, my father was paid thirty-one cents an hour to work ten hours or more a day on the assembly line at the huge Chrysler plant near our small house in south central Los Angeles. That didn't pay the bills, so he set up a little auto body repair shop in our garage, where he worked after he got *done* working at the plant, late at night and on weekends.

When I was a teenager, I had to work with him on many of those evenings and weekends, long hours into the night helping him out. I hated it, but he taught me the connection between hard work and survival, between survival and success. Dad taught me that. His work ethic became *my* work ethic.

He paid a tremendous price for his willingness to work. It may have shortened his life—a life that offered little in the way of fun or material reward—and kept him from connecting in any meaningful way with his son. I never really got to know my father; he didn't have time. It was all work for Dad, or his family wouldn't survive.

Over the years, I've heard many theories, often complex or convoluted, on what it takes to be an outstanding leader. Most of the theories seem to take a monumental work ethic for granted, as if it is assumed or something, as if people automatically know what it is and do it. I didn't assume it. The majority of people out there don't know what it is. They need to be shown, and you're the one who must show it.

Some of our great leaders come from the military, not just America's, but those we fought against. General Erwin Rommel, the Desert Fox, as he was known commanding Germany's tank brigades in North Africa during World Ward II, understood the power of example in the area of effort. Here's what he said: "A commander must accustom his staff to a high tempo from the outset, and continuously keep them up to it. If he once allows himself to be satisfied with norms, or anything less than an all-out effort, he gives up the race from the starting post, and will sooner or later be taught a bitter lesson."

A high tempo from the outset and continuously throughout; dissatisfaction with the usual norms; insistence on all-out effort? Rommel understood hard work and the importance of *demonstrating* it to his troops. The same applies to your troops. You're the one who shows them what all-out effort really means, what hard work looks like.

You cannot do that if you're invisible, cooped up in your office instead of being out there with your team. A leader's great work ethic must been *seen* to be perceived, must be perceived if it is to be the organization's *norm*.

The Perfection of the Puzzle

I hate to see bad football. I hate to see a team play bad football, even on a single play—in practice, in a game, anywhere. Bad football makes me ill in the same way, I suppose, a symphony conductor hates to hear an orchestra mangle Bach or Beethoven. There's a reverence for the art. For me, it can be described as a reverence for football as it *could* be played—the exquisite beauty of what can occur at its uppermost level. I think top performers in all professions have that same deep respect—even reverence—for their work.

One player, a guard, for example, making every small move perfectly on a play is a little work of art that I can watch on tape over and over again with satisfaction. Imagine then, when on a single play each one of our players does his job exactly, perfectly, totally *right*. It can be breathtaking. If it scores a touchdown, the points are almost incidental, frosting on the cake (unless the frosting wins a game).

When it's done perfectly at its highest level, football is art and gives me such great fulfillment. Anything less, the botched play, casual effort, sloppy execution, inept play calling, even if it gains ground or scores points, was very disturbing—painful—to me on an aesthetic level. I was never able to take refuge in a winning score if it was produced by shoddy performance—bad football.

Thus, if we won, I cared about *how* we won; if we lost, I cared about *how* we lost. I didn't want to lose by forty points; I'd prefer to lose by thirty-nine. If we won by twenty, I'd wake up in the middle of the night and try hard to figure out how we could have scored twenty-one points. It wasn't increasing or decreasing the point differential that was so intriguing to me, but rather increasing the quality of our execution and decision making—the quality of the football we played.

Had I miscalculated or ignored information that was there for me to see and evaluate? Why and where did our execution break down? Where were our decisions—my decisions—flawed or dead wrong? On and on and on. It was, I think, perfection that I was pursuing.

Whatever it was, beyond the score I had a passion for figuring out how we could have performed at a higher and higher level of excellence. Good or bad, win or lose, "What caused what, and how can it be improved?" was my recurrent question, an obsession.

At 2 A.M. I'd be staring up at the ceiling or tossing around in bed. Eventually, I'd get up, pace around, sit down in the next room to write some notes. Then back to pacing, slowly analyzing before writing down additional observations or ideas.

Finally, as the sun was getting ready to come up, I'd go back to bed and try to get a few minutes of sleep. It was like this after every single game I coached at San Francisco for ten years, close to it on many other nights. By the end of the season, I was a mess physically and emotionally.

All of this had less to do with running up the score or trying to lose by fewer points than with how I perceived the entire process of leadership and striving for success. To me it was a puzzle to be solved, pieces to be found and put in place, solutions to be figured out. I had a passion for trying to determine how we could have performed at a higher level, how we could achieve perfection, or at least get closer and closer and closer.

Of course, losing is monumentally—traumatically—different from

winning, but in both cases I was extremely and, at times, perhaps overly analytical of our efforts in searching for a means of closing in on perfection.

In Super Bowl XIX—the closest I've ever come to coaching a perfect game—two events occurred that marred it for me to this very day.
Although they may seem trivial or illogical to you, they illustrate my
all-consuming desire to set every single piece of the puzzle perfectly in
place.

The game was played in front of 84,059 fans at Stanford Stadium,
thirty minutes south of San Francisco in Palo Alto, California. Our opponents, the Miami Dolphins, were led by Dan Marino, a quarterback
whose arm was so strong he could supposedly throw a football sixty yards
behind his back. Additionally, he had an uncanny ability to read defenses,
a trigger-fast release, and two of the greatest receivers of the time, Mark
Clayton and Mark Duper.

Some viewed Miami and Marino as unstoppable, and the results supported it: a regular-season record of 14–2. While our regular season record
was even better, 15–1, there was a troubling fact within those numbers;
namely, in the AFC championship game to advance to the Super Bowl,
Marino had thrown twenty-one completions for 421 yards against the
Pittsburgh Steelers. It was an easy win for the Dolphins: 45–28. This was
relevant and very troubling because Pittsburgh had been the *only* team to
beat San Francisco during our 15–1 regular season.

That's why it concerned me so much—the only team to beat us had,
in turn, been beaten easily by our upcoming Super Bowl opponents, the
Miami Dolphins, and their young superstar quarterback, Marino. While
the oddsmakers had us favored by three points, lots of bettors thought it
should have been the other way around and placed their bets accordingly.

Nevertheless, after trailing 10–7 at the end of the first quarter, we
began to gradually take over on both offense and defense. With less than a
minute remaining in the first half, San Francisco seemed to be in control
of the game and held a big lead: 28–10.

With time running out on the half, the Dolphins' kicker, Uwe von
Schamann, nailed a field goal from thirty-seven yards to bring the score
to 28–13. As Miami prepared to kick off, I instructed our kickoff return
team to simply fall on the ball to remove all risk of a fumble: "No runback!
No runback! Fall on the ball! No runback!" I would be very happy to let

the first half run down and head into the locker room with a fifteen-point lead.

The Dolphins' kick went to Guy McIntyre, a blocker, who grabbed the ball and immediately fell to the ground, exactly as I had instructed just seconds earlier. The clock would now run out on the first half in a very orderly manner and send us into the locker room to prepare for the second half with a solid advantage.

But suddenly 49er rookie Derrick Harmon ran over to McIntyre and began screaming, "Get up! Run! Run, run, run!" Guy got up and ran. Or tried to. He immediately got hit by a Miami defender who'd been building up a full-speed head of steam for twenty yards. In the resulting collision, Guy fumbled; Miami recovered and quickly kicked another field goal. The first half—*suddenly*—was over.

It happened in a flash, and it was stunning to me. I felt like I'd been hit hard on the head with a metal baseball bat. Even though we still had a comfortable lead, in a space of ten seconds the Dolphins had scored twice on field goals, narrowed the margin, and completely turned things around *psychologically*. But in retrospect there was something else that was equally upsetting.

I felt that if our coaching—*my* teaching—had been better, the breakdown in discipline and execution would not have occurred. I didn't blame Guy, nor did I really blame Derrick. I blamed myself for that high school level of execution and still do. It was bad football.

The second blemish on this otherwise near-perfect game occurred as the clock was winding down very late in the fourth quarter, with the 49ers leading 38–16. At that point, I made a decision that still gnaws at me.

With second down and less than a yard to go for a touchdown, I called off the hunt, ran the same play three consecutive times, knowing it probably wouldn't score—variations of Roger Craig going over the top—because I didn't want to create the impression we were pouring it on, running up the score.

As intended, we didn't make a touchdown. Miami took possession as the clock ran out, and the 49ers won our second Super Bowl in four years: 38–16.

My decision obviously didn't affect the final outcome of the game, but I believe it was wrong to do what I decided to do; namely, force a team dedicated to competing to stop competing. It was wrong to do that, to take the bullet out of the chamber. It was bad football, and it was my fault.

Now, those two incidents might cause you to say, "Why in the world would you worry about it, Bill? Guy McIntyre's response to Derrick Harmon's yelling to get up and run was just good aggressive instinct, and your calling off the hunt at the end of the game was just good sportsmanship."

But as the years have passed, both situations have come back to me in a negative way that I don't feel good about. Neither should have occurred; both marred an otherwise perfect game. And that's the point: Our game was very close to perfect.

Those two incidents will live with me forever because otherwise it was as flawless a football game as I've ever coached, as close to putting all the pieces in place for the full four quarters of a game.

Achieving success in a competitive environment requires solving a very complicated puzzle. This is true in all big-time competition. The winners know how to get more pieces of the puzzle in place than the losers. I still regret that those two final pieces of the puzzle prevented it from being solved perfectly.

I also know that the degree of drive an individual has to solve the puzzle perfectly, no matter how complex or difficult, is directly related to attaining higher and higher levels of success. It's that desire that wakes you up in the middle of the night reaching for a pen and paper next to your bed—an insatiable hunger to capture inspiration and answers that all highly driven people share.

Where that drive comes from is often a mystery. Here's what Arthur Ashe, one of the greatest tennis players in history, had to say about it: "Who knows what force gnaws at us, telling us that our accomplishments, no matter how sensational, are not enough; that we need to do more?" (Arthur Ashe, *Days of Grace*.)

I sought perfection, and 99 percent isn't perfection. Why "almost perfect" wasn't enough for me is something I can't explain.

The Gladiator Mentality: Get Your Mind Right

The gladiator mentality is common in sports, especially football at all levels. Although it's played out differently in business, I think there is a similar phenomenon—that is, the effort to "get your mind *right*," totally focused—before a significant event, whether it's a major sales presentation or something else. Among other things, it involves the preparation, the "ceremony" before the main event. Top performers utilize this opportunity to get ready for battle.

There is a ritual, sort of a crescendo, that takes you to the very peak of preparation and readiness. The gladiator is thinking, mentally narrowing his focus, as he goes through the ritual before the game. It draws him upward smoothly into the increasing intensity and pressure of the event like a high-performance car going from zero to sixty, the gears shifting seamlessly and without notice.

In addition to our pregame discussions, I had my own ritual as a coach before each kickoff and did it almost unconsciously. I always went to my locker first and then walked through the locker room, taking exactly the same route each time. I would sit in my office and watch another NFL game on television for five minutes or so—not really paying much attention to it, just distracting myself. Then I would leave my office, and just before going out to the field I would shake hands with every single player on our team. If I got done and had missed one of them, I somehow knew it and would search him out and shake hands.

It was that ritual that helped me to create the mind-set I wanted before each game. It helped me to focus on what I was about to do, allowed me to methodically narrow my concentration to the point where I could block out everything but the game plan and its execution. The routine was part of the grounding process in which I sought to eradicate worry, excitement, stress, distractions, hopes, fears, and all personal issues. It was like walking into a completely different room mentally, like being on a different planet. And it didn't end when I left the locker room.

I Never Sang "The Star-Spangled Banner"

During "The Star-Spangled Banner" before the opening kickoff, I would stand at attention with my hand over my heart, but I wasn't singing. It was during this brief moment that I would remove myself mentally from the activities and considerable energy around me on the sidelines—compose and focus myself, extend what I had begun in the locker room.

I visualized that I was looking at the football field through a big plate-glass window, removed, in a sense, so I wouldn't get overly involved emotionally and could stay with what I had prepared prior to game. Clear thinking and overly charged emotions are usually antithetical.

I actually think my heart rate may have gone down as the opening kickoff approached. Rather than getting more and more excited, pumped up and emotional, a sense of calm came over me. If a person can be extremely intense, extraordinarily focused, *and* completely composed all at the same time, I guess that's the state I was in by the time I was through *not* singing the national anthem.

By the opening kickoff, I had blocked out crowd noise (and the crowd) and all the crazy energy and activity on the sidelines, which are disruptive to good decision making. It may have been as pleasing a sensation as any I ever got as a coach. Winning a Super Bowl championship was great, but the emotion I felt in victory was often more relief than anything else, especially as the years went on.

The state of mind I could achieve as a game was about to begin was pure, so free of dissonance—it was just the best. The ritual created it. It was the gladiator mind-set, free of stress, distractions, and emotionalism, that got me ready for the competition and allowed me to work at my highest level.

"Getting your mind right" has application beyond a football game. Those events where you're putting it all on the line—a big sales presentation, an important conference with your team (or your boss), and many other occasions—all require that your thinking be at its best. The preperformance "ritual" that you develop can help make it happen just as it helped me to do my job to the best of my ability.

My Strengths?

I have a passion for what I do. Also, if I'm honest about it, I'd say that I have an ability to communicate and relate to others in the context of work, to express myself clearly, and to do that in all circumstances, especially under extreme pressure.

If I have a gift, it is the imaginative strain in my system, my makeup. I'm excellent at coming up with concepts and then finding a way to make them a reality. If I have a vision, a concept, I know how to find a way to implement it and not back away from it, a determination to see it through and, if necessary, take risks to make it happen.

If I had an idea for a certain new formation or play, or a way of using a particular player, I would find a way to make it work. (This is what I did when I utilized John Ayers to take on the task of neutralizing the great threat presented by New York Giants outside linebacker Lawrence "L.T." Taylor.) And if my idea failed, I knew whether to drop it and move on to something else or to continue to develop it. You could call me a good problem solver. Of course, before you solve a problem, you've got to spot the problem. I was good at that too.

I had this ability even when I was coaching high school football in Fremont, California. I just couldn't stop trying to figure out new ways of doing things, coming up with novel solutions to problems, different plays. It fascinated me. That part of it never stopped—looking for innovative ways of doing things. I was always looking to build a better mousetrap.

Unleash Mentors: Tell Your Team to Teach

One of the reasons the 49ers won five Super Bowls in fourteen years is that we expected veterans to do everything possible to bring along rookies. In effect, they were expected to train their own replacements, and it was one of the reasons I prohibited hazing. I wanted new players, new staff members, new scouts, and everyone else who joined us to sense immediately they had joined an organization with a unique environment.

I stressed to veterans that we should take pride in welcoming the new arrivals who could help the team win and create and carry on the 49ers tradition. To help us accomplish this goal, the veterans were instructed to help others learn the ropes, do the job better (even if it was their *own* job they were training someone else to do). Thus, the body of knowledge a veteran player had accumulated—especially as it pertained to my Standard of Performance—was being assimilated by new employees, rookies, and first- and second-year players in a very effective manner. In a sense, I made teachers out of my students. The players became coaches. This built-in crew of teachers exists in your own organization. Tap into it.

I applied the same expectations—teaching and training others to do one's own job—to myself. When I retired as head coach after Super Bowl XXIII, my replacement and longtime assistant coach, George Seifert, had been well schooled in the Standard of Performance that had become the 49er way. Seifert's San Francisco 49ers won Super Bowl XXIV the year immediately following my departure. It was his team, but I felt ownership and pride in it.

There was, however, great ambivalence in my pride. At the moment of San Francisco's fourth Super Bowl title, as I watched the commissioner of NFL football, Paul Tagliabue, hand the Lombardi Trophy to George Seifert and Eddie DeBartolo, I was filled with deep remorse and great sadness.

By retiring at the end of the previous season I had denied myself the opportunity to equal the all-time record for a head coach of winning four Super Bowls, as Chuck Noll's Pittsburgh Steelers had done under his leadership. It is perhaps the most illustrious of all NFL records. I quit at three, "voluntarily" walked away from my chance to make history. I never got over that one.

My philosophy of team members teaching new arrivals the organization's system, not just *X*'s and *O*'s but the attitudes and actions of performance, is essential to a self-sustaining winning organization. It is accomplished through mentoring within your organization. And for mentoring to exist, members of your team must truly believe that their first loyalty is to furthering the good of the group: "What is good for *us* is good for me." That's tough to teach, but it's part of the connection and extension principle that was built into my Standard of Performance.

I am not naive. Intense rivalries existed between players fighting for the same position, and they did *not* want to train their own replacements. The best example in my experience is perhaps Steve Young and Joe Montana—two of the greatest quarterbacks in NFL history, who are both in the NFL Hall of Fame. When Steve was acquired from Tampa after Joe had led San Francisco to two Super Bowl championships, Montana didn't like it one bit. He felt threatened, perhaps insulted and embarrassed. Nevertheless, my goal was to help both of them put aside personal ambition and accept my decisions regarding what was best for the team as I looked into the future. Good luck with that.

Obviously, it was impossible for them to literally do this, to forget about their rivalry. After all, they were both thoroughbreds by nature and nurturing, born leaders who felt diminished standing on the sidelines watching the other guy do a job each felt he could do better. Nevertheless, I wanted to get close to a situation where they were able to coexist and not be disruptive to the overall environment of the organization.

An overall workable "truce," which was uneasy at times, was held together, and each player made some efforts to help the other. They were never buddies, and in fact to this day view each other with a wary eye. But it held together. We—*they*—kept the peace. In my opinion, overall they did help each other. Perhaps it's wishful thinking, but that's how I would like to think it was. It certainly was that way for other players throughout most of the organization.

Everyone must have an attitude of helping one another. Are you teaching that to those you lead? Do you teach that being on your team includes sharing their knowledge? That an employee strengthens himself or herself when he or she strengthens another member of the organization?

It's a powerful force when you unleash it. I unleashed it during my years as head coach of the San Francisco 49ers. It was one of our great assets—unseen by those outside the 49er organization.

Don't Do unto Others (What Paul Brown Did unto Me)

Paul Brown, the only man in history to have an NFL team named after him—the Cleveland Browns—was also one of professional football's most powerful and creative forces, a football genius whose absolute commitment to his team's welfare was an obsession. He was willing to do virtually anything for the good of the team. This caused him to deal severely and, at times, unscrupulously with anyone acting in a manner he viewed as contrary to the best interests of the Browns (and later the Cincinnati Bengals).

I know because at a very important point in my career I was subjected to this dark side of Paul Brown's character. Ultimately, it became one half of a crucial lesson I learned about dealing with people.

When Paul Brown decided to retire, I had been his assistant offensive coach at Cincinnati for eight years. During that time, he'd led me to believe I would replace him as head coach when the time came for him to step down. But when the time came, he chose Bill "Tiger" Johnson, a talented offensive coordinator I had worked with during my years on the Bengals' staff. I was devastated and felt it was time to look elsewhere if I was going to advance my career in the direction of eventually becoming a head coach.

Very soon I discussed job openings with the Seattle Seahawks and the New York Jets, neither of whom showed any interest at all. This struck me as unusual, since both teams needed to make improvements in an area where I had proven expertise and a good track record; namely, figuring out how to score more touchdowns.

Later, during an interview with the San Diego Chargers about the job as their offensive coordinator, I began to understand why I had received such a cool reception in those earlier job interviews: My efforts to find employment outside the Bengals football organization were being aggressively sabotaged by someone from *inside* the Bengals organization: my boss, Paul Brown.

Tommy Prothro, head coach of the Chargers, casually mentioned during my job interview that Paul had called him two days earlier and made very critical remarks about my work at Cincinnati, including the observation that I was too passive to really motivate and lead a large group of players. He strongly urged Tommy not to hire me. (Simultaneously, I was being offered the job as offensive coordinator of the Bengals, the same position the Chargers had been told by Brown that I couldn't handle.)

This backstabbing was confirmed shortly afterward by Al Davis, the crafty owner of the Oakland Raiders, who told me that other owners and executives around the NFL were also getting negative critiques about me out of Cincinnati. "The word going out on you isn't so good, Bill. People are hearing that you're great with X's and O's but not really a leader. Maybe that's why you're not getting offers," he suggested.

Al was correct. In spite of my loyal and very productive years as an assistant coach with the Cincinnati Bengals, Paul Brown wouldn't recommend me to other teams and was, in fact, aggressively reaching out to prevent me from getting a job elsewhere. (It also explained why during my eight years at Cincinnati I had received no serious job offers. Brown had turned aside inquiries about my availability and downplayed my leadership abilities. In all those years, he never mentioned that others were expressing interest in hiring me, that other teams wanted to talk to me about a job.)

In one way, it was understandable. Brown had a fanatical desire to protect the Cincinnati franchise at all costs, even if it meant dishonestly denigrating my ability to other NFL owners and coaches. Obviously, this was a personal betrayal, even if he believed it was somehow in my own best interests to remain with the Bengals.

Added to everything else, this made it imperative that I leave Cincinnati as soon as possible. Subsequently, I joined Tommy Prothro's staff in San Diego and soon learned the other half of an important lesson in how to treat people if you want a productive organization filled with true team spirit and vitality.

One year after I was hired by the Chargers, Stanford University called and inquired about my availability to take over as its head coach. When Tommy heard about the offer, he immediately came to me with the following advice: "Take the job, Bill, because a head coaching position in the Pac-10 is significant. For the good of your family and career and peace of mind, go to Stanford."

Tommy felt that I had done outstanding work for him during the previous season—my efforts with future Hall of Fame quarterback Dan Fouts and the subsequent improved offensive attack had produced excellent results, and there was every reason to expect more of the same. Nevertheless, Tommy put *my* best interests ahead of his own and his team's. He was a man of the highest ethical standards.

My subsequent work as head coach at Stanford University led directly to being hired by the San Francisco 49ers, and it was due in great measure to his encouragement and selflessness.

However, the following question should be addressed: If the bottom line, winning, is all that counts, didn't Paul Brown make the smart choice—doing everything possible to keep a valued employee on staff, even if it meant hurting that individual's chance for advancement elsewhere? No, and ethical considerations aside, here's a very practical reason why.

I believe that character-based leaders tend to seek and attract character-based employees in sports, in business, or anywhere else. As my own career progressed, I tried hard to emulate the example of Tommy Prothro, who believed in treating people right, whose leadership was founded on ethics. Here's just one example of how it played out for me.

When I was head coach of the 49ers, one of our defensive coaches, Ray Rhodes, began attracting attention from other teams because of his uncommon abilities—highly informed, enthusiastic, straightforward, a good teacher and communicator who got exceptional results. He was a very important factor in the early years when we were trying to turn things around and then later in winning Super Bowls.

The New York Giants, already familiar with Ray's outstanding qualities because he was one of their former players, requested permission to talk to him about a coaching position (he still had a one-year obligation left on his San Francisco contract).

In spite of the fact that we greatly valued his ability, character, and importance to our team, I recognized what Tommy Prothro had done for me. I gave New York permission to talk to Ray with the understanding that if he ultimately wanted to break his contract with the 49ers and join the Giants, he would be free to do so. Additionally, I told New York the truth about Ray Rhodes; namely, that he was a terrific coach and solid citizen. The Giants soon offered him a job.

Now it was our turn. To keep Ray in the organization, we prepared a very strong counteroffer, including a three-year contract for a lot more money. It was not an easy decision for Ray, because he had received two outstanding offers, but after giving it careful consideration over a period of several days, he decided he would benefit most by staying with the 49ers. Ray remained with us and continued to do great work. A few years later, he became head coach of the Philadelphia Eagles.

There's a phrase that sums it up fairly well: "What goes around comes around." I believe that word of what Paul Brown had done to me (and probably others) when I was attempting to leave Cincinnati got around the league and ultimately hurt the Bengals in a variety of predictable ways. After all, how eager would you be to join an organization that might not look after your interests, that might betray your loyalty?

Conversely, I know for a fact that many talented players and coaches—individuals who eventually helped us win NFC conference championships and Super Bowls, such as quarterback Steve Young, Wendell Tyler, Jack "Hacksaw" Reynolds, Paul Hackett (later head coach of USC), and others—*sought* to join San Francisco in large measure because they knew their career aspirations would be addressed and respected.

While they were with us, we expected them to give us everything they had, but in turn, we gave them our recognition that they had the right to advance their own careers. Word got around that the 49ers treated people right.

In your own professional activities, remember that a reputation for fair play—treating people right—can be a big part of a potential employee's decision to join you or a current and valued employee's desire to remain. It can infuse your team with strength in creating a self-image that transcends a sense of being in a band of mercenaries. It can matter more than money.

When it comes to deciding how you treat people, exploitation, expedience, and self-interest are a formula for creating a team of individuals who will soon be looking to join another team. I learned many great lessons from Paul Brown, but "treating people right" was not among them. That lesson was one I learned from Tommy Prothro.

Nine Steps for a Healthy Heart

People matter most—more than equipment, investors, inventions, momentum, or X's and O's. People are at the heart of achieving organizational greatness. Too often aggressive leaders forget the human part of the equation—the most important part. Let me suggest nine steps you can take that involve treating people right, for having a healthy heart in your organization:

1. **Afford each person the same respect, support, and fair treatment you would expect if your roles were reversed.** Deal with people individually, not as objects who are part of a herd—that's the critical factor.
2. **Leadership involves many people, each with their own need for role identity within the organization.** Find what a person does best, utilize and emphasize it, and steer clear of his or her weaknesses.
3. **Demonstrate a pronounced commitment to employees** by providing a work environment that enables them to achieve their maximum potential and productivity.
4. **Acknowledge the uniqueness of each employee** and the need he or she has for a reasonable degree of job security and self-actualization. You don't own him or her.
5. **The most talented personnel often are very independent minded.** This requires that you carefully consider how you relate to and communicate with this type of individual. Creative people usually bring a passion to seeing their ideas put into play as quickly as possible. They must be helped to understand that not every idea is appropriate and that coming up with a new concept is just the start of a process that includes evaluation, comparisons, practicability, and more. But be careful not to quash an idea-friendly environment in your organization.
6. **While at times a divergence may exist between the good**

of the group and the good of the individual, in a best-case scenario the group's and the individual's "good" should be the same. When this is not the case, you are well served to explain the reasons behind the divergence to the person who feels badly treated—for example, when he or she is passed over for promotion. (For me, occasionally a player wanted to play one position when, in fact, he was better suited to another. I attempted to explain this to the individual whose goal was being denied. You may have an individual who similarly needs direction to play to his or her strength within your organization. And you may have to explain how this benefits the goal of the team.)

7. **People are most comfortable with how they are being treated when their duties are laid out in specific detail** and their performance can be gauged by specific metrics. The key is to document—clarify—those expectations. In my initial year at San Francisco, our starting quarterback, Steve DeBerg, was outstanding in many areas. The category that he came up short in, however, was critical—throwing interceptions at important junctures. It cost him his job because it was right there on paper, a quantifiable statistic that verified what I already knew. In a very easily seen way, he could be shown where he was underperforming.

8. **It is critical that employee expectation levels be reasonable, attainable, and high.** While you should exhibit flexibility in the work environment to accommodate the needs of employees, you should be inflexible with regard to your *expectations* of their performance.

9. **Establish a protocol for how members of the organization interact with one another.** This is essential to preventing compartmentalization and "turf protection." Let them know their first priority is to do their job; their second priority is to facilitate others in doing their jobs.

Seriously, Don't Be Too Serious

There's not a lot of room for joking around in the midst of competitive challenges, whether on the football field or in the marketplace. Humor is often a sign of being removed from the focus and commitment necessary to do the job well—a casual attitude about a serious endeavor.

But a leader also runs the risk of pushing so hard, with deadly solemnity and grim-faced determination, that he or she creates an oppressive and performance-limiting workplace. You need to recognize when it's time to lighten up and let some of the steam—pressure—vent. This requires the ability to gauge when and how it is appropriate to utilize humor.

We encountered that kind of situation in the week prior to playing in our first Super Bowl. The incredible experience was brand new to all of us, but I was especially concerned that our young players would be adversely affected by the media gauntlet and fan frenzy, not to mention the requirement that they perform at their absolute best. It could be crushing, and in fact, oddsmakers generally give an edge in the Super Bowl to a team that has been there before—experienced the near-trauma of the week's media circus and ultimate-game pressure. (In this instance, neither team had appeared in a Super Bowl before.)

I arrived in Detroit several days before the rest of the team to do interviews and participate in league meetings. My plan was to meet the players when they arrived at our hotel after their bus trip in from the Detroit airport. Consequently, I was looking for something for our guys that would crack the tension, something where they could just enjoy one another in the incredible hype they would encounter immediately after stepping off the buses in front of the hotel.

I had about thirty minutes before they arrived and came up with this idea: I would put on a bellhop's uniform and cap—disguise myself—and help the players with their bags as they got off the bus. I paid a bellhop thirty bucks to let me wear his outfit and stood on the curb as the first San Francisco 49ers bus pulled up right in front of me. My disguise was effective because crowding behind me on the sidewalk were hundreds of fans, friends, reporters, and photographers who distracted the players as they got off the bus.

As team members stepped to the sidewalk I kept my head kind of looking down at their luggage so they couldn't see who it was—their head coach handling their bags. The whole point, of course, was to break the heat of the experience and remind them, "Hey, we're still *us*." I wanted to let them know that it was okay to be comfortable and even enjoy what was going on, that they didn't have to go into some hyper level of tension and stress because it was the Super Bowl.

My disguise worked so well that Joe Montana actually got into a tug-of-war with me over his duffel bag. He was trying to keep me from taking it when suddenly he saw who the "bellhop" was—his head coach. The whole team started breaking up and joking with one another—a big shift for the positive in team attitude. They saw the guy in charge— me—having a little fun. It gave them an important message: Don't get all worked up and stressed out by everything. Stay loose.

The little stunt went to my understanding that in a crucible of pressure a safety valve is valuable, something that will release tension. And I could see that the pressure immediately reduced in the 49ers as they got off the buses.

The same kind of opportunities exist for you if you're alert and recognize that puncturing pressure with *appropriate* humor can be beneficial under the weight of deadlines and other stress producers.

A more outlandish situation occurred a week later on the way to the Silverdome in Pontiac, Michigan, where we would play in Super Bowl XVI. We traveled in two buses, and I was on the second one with Montana and half of the team. The first bus made it to the Silverdome without a problem. Our bus got caught in a massive traffic jam caused by a motorcade for Vice President George Bush. It was made worse by a snowstorm that had hit a few hours earlier. At one point, it looked like we might be thirty minutes late for our own Super Bowl game.

It would have been easy to sit in silence and stew, to let the extreme pressure go even higher. Instead, I intentionally made some lighter comments and a few jokes, including my announcement over the bus's loudspeaker that the game had started without us using just the players of the first bus: "May I have your attention, please. This just in from the

Silverdome: 'Early in the first quarter, San Francisco is trailing Cincinnati 7–0. 49ers trainer Chico Norton is calling the plays." This loosened people up, and the energy returned to something approaching a "normal" level of enthusiasm and eagerness to go into battle. We arrived at the Silverdome just ninety minutes before the kickoff.

I certainly am not suggesting that a joke or lighter comment is why we won that game. But I know for certain that tightening of nerves in an atmosphere of increasing uncertainty and anxiety is counterproductive. I defused or changed it to something more productive because I knew that humor, used in the right way at the right time, could provide that valuable safety valve. (By the way, after nearly being late for the Super Bowl because he was on the second bus, Joe started taking a taxi to the stadium for all future road games. That way he could leave much earlier and guarantee that he wouldn't miss the opening snap.)

Does pressure improve performance? Yes, up to a point, but let me suggest the following: Regardless of context, those who are able to perform best are those who are best able to *remove* tension, anxiety, and fear from their minds. There's a phrase for it: "being in the zone." And, there is no tension, anxiety, or fear in the zone, whether on the football field, in the conference room, or in a multitude of situations where you are called on to really produce.

You want your team to push hard, to feel as if they will come up short without total effort. But total effort doesn't mean total anxiety. I believe optimum creativity and high performance—a sales presentation, for example, or a complex pass play from Joe Montana to Jerry Rice— are most likely to succeed when the individual or group has an attitude that is seemingly a paradox; specifically, both relaxed *and* intense. That's when things really happen. Here's an example that many people still don't believe is true.

In Super Bowl XXIII the 49ers took possession of the ball late in the fourth quarter—with less than three minutes left—on our own eight-yard line. We needed to drive the length of the field and score a touchdown to win the ballgame. A single mistake along the way could cost us the Super Bowl. This is about as much situational pressure as exists in NFL football.

As our offense huddled in the end zone to hear Joe Montana call the first play, they noticed his head turn; something had caught his eye. "Hey," he said to his teammates huddled with him, "isn't that John Candy, the comedian, standing over there by the exit in the stands?" Everybody looked up, and sure enough, it was Candy. Then they turned back into the huddle and got back to business.

How was it possible for Joe (and his teammates) to be comfortable—relaxed but intense and focused—in the middle of that cauldron? With all due respect to Joe and his teammates, that's what a leader tries to teach—how to be in the zone.

Wisely applied humor—even something as silly as putting on a bell-hop's uniform—can be a useful device in allowing your team, staff, or organization to get past anxiety and into the zone. Don't overdo it, but don't underestimate its effectiveness.

The Last Word on Getting in the Last Word

I have been accused of being overly sensitive to criticism—thin-skinned. Maybe it's because I've seen too many examples of so-called experts and critics who didn't have much of a clue. Unfortunately, what they say or write becomes part of the public record and is subsequently perceived as fact. This can really hurt when it's hogwash.

Here's an example. A Seattle sports writer published a book that singled me out as "a most stupid coach." He gave as evidence a game against the Seahawks in which the 49ers had executed a series of well-crafted running plays to get inside Seattle's ten-yard line. I then called three *passing* plays in an attempt to score. We failed. The writer suggested this was the work of a coaching moron.

What this "expert" didn't recognize was that while Seattle had a much weaker team, they did have one outstanding asset: the NFL's best goal-line defense against the run. You just couldn't expect to score on the ground against the Seahawks inside the ten-yard line. So we went to the air. Again and again and again.

When I read this critic's analysis of me, it hurt. Not because he was right, but because tens of thousands of his readers would accept his mis-guided evidence as proof and his opinion as fact: "Bill Walsh is a most stupid coach."

If you care about how you're perceived by others, including the pub-lic, it's good to remember the following: Criticism—both deserved and undeserved—is part of the territory when you're the one calling the shots. Ignore the undeserved; learn from the deserved; lick your wounds and move on.

Sometimes you can't have the last word.

Thinly Sliced Baloney (Can Make a Good Sandwich)

There's a certain amount of "larceny" that goes on with competition—gamesmanship both intentional and unintentional. Whether you're pro-active or reactive, how you deal with it can affect the outcome in sports or elsewhere.

For example, the week prior to each of our first three Super Bowl appearances, a key 49er receiver came down with an unexpected injury—a legitimate but not debilitating one. I understood the media frenzy that goes along with a world championship Super Bowl game and the des-perate need of the media to supply all kinds of "news," including gossip, conjecture, and rumor. Of course, an injury to a primary receiver in a pass-oriented offense like ours becomes very big news.

One year it was Freddie Solomon, who twisted his knee in practice. I said publicly he could miss the game because of it. *Could* he miss the game? Yes, it was a possibility, but an unlikely possibility.

All I cared about was the Bengals reading the injury report about Fred-die and wondering whether or not he was going to play. I was hoping it might upset their preparation slightly, make them prepare for what we might do without our star receiver, perhaps get overly confident that they had an advantage going into the game. I was using a little gamesmanship.

In Super Bowl XIX the same sort of thing happened with Dwight Clark—a sprained ligament. Then in Super Bowl XXIII it was Jerry Rice, who came to me after a practice at Joe Robbie Stadium in Miami and said, "Bill, my hamstring is really tight. I hope it doesn't get any worse." That's all I needed to put him on the questionable list and express my concern publicly about his being fully recovered in time for the kickoff.

In duly reporting the status of these top receivers to the media—always with the look of a graveside preacher—I knew the story would get blown out of proportion as it worked its way through the news process: "Will San Francisco's offense sputter if Solomon (or Dwight Clark) can't play?" "Can the 49ers win with a hobbled Jerry Rice?" These and scores of variations would dominate the sports news for at least twenty-four hours, because this kind of story is like catnip to the media.

I was taking the "rules" right to the edge, flirting, going as far as I could legitimately go. And of course, other than those who were somewhat naive, I think all of us did it. You use the resources and remedies that are available within the boundaries of the law.

Seeing the story evolve from an update on a player's condition to the center of a media storm was predictable and somewhat amusing. I also recognized that opposing players and coaches would perhaps read or hear the "news" and tend to be distracted as they evaluated any potential advantage to be gained. It takes tremendous discipline to avoid this kind of speculation.

As a result, I constantly warned our own players to ignore any and all media "updates" coming out of an opponent's camp or anywhere else. If the papers reported that the entire opposing team had gotten the flu and been rushed to a local hospital in a Mayflower van, I didn't want us to be distracted by it; I didn't want us to speculate on anything other than the assumption that the Dolphins, Bengals, or anyone else would be 100 percent ready to go at game time. All else is usually thinly sliced baloney, which can take away from the intense concentration needed to achieve maximum results.

A similar kind of distraction crops up in business. A sales representative will learn that a competitor has just reduced the price on a competing product or introduced a new feature that may offer a significant benefit; an individual will hear that someone is being groomed to replace him or her or that a much desired promotion is going to someone else (exactly the same situation many players and coaches face every day of their professional lives).

True or false, these rumors can cause great uncertainty and create a distraction that can grow into anxiety and fear. In a worst-case scenario in sports, it can be crushing to a player and even lead to his professional demise because his self-distraction leads to plummeting performance. Even superstars—franchise players—such as Steve Young and Joe Montana heard occasional rumors and undercurrents that they were going to be traded. Both were subject to uncertainty and the embarrassment a trade would bring to them when, in fact, neither one was seriously being offered for trade during his peak years with the 49ers.

The fact is that I was in a continuous dialogue with other teams about trades, or, at times, exploring trades without even being serious—throwing out the name of one player in hopes that the other side would express interest in a player I wasn't offering. I was just throwing the bait out, hoping the other side would come back and express interest in someone else: "We don't want this one, but we will take that guy." This gave us information as to the level of interest the opposing partner in the trade talks had.

In fact, I offered to trade Joe and Steve at various times knowing it would get the attention of the team I was talking to—hoping I could move them to another player off that opener. During all of this, I was careful to reassure those players whose names were offered that nothing was in the works. I suspect that my comforting words provided little comfort—football is a game that induces paranoia.

In all cases, I emphasized to the people in our organization that their response to rumors, gossip, and hearsay should be the same: Focus only on doing your best to maintain and improve your level of performance; concern yourself only with that which you can control, and you can't control rumors. Ignore thinly sliced baloney.

Surprising News Re: The Element of Surprise

The surprise tactic has its place—very limited—in any competitive endeavor. However, I believe surprise for the sake of surprise is often a trap. There's a mistaken mentality, a kind of thinking that leads you to a faulty conclusion: "They won't expect us to do *this*." It's very dramatic but often reveals recklessness—"Let's try it. No one will ever anticipate it."

The media glorified this attitude in movies such as *The Great Escape*: "They'll never expect us to do it in broad daylight," or something to that effect. That idea—"nobody will expect it"—is grossly overrated and often the manifestation of poor strategic planning. Surprise is often simply a default device, something in lieu of strong thinking. Innovation is something else.

Innovation—according to the dictionary, "to advance or improve"—is an intrinsic part of achieving dominance in a given profession. In my own work, it was innovation regarding the use of the forward pass that led directly to a breakthrough in performance results. What our team did, though innovative, was usually not based on surprise tactics, although opposing teams were often surprised by the complexity of what they faced.

Innovation that works is based on solid integral logic and applied performance. *Calculated* risks are part of what you do, but the idea that something completely crazy will work just because it's completely crazy is completely crazy. It fails dramatically more often than it succeeds, but when it does succeed you're tempted to do it again, and that's when you get caught. By taking a reckless approach you think you'll fool people. You hear commentators talking about it: "They really caught 'em with that one," or "They never expected that." It's glorified, just like in the movies.

The principle of assuming the other person is unprepared, believing the competition will not adjust or is inflexible, or being convinced you can just outsmart the opposition with the element of surprise, is bad. In football terms, it's comparable to running a reverse on third-and-goal, thinking, "They'll never expect it." That's poor logic.

If it works, that might be the worst thing that can happen, because you'll be tempted to make other equally ill-advised and risky decisions. High-risk decisions are very necessary at times but should not be an ongoing course of action. Finding yourself in a position where you believe your only option is to pull off a big surprise often means you haven't prepared, haven't done your homework. The "big surprise" option eases the internal pressure to come up with solid planning and preparation that can force your opponent to resort to high-risk options.

I preferred the position of being able to take lower-risk actions with higher reward potential. That sounds like a situation that rarely exists—low risk, high reward—but it's exactly what my pass-oriented, ball-control system offered on the majority of our plays. In order to make it work, I applied great energy and expertise to a methodical process of anticipating, planning, and practicing for every conceivable situation.

This sounds rather easy, but we both know that "walking the walk" is harder than "talking the talk." Just "talking about it" will too often put you in the position where your only option is the element of surprise.

Don't Delay Delegating (Famous Last Words: "I'll Do It Myself")

My stated philosophy as head coach was that the person in our organization best suited for a specific job should be the person heading it up or doing it. The best play caller should be calling plays, the best offensive coordinator should be coordinating the offense, and so on. That was my theory, but not my practice.

Somehow in my mind I believed that I was the best qualified to do almost every job, especially when it came to the offensive part of our game. In one sense, it stemmed from confidence; I was absolutely sure that if I did the job it would not get screwed up. Well, that can only take you so far. Pretty soon you're on overload while very talented people in the organization are being underutilized.

For example, Mike Holmgren, a superb assistant coach who eventually won a Super Bowl while head coach of the Green Bay Packers, was on my staff and could have taken on much more responsibility than I gave him. (The year immediately following my retirement, the 49ers won Super Bowl XXIV against the Denver Broncos 55–10, an all-time scoring record. Mike was calling the plays.)

There were others, too, on my staff who were able and willing to take on more responsibilities. *They* were willing; I was reluctant, even unwilling—unable is perhaps more accurate. Of the various failures I cite myself for, one of the most problematic may have been my inability to delegate to the extent I could, and should, have. Increasingly, I continued to take on massive responsibilities. I appeared to be in full control—and I think I was—but the exhaustion I experienced, the track I was on, offered no escape. I couldn't take a real vacation because there was always more and more to do, and I felt, rightly or wrongly, that Bill Walsh was the one best able to handle too many of the various responsibilities. Well, that kind of thinking can only take you so far. Eventually, you're working seven days a week, sixteen hours a day with little good sleep, eating poorly, and dealing with all kinds of forces. You burn your energy like an acetylene torch until your nerves are completely stretched and then virtually destroyed. It took me years to figure this out, to learn it, to understand it. By then I was no longer head coach of the San Francisco 49ers.

You may suspect you need to be delegating more, but you can't bring yourself to do it; you can't summon in yourself a trust in others whose talent you respected enough to hire them. I should have had more of a plan or commitment to move other people into different roles and to let them emerge, to loosen my grip on control, but I couldn't, and the exhaustion I experienced, the track I was on, was partially the direct result of not being able to delegate more intelligently.

There was always something to do, and I was the one most capable of doing it—or so I thought.

Cut Your Losses Before They Cut You

Thomas Henderson was not only one of the best linebackers in NFL history, but a very intelligent man—one of the great athletes to play the game. He was also one of the most flamboyant during his years with the Dallas Cowboys. His nickname was appropriate: "Hollywood."

Unfortunately, by the time he joined the 49ers during my first year as head coach, a more apt moniker would have been "Cocaine" Henderson, because he was a serious addict whose life was coming apart.

In fact, when my wife, Geri, and I had Thomas and his wife, Wyetta, over for dinner at our home in Menlo Park, California, shortly before he officially joined San Francisco, he excused himself briefly while the apple pie and ice cream were being served. Later, I discovered he had gone into our bathroom to snort cocaine.

I was aware that Thomas had become somewhat difficult during his final years with Tom Landry's Cowboys—violating curfews, breaking dress code rules, increasingly contentious and criticizing the coaching staff, even mugging on the sidelines for the television cameras—but I thought that with my supposed ability to work with problem players, I could get him back on track. Plus, in that first year as head coach, I was desperate for talent—especially on our defensive team.

However, it soon became evident that my abilities were no match for the destructive power of Henderson's addiction. (In fact, in those days most coaches were ignorant when it came to hard drug use among players. The most common drug being abused was alcohol. When a player had a problem with it, the symptoms were evident the next day—a big hangover. The cure was simple: Work him hard and make him suffer. Throwing up over on the sidelines in ninety-degree heat usually solved the problem for a while. Cocaine was much more insidious.)

When it soon became apparent that things weren't going to work out between "Hollywood" and the 49ers, he began talking about injuries— most of all a neck problem that kept him out of practice. Keep in mind that neck injuries are often difficult to diagnose and consequently easy to feign.

In truth, and in light of "Hollywood's" recent behavior, we had no idea whether or not he was injured or faking it. Thus, it appeared the 49ers might not only be unable to trade him, but have to pay for an "injury" that was imaginary or had happened when he was with Dallas.

It all came to a boiling point during practice one afternoon, with "Hollywood" stretched out and moaning on our locker room floor— spread-eagled while players gingerly stepped over him to get out to the practice field. It was completely disordered and a serious distraction. I realized we needed to remove him from the environment—that is, get him off the roster—quickly, while at the same time avoiding a lawsuit related to his neck issues.

I used his ego to solve the problem. "Hollywood," I said, leaning over him, "this next game of ours is televised nationally. The whole country is going to be watching, and you're one of the guys the cameras are going to be zooming in on. We absolutely need you out on the field to run through some plays today. Otherwise, you won't be ready to go into the game and your family and friends are going to be very disappointed when they don't see you on network television."

"Hollywood" loved attention. With the prospect of national television exposure in the balance, he "struggled" to his feet and ran out to the practice field.

Meanwhile, my assistants were ready. Three cameras had been set up in the stands to tape "Hollywood" slamming into people with great zest and without the slightest discomfort. We had our evidence and released him immediately. I don't know if "Hollywood" ever found out that our upcoming game was not scheduled for network television.

The lesson is simple: When you make a mistake, admit it and fix it. Don't let pride, stubbornness, or possible embarrassment about your bad decision prevent you from correcting what you have done. Fix it, or the little problem becomes a big one.

The ending to this story about Thomas Henderson is positive, although it took a while. Soon after his release from San Francisco, he was out of football and in trouble, including serving time in jail. Eventually, however, he overcame his addiction to drugs and alcohol and got his life back on track. That's the biggest game Thomas Henderson ever won. I'm only sorry he couldn't have achieved that victory while a member of the San Francisco 49ers.

Look Below the Surface: There's More Than Meets the Eye

You must be willing to account for a person's emotions and state of mind when you judge his or her actions. Frequently we misinterpret behavior because we don't allow for explanations other than what is most obvious; we don't look below the surface. Here's an example from my own experience.

During my last season as head coach, I began suffering from emotional and mental exhaustion brought on by the demands and pressures of my job that had been building up in my mind for several years. The inner toll this took is indescribable. It became almost torturous and manifested itself during the last months in my becoming increasingly sentimental about things and, at times, maudlin. All of it was, of course, related to exhaustion.

I would frequently be on the edge of breaking down in tears and started to protect myself to keep it from happening. Consequently, and without telling anyone, I decided I had to retire at the end of the season.

A week before we played in Super Bowl XXIII, I did a television interview in which the topic eventually turned to my feelings about the team. Well, this really got to me because of my fragile emotional state. The woman interviewing me had no ulterior motive; she was simply interested in knowing if I felt any different about these players compared with earlier 49er teams and had no idea her question would evoke overwhelming emotion in me.

I could feel myself starting to come apart as I considered her question and realized if I said even one word I was going to break down and start crying in front of a camera. Since I had no interest in sobbing on television, I abruptly stood up and walked off the set. The studio personnel were stunned, and the story subsequently went out that Bill Walsh, in becoming a successful coach, had also become arrogant and uncivil, a person who would truncate a conversation by standing and storming out of the room. This, of course, was incorrect.

It's important to understand a person's response in the context of his or her state of mind, where he or she might be emotionally; this often connects directly to his or her answers and actions. This reporter decided I was an arrogant, strutting personality who would simply walk out when I had had enough. In reality, she missed the point. Something big was going on, and she didn't get it, didn't go beneath the surface of what she saw.

She didn't even consider any other explanation. She missed the larger story in settling for the obvious answer.

A Pretty Package Can't Sell a Poor Product

Even before I joined the 49ers, it was apparent that their public image was deeply damaged, almost as bad as their won-lost record. In a sense, I had a front-row seat, because I was coaching at Stanford University, which is right in the middle of the San Francisco 49ers' fan base.

Subsequently, when I came aboard as head coach and general manager of the 49ers, I was concerned not only with the specifics of what happened on the field, but also with crucial off-field matters such as selling tickets, in particular season tickets. Our season ticket sales were awful, the worst in the league—7,012 in a stadium that held over 60,000 people. I immediately set to work beefing up those sales so that our 2–14 team would have bigger crowds to play in front of and the owner would have larger gate receipts.

In an attempt to do this, I tried to reach out to the community, to repair the damaged image the public had of us. I made sure the players and staff lent their support and presence to good causes, were available for interviews, and responded to correspondence.

To promote sales of season tickets, I came up with an ambitious (and time-consuming) plan called "Pick-a-Seat Day" in which we put bright red ribbons on all available season ticket seats and invited the public to buy their favorites. And that's not all.

On the big promotion day we offered balloons, free donkey rides, ethnic foods, and clowns for the kiddies. Also, free popcorn, soft drinks and hot dogs, jugglers, a Dixieland band, and magicians. It was really a great family event for the thousands of folks who came out to Candlestick Park.

The next morning I arrived at the office early to see what the results of my "Pick-a-Seat Day" promotion were. Or, more accurately, weren't. Total season tickets sold: seven. (I bought three more myself on the fifty-yard line, just so I could report that we'd hit double digits. In fact, our family still has those seats.)

"Pick-a-Seat Day" was a total flop, but it was a flop that taught me something very important: A pretty package can't sell a poor product. Results—in my profession, winning football games—are the ultimate promotional tool. I was trying to sell a bad product, a team that was the worst franchise in sports, that had lost twenty-seven straight road games, and whose record at home wasn't much better.

From that point on, I focused my energies exclusively on creating a quality product, a team that was worth spending money to see. When that was achieved, we also achieved a ten-year waiting list to buy a 49ers' season ticket.

In your efforts to create interest in your own product, don't get carried away with premature promotion—creating a pretty package with hype, spin, and all the rest. First, make sure you've got something of quality to promote. Then worry about how you're going to wrap it in an attractive package. The world's best promotional tool is a good product.

Zero Points for Winning (Means You're Losing)

Part of the makeup of many people with a very strong competitive instinct, whether in sports or business—especially those who are more intelligent— is that they know just how much losing hurts and don't like that feeling; they just can't accept it.

Losing is so devastating to them that it's just *thorough*; there isn't anything that can stop the pain except winning. For those people, I think probably in the majority at the top end of the competitive scale, it's almost impossible to accept defeat and the feelings of desolation that go with it. Consequently, we'll do almost anything to avoid it.

That anxiety about failure, that disgust with failure, that fear of failure is really a distinct part of competition and must be absolutely under your control. Unfortunately, this is often very hard to do—at least it was for me and took four or five years off of my coaching career at San Francisco.

Losing, however you define it, even the *thought* of losing, can become so psychologically crippling that winning offers little solace and no cause for celebration because you've imposed an internal accounting system on yourself that awards *zero* points for winning and minus points for losing. You can never get ahead on points. That's exactly what happened to me.

I see the symptom all the time in business. Study the faces of some executives or salespeople when they achieve a big "win." The best description of their demeanor is "grim-faced," and grim-faced they trudge cheerlessly on to fight without comment. They have allotted themselves zero points for victory.

This can occur as your expectations and the expectations of others get higher and higher—they keep raising the bar on you, and you keep raising it on yourself.

In my early years as an assistant coach, and then later in the beginning with the 49ers, simply teaching our personnel how to execute and perform at higher levels provided satisfaction and gratification. Seeing areas of our game reflect that improvement—increased yards per carry, fewer turnovers, higher pass completion percentages, and fewer penalties—allowed me to take pride in various elements of a loss. We hadn't yet reached the point of being expected to win every game, every Super Bowl.

Later, good play and execution were still able to produce satisfaction, but only if accompanied by a win. Eventually, good play and execution, even when accompanied by victory, produced virtually no ongoing satisfaction or pleasure, just momentary relief. I got zero points for winning.

Victory meant little more than delaying the pain of loss, as I quickly turned to the next game and the next one and the next one, each offering no more than the opportunity to postpone the awful feelings that accompany defeat while doing nothing to remove the fear of it.

When this happens, any kind of loss, mistake, or setback becomes very disturbing, even devastating, because you've attached your self-image to the results of the competition. Winning can become insidious for the same reason, that is, you allow the victory to begin determining your self-worth, how you feel about yourself.

Either way, you are putting yourself on a slippery slope when you start believing that the outcome of your effort represents or embodies who you really are as a person—what your value as a person is. I speak from personal experience.

For me, the San Francisco 49ers increasingly became who "Bill Walsh" was on the inside. Any mistake or loss became *me*. Any setback—big or small—reflected back on me, and I personalized it. If Jerry Rice dropped a pass, I dropped it; if a play didn't work, it was my fault, instead of the fault of the assistant coach who called it or the opposing defensive player who made an outstanding stop; if Steve Young or Joe Montana threw an interception, it was my poor pass. This is a dangerous way to run your professional life because it seeps into and contaminates your private life. Eventually, it led me to make some horrible choices in my personal behavior that I deeply regret and am embarrassed by—even ashamed of.

Ultimately, because failure had been personalized to such a degree, I was tormented by the very thought of errors of execution, mistakes, or loss. Winning, winning, winning—perfection—was the only solution.

Except it was no solution—even winning a Super Bowl couldn't remove the knowledge that failure *was* in the future, because nobody wins all the time.

In part, I brought the situation on myself, because our team was so bad in the beginning that all of us, including the owner, Eddie DeBartolo Jr., were grateful for the slightest signs of improvement. Eddie did not come from a football background, so he left me totally alone, free to fail or succeed without interference. This changed when I achieved results.

When San Francisco won a Super Bowl championship, the owner's involvement began to show itself in various ways, including a willingness to pay top money for talent. Eddie Jr. opened his pocketbook, and the 49ers went from the bottom of the spending charts to among those at the top.

Salaries were high, and the players (and their families) were given first-class treatment in travel and accommodations, including being flown to luxurious resorts for our Super Bowl ring ceremonies. When we needed him to write a check to acquire top talent from another team, Eddie didn't bat an eye. He was the best in the NFL in that regard and was known to occasionally hand an envelope stuffed with cash to a player who had done well during a game.

That part of it was great. Unfortunately, it was accompanied by something else that became destructive. Increasingly, Eddie kept raising the bar. Soon enough, if his team didn't win that year's Super Bowl, he was distraught, enraged. Just getting to the play-offs each year was insufficient; in fact, it drove him crazy—it was unacceptable to him, perhaps because his pride was involved.

When we lost, he felt helpless, since I was the coach, the one in charge who was running the show, not him. At the same time he was loosening the purse strings, he was beginning his heavy-handed approach to micromanagement, occasionally offering ideas to me, which was certainly his right. But then he began questioning my decisions, occasionally belittling them, wondering out loud to anyone who cared to listen whether there wasn't a better way than what I did—whether he, perhaps, knew more about it than I did.

This was embarrassing because, among other reasons, when it came to technical football, Eddie knew about as much as the average fan, which is to say, not too much. It reached a point, after one loss in a season during which we struggled, that he called me into *my* office for a ranting critique of the game and my coaching of it. The team knew what was going on because they could see and hear it; it was embarrassing—more than that, humiliating.

Eddie's background in football, his knowledge of football, was limited, but he felt peer pressure from his friends when we lost, and he occasionally reacted in an uncontrolled manner, usually after overindulging.

When people are frustrated, they look outside themselves for someone to blame; it was someone *else* causing his problem, others are making bad decisions, not him. "I'm being criticized unfairly," Eddie may have thought. It's human nature when your deep emotions are involved in something that you lash out at anything or try to reach in and fix it even if you don't know what's going on.

Looking back, it was something I should not have allowed. I let him haul me over the coals in regard to my effort or performance when he had no basis for doing it. His only basis was that he owned the team, a pretty good basis, but not enough for me to let him excoriate me without significant cause in front of the team even once.

I regret that I didn't back him down. Or leave. Ironically, it *was* part of the reason I left, for good. By then I had lost my taste for the job. I'm not sure I ever got it back, and in some way Eddie was part of the reason. I let him set a preposterous standard and then humiliate me when I couldn't reach it.

Looking back on it, I concluded that there are times when you must stand up for yourself even if the consequences include being fired. That's easier said than done, as evidenced by the fact that I didn't do it.

For Eddie—and I admit, for me too—eventually only a Super Bowl championship was acceptable; anything less was failure and cause for disgust and dismissal. (George Seifert, my immediate and able successor as 49er head coach, won two Super Bowls in eight years and was fired two seasons after the second championship in spite of having the highest winning percentage of any coach in NFL history: .766 with a 98–30–1 record. Eddie wanted a Super Bowl. Every year.)

All of the above, in a nutshell, contributed to why I had to retire. The pursuit of the prize had become an exercise in avoiding pain; the expectations had become unattainable; the behavior of our owner had become—on occasion—unacceptable; and the responsibilities I took on, coupled with the pressure I put on myself, were unmanageable. Or so it seemed.

A profession I loved and had worked for all my life had gone from being joyful to unenjoyable to unendurable. I couldn't win when I won; there were no points in winning and thus no point in continuing.

Later, when I became a commentator for NBC after I got out of NFL coaching, I would see similar pain when I'd interview some coaches at the beginning of the regular season. They were hanging on for dear life after a bad year and had just been through eight weeks of training camp working eighteen-hour days with no sleep, bad food, and all kinds of forces pounding them, including decisions on which players stay, which players go, and how to deal with the press, injuries, holdouts, agents, owners, media, and everything else.

On some of those occasions, a coach would see me and just break down. Marty Schottenheimer broke down one time when I opened the door to his hotel room after he had lost two consecutive games early in the season. He came to me and put his arms around me and quietly cried. Why? He looked at me, a former coach, and saw relief, someone who had been there, who understood and sympathized.

Football coaches, just like executives who push themselves to the brink and beyond, often have no support system and become isolated from family, friends, and normal interactions. I've described it as being in a submarine, submerged and cut off from the human race.

My good friend Dick Vermeil did it as head coach of the Philadelphia Eagles. In his quest for a Super Bowl title, he ultimately began living full time in his cramped little office deep inside Veterans Stadium, working to the exclusion of everything else. His team reached Super Bowl XV only to lose to the Oakland Raiders (led by Jim Plunkett). Dick then pushed himself even harder.

Not long after, he was finished—"burnout," as he described it to reporters at a very emotional press conference when he announced he was quitting. Dick retired for *fourteen* years before returning in triumph by leading the St. Louis Rams to victory against the Tennessee Titans in Super Bowl XXXIV. Later he told the story of having a sign on the wall while he was the Eagles head coach. It said, "The best way to kill time is to work it to death." He told people, "I worked time to death until it killed me."

Can you imagine how burned out you must be to wait fourteen years to return to doing something you love? I don't have to imagine it. I never returned to the NFL as a head coach, in spite of offers where I was given a blank contract and told to fill it in with whatever I wanted and then sign it.

In professional football, just as in corporate life, as you press harder and harder the ownership (shareholders or the board of directors) may or may not support you. At midnight, while an exhausted coach is staring at a screen watching game video inch by inch by inch, back and forth, over and over, eating stale, cold pizza in the dim light, they're deciding over martinis and a steak dinner by candlelight whether he's worth keeping around: "Does he measure up?" they're asking over dessert while you're killing yourself with work. "Poor bastard looked pretty beat up last time I saw him," somebody says with a chuckle. Everybody nods. I didn't want to be that "poor bastard" again.

Nevertheless, that's part of *their* duty—to plan ahead, to be ready for whatever the future brings, to decide when their "poor bastard" should be gotten rid of. But the volatility and emotional exhaustion of the environment can just drain you totally, and you're living with it continuously. It can make you very vulnerable, fragile.

I was in Columbus, Ohio, to receive an NFL award just after the 49ers had won a Super Bowl. I got up, started talking, and lost it because I was still emotionally exhausted from the season. Most of the folks in the crowd didn't really care. Some did, some didn't.

I sat down afterward, and it occurred to me, "Most of these people don't give a damn about me. Why am I exposing my emotions to them? For what?" In that situation you can become a walking basket case for people to gawk at. When this happens, you must have the extreme discipline to alter your perspective. You must change things, but, oh, boy, is that tough to do.

Aggressively looking for the positive elements, however small, can dilute the toxic pressure of personalizing the results by allowing you to take pride in your strategies, tactics, effort, and execution even when they don't produce victory every time. It can provide comfort and ease the severity of an ever-growing loathing of failure, which, uncontrolled, can eventually take over to a point of making you almost dysfunctional.

And, of course, you must derive satisfaction and gratification from winning without letting it define your self-worth, just as you cannot allow defeat to define you as a person. There has to be a balance. You can't put yourself in a smaller and smaller box where there's only the infliction or avoidance of pain—a personal torture chamber.

I was increasingly unable to do this. Consequently, during my tenth season with the 49ers, I knew I had to get out. We had achieved great success, gone beyond anything we or anyone else could have imagined early on. In the eyes of many, a San Francisco 49ers dynasty had been created in which a Super Bowl championship was now a given. Imagine that. Winning a Super Bowl was a given. But I bought into it and thought anything less was utter and contemptible failure. I believed it, but I didn't really believe it.

I was suffering from the emotional and mental exhaustion of having been at various times head coach, president, general manager, offensive coordinator, and play caller, in addition to having other unofficial titles and responsibilities for various parts of a decade. But much of it had to do with our ultimately unattainable expectations and my inability to deal with the prospect of failure. All of it put together became too much.

Had I been able to avoid the dead-end calculation of "zero points for winning," I would have continued to coach the 49ers and, I believe, won additional Super Bowl championships. That is something that has never stopped eating at me. But by the end I wasn't thinking straight. When CBS announcer Brent Musburger interviewed me in the locker room in the middle of the wild celebration immediately after our third Super Bowl victory, he asked me, "Will this be the final game on the sidelines for Bill Walsh?"

Before he could even finish the sentence, I dropped my head and began weeping. I looked for my son Craig in the crowd and put my arm around him for support; we walked away. Somebody took a picture of us at that moment. I saw it the other day. I looked like an old man—frail, weak, almost bewildered.

Like my dear friend Dick Vermeil when he left Philadelphia, I had nothing left in the tank. In retrospect, it seems so simple; that is, the steps

I could have taken to remain the productive and enthusiastic head coach of the San Francisco 49ers.

Let me share some thoughts on avoiding the trap I fell into, some ideas on how to deal with escalating expectations that become preposterous, personalization of results, and "zero points for winning." I must admit that I'm not sure any of this would have benefitted me by the time I reached the end of my rope. The time to do it is before your tank is empty.

1. **Do not isolate yourself.** While your spouse and family can be extremely important for support, they may not be equipped to deal with the magnitude of your professional issues in this area. Thus, develop a *small*, trusted network of people whose opinions you respect and are willing to honestly evaluate. My own make-up resisted this. As I marched forward as head coach, I became isolated, increasingly separated, even lonely. Keep your lines of communication open with mentors and professionals in your business whom you trust, even a professional counselor. (I had one for a while.) They can help you restore perspective and help clarify and prioritize situations and responsibilities. Be very discreet about whom you confide in. Crying on somebody's shoulder, if it's the wrong "somebody," can have negative repercussions.

2. **Delegate abundantly.** If you've done your job in leadership, you've brought on board individuals who are very talented. Allow them to use their talent in ways that serve the team and lighten your load. If you've hired and taught them well, they will do their job. I confess it was hard for me to amply delegate, even though I was surrounded by exceptionally talented people. I hired them, added to their expertise, and then had trouble turning some of them—especially on the offensive side of the game—fully loose to do their jobs. I was like a man dying of thirst who was sitting on the edge of a mountain stream. I denied myself what was available.

3. **Avoid the destructive temptation to *define* yourself as a person by the won-lost record, the "score," however you**

define it. Don't equate your team's "won-lost record" with your self-worth.

4. **Shake it off.** Marv Levy lost four straight Super Bowls as head coach of the Buffalo Bills and was able to keep it in perspective: "It hurts like the devil for ten days or two weeks and then you bury it and go back to work and look ahead." Bud Grant lost four Super Bowls as head coach of the Minnesota Vikings and was able to keep it in perspective: "I've got a 24-hour rule. You only let it bother you for 24 hours and then it's over."

As you may have noted, I was unable or unwilling to utilize any of the prescriptions that I've just suggested. It would be facile to say it was because I didn't know about these options while I was head coach. In honesty, I did know—at least I think I did—but I didn't have the strength or intelligence to use them, to protect myself. Like many who wear blinders and focus on victory to the exclusion of everything else, I barreled down the highway until the engine burned up.

One of the common traits of outstanding performers—coaches, athletes, managers, sales representatives, executives, and others who face a daily up/down, win/lose accounting system—is that a rejection, that is, defeat, is quickly forgotten, replaced eagerly by pursuit of a new order, client, or opponent. They know that a defeat, whether a lost account or a loss on the field, can't be taken personally. Like Bud Grant, they shake it off and go forward. And so must you.

In my early days, I did this too. I firmly believed that if I took care of my job the score would take care of itself. When it didn't, I worked even harder to improve my coaching and elevate the Standard of Performance of our team. This was one of the reasons I drove myself so relentlessly. But gradually I found it harder and harder to accept my concept that the "score will take care of itself." I became consumed with *how* the score would take care of itself, whether it would be in a manner that resulted in victory for me. I became overwhelmed with worry about that score and lost sight of the fact that in a fight you go as hard as you can, do all you're capable of doing, knowing that ultimately, while you can influence the result to a greater or lesser degree, you do not *control* the result.

If your hard work is coupled with intelligence and talent, you may win.

If not, you go back to work and get ready for the next fight without feeling that somehow, having given it everything you've got (as I did for ten years), you are somehow inadequate as a person, that you didn't measure up. You can't let that happen to yourself.

What Do I Miss Least?

The cruelty of the sport, both mental and physical, was almost repellent to me—not what occurs during a game so much, but the brutal attitudes and practices I saw when I was coming up: treating players in an almost thuglike manner, working them to death in practice, pitting one against another, disrespecting their intelligence, dehumanizing them, and all the rest of it. It just seemed to be a crude model of leadership, an ineffective way of bringing out great performance for an organization filled with highly competitive and usually intelligent individuals who just happened to be fantastic athletes. I changed that completely when I became a head coach in charge of everything.

Even more, it was disgusting to see how people under stress can turn on one another and how those satellite and peripheral people will try to take credit for what you've done. I've got a list of people—albeit short—who claim *they* discovered Joe Montana and had to talk me into drafting him because I didn't think he had what it takes. One of the lessons I learned was how people change with success or failure. People's behavior and attitudes can be transformed in the most positive *or* most disturbing ways.

Also, it was unpleasant to know that doing a good job in the NFL wasn't much different from doing a bad job. Both will get you fired; the latter just gets you fired sooner. You know you're there as a coach temporarily, only while you're very successful, only when you do a fantastic job. Then you learn that even a fantastic job is inadequate. The norm becomes the impossible, and when you don't achieve the impossible, your head's on the chopping block.

Good and bad are about the same in the NFL, perhaps in corporate America too. You're gone if good is the best you can do. Good just buys you time; great buys you a little more time. And then you're gone. In the NFL, a head coach is on a very short string.

What Do I Miss Most?

I will start a list like this with the athletes and the relationships I had with others in the organization, especially assistant coaches and staff such as John McVay, Bill White, Bobb McKittrick, George Seifert, Norb Hecker, Denny Green, Ray Rhodes, Bill McPherson, and so many others—sharing a common goal, sacrificing, interacting, navigating the dynamics of dealing with other people in moving toward our goal. In fact, even though my relationship with Eddie DeBartolo became almost toxic at the end, during the early years it was wonderful. (And by the way, we repaired things in the years after my retirement and became very good friends. Eddie DeBartolo did what nobody else was willing to do; namely, he gave me a chance. I will always be indebted to him for seeing in me the potential that others did not. Eddie and I were partners in one of the great success stories in the history of sports.)

I also really miss the strategy and tactics of the game—designing plays and seeing them work. Nothing is more gratifying than creating something that you're sure no one else has ever seen or thought of and having it succeed. Then later to see it become a commonly used device throughout football is really something that is satisfying.

The offensive system I came up with was like that, what they called the West Coast Offense. As variations of it spread throughout the NFL and college football, it was very nice to see. I felt good about it, perhaps because it was the ultimate compliment, something along the lines of, "If you can't beat 'em, join 'em." Many started "joining" my approach to offensive football. It was in some sense a validation of what I'd created at Cincinnati and then been mocked for at San Francisco even after we won a Super Bowl. (I've never forgotten the dismissive comments, even ridicule, by many who thought that the kind of football I was teaching wasn't "real" football, that it was a gimmick. For reasons that I've never totally figured out, there was a reluctance to acknowledge the legitimacy of what I was doing.)

I also got a kick out of seeing opposing coaches start using the situational advance planning of plays, written out on a clipboard (usually covered in clear plastic to protect against rain and snow). I started it in response to Paul Brown's question at Cincinnati, "What've you got for openers, Bill?" and then developed and greatly expanded it as the benefits became more obvious.

And of course there was the deep fulfillment of climbing the mountain, of going where few in my profession were able to go. Our first Super Bowl championship was profoundly meaningful and satisfying—thrilling beyond my ability to fully articulate. *Thrilling*.

I miss all of that.

Quick Results Come Slowly: The Score Takes Care of Itself

The Fujian Province of China is known as the Venice of Asia because of the superb stone sculptures created there over the centuries. Hundreds, perhaps thousands of years ago, near the city of Sichuan, artists—stone sculptors—worked in a time-honored and time-consuming way. Legend has it that when their sculpture was completed, the artist immersed it in the shallows of a nearby stream, where it remained for many years as the waters constantly flowed over it.

During this period, the finishing touch was applied by Mother Nature (or perhaps Father Time). The gentle but constant flow of water over the stone changed it in subtle but profound ways. Only after this occurred would the sculptor consider it complete—only when time had done its work was the sculpture perfect.

I believe it's much the same in one's profession; at least it was in mine. Superb, reliable results take time. The little improvements that lead to impressive achievements come not from a week's work or a month's practice, but from a series of months and years until your organization knows what you are teaching inside and out and everyone is able to execute their responsibilities in all ways at the highest level.

Your team has absorbed and assimilated not just the mechanics of your own Standard of Performance, but the attitudes and beliefs that are central to it. I believe that every organization has a cultural conscience that it carries forward year after year. That ethos may be good or bad, productive or unproductive. Some leaders are able to create the former, others the latter. But productive or unproductive, it exists, and it is guiding ongoing personnel and informing new arrivals as they come on board.

The attitudes and actions I installed, including the inventory of San Francisco's football plays—offensive and defensive—were the result of the same guys (or their similarly trained replacements) doing the same thing for years and years. Subsequently, it became almost routine to execute at the highest level when the heat was on. Excellence in every single area of our organization had been taught and expected from the day I arrived as head coach.

The "big plays" in business—or professional football—don't just suddenly occur out of thin air. They result from very hard work and painstaking attention over the years to all of the details related to your leadership.

Talent, functional intelligence, experience, maturity, effort, dedication, and practice may not be perfect, but they will get you so close to perfection that most people will think you achieved it. And the results will show it.

It takes time to develop this Standard of Performance; it is not just a seminar or a practice or a season's worth of seminars and practices, but thoughtful and intense attention over years and years. Then, when you've got to score on the last play of the game to win, you know it can happen. This is a powerful force to have within you.

In Super Bowl XXIII, the final game I ever coached in the NFL, the Cincinnati Bengals led San Francisco 16–13 when we took possession of the ball on our own eight-yard line with 3:08 remaining to play. Most smart observers assumed a Cincinnati victory was now almost a given. What followed has become legendary in the NFL: the Drive. It is a wonderful example of the principles demonstrated by the stone sculptors of China as applied to one's profession.

The 49ers methodically—and artistically—marched ninety-two yards in eleven plays, culminating with orderly precision in an eighteen-yard pass from Joe Montana to John Taylor ("20 halfback curl X up") for a touchdown and a Super Bowl championship. There was hardly a hiccup as Joe and the team looked up from our own eight-yard line and saw the mountain's summit ninety-two yards away, then calmly—almost nonchalantly—climbed to the top.

As the Drive unfolded—those eleven plays—I had a deep sense that what I was witnessing was the manifestation, the expression, of everything we had done along the way in the previous decade, culminating with this final opportunity for a grand victory. Everything that was happening in front of me went back to the beginning, the first day of practice at training camp ten years earlier, and was linked by all the years of effort and intelligence by all the people in our organization during the decade since then.

From my first day at 49er headquarters, I had begun imbuing individuals with a sense that a higher standard was being taught and learned, executed and expected in all of our actions and attitudes. My Standard of Performance and the hard work all of us put into achieving it had created a deep sense of organizational character, commitment, and ability—a sense that every individual was connected to the entire team, and that this group fighting its way to the summit against Cincinnati was a natural extension of those that had preceded it—culminating now in a work of near perfection.

There was almost a sense of inevitability. We seemed certain, almost destined, to drive the length of the field against a ferocious Cincinnati Bengals defense. At least, that's how I remember feeling—no panic, no anxiety, no uncertainty. All we had to do was exactly what we had been doing for years and years: adhere to the Standard of Performance we had been sculpting for a decade.

The Drive became the final offensive series of plays in my career as a head coach in the National Football League. As it unfolded on the field in front of 75,129 fans in Miami's Joe Robbie Stadium, I was filled with an appreciation that what these players and the members of our organization who were not on the field were doing was a work of art, one that had been created over many years—similar, in a way, to the sculptures in China. It was a thing of beauty.

I believe it's true in your profession. Your effort in the beginning is part of a continuum of effort; your Standard of Performance is part of a continuum of standards. Today's effort becomes tomorrow's result. The quality of those efforts becomes the quality of your work. One day is connected to the following day and the following month to the succeeding years.

Your own Standard of Performance becomes who and what you are. You and your organization achieve greatness.

For me, the road had been rocky at times, triumphant too, but along the way I had never wavered in my dedication to installing—teaching—those actions and attitudes I believed would create a great team, a superior organization. I knew that if I achieved that, the score would take care of itself.

As you've seen, there were stretches where I found it impossible to truly allow that to happen, when I became almost terrified of losing, of letting the score take care of itself. But ultimately, I got back to it. On that final San Francisco 49er drive, ninety-two yards to a championship, I was at peace knowing the score—one way or another—would take care of itself.

And it did.

A Complex Man. A Simple Goal.

Craig Walsh

I was with my father on that final day, experienced with tens of thousands of others the incredible conclusion not only to Super Bowl XXIII, but to the NFL coaching career of Bill Walsh. "The Drive," ninety-two yards against Cincinnati for his third Super Bowl championship in eight years, has become legendary—a point of perfection when experts talk about how great teams perform under pressure.

Moments after the final gun sounded and victory was secured, my father found himself in the midst of total pandemonium. The San Francisco 49ers' locker room was exploding with joy and manic energy—reporters, players, staff, and many others all jammed inside to celebrate. Amid the wild crowd, Bill Walsh was an anomaly—quiet, withdrawn, almost melancholy. As he stepped off the podium after receiving the Lombardi Trophy and trying to give a short speech—shortened because of his overwhelming emotion and fatigue—he found me in the crowd, put his arm around my shoulder, and wept. "Let's go," he said quietly. My father was stepping down at the top, like he had asked his players to do when it was their turn.

The Score Will Take Care of Itself is an appropriate title for his book on leadership. As head coach he was tireless—even obsessive—in his drive to intelligently prepare himself and his entire organization (players, assistant coaches, trainers, staff, and everybody else) so that they were in a position to prevail in one of the most fiercely contested professions—the National Football League. A man of great logic, he truly believed that in the end, your ultimate assignment as a leader is getting those on your team totally ready for the battle. After that, you have to let winning take care of itself. His ability to do that contributed to his success; his inability to do that, increasing as the years went by, forced him to leave the game as an NFL head coach.

Having said that, I will share an interesting and revealing and little-known fact about my father: When he started his coaching career, the approval of and acceptance by fans meant very little to him. Football was in large part an intellectual activity in which he completely immersed himself—almost like a scientist searching for, and fascinated by, a mathematical solution in quantum physics. For Dad, "quantum physics" was about leadership, team building, and extraordinary performance in the context of football. (Of course, he also had a competitive streak a mile wide.)

How football could create devotion, fan frenzy, and be America's number one sport was something of a mystery to my father. When he did the impossible and won Super Bowl XVI in his third year as head coach, he quietly argued *against* a victory parade in San Francisco because he didn't think many people would show up; he feared that it would be an embarrassment for his players to be riding down empty streets waving at nobody.

He was surprised, but delighted, when over five hundred thousand people lined Market Street in downtown San Francisco to wildly cheer their newly beloved 49ers. Nevertheless, he could never fully comprehend what all the excitement was about. *His* excitement was drawn from a completely different source than the average fan's.

However, after the rallying point of that first San Francisco 49er Super Bowl victory, my father realized what a dramatic role the team had played in bringing the city back together as one following the public trauma of the murders of Mayor George Moscone and Supervisor Harvey Milk, and the Jonestown massacre a few years earlier. The "Niners" had become the common ground for the entire city of San Francisco and much of the Bay Area—a wildly diverse group of people. Dad took immense pride in this.

In a sense, Bill Walsh introduced twenty-first-century playmaking and management in the NFL two decades before the new century arrived— starting in 1979 when he was appointed president, general manager, and head coach of a lowly franchise in San Francisco, a distant outpost in the eyes of many throughout the league.

While most observers focus on his "genius" when it came to figuring out how a football team gains ground and scores touchdowns, few understand the complex psychological make-up of this remarkable man, whose need to prove himself, while almost self-destructive, was the fuel in the engine that helped catapult him to the top.

I've come to understand that, in some ways, my father's life was almost Shakespearean, because what got him to the top professionally was his downfall personally; in spite of his incomparable achievements, he had trouble ever feeling fulfilled on a continuing basis. While he learned from each loss and every win, my dad increasingly took something away from a defeat that he couldn't shake. Driven by a desire to gain the stamp of approval from his peers (but not necessarily the public), he was consumed by work and winning, increasingly haunted by losing. When you achieve what he achieved, the inability or unwillingness to grant yourself happiness and satisfaction is perhaps tragic.

By the sixth and seventh year of his decade as head coach with the 49ers, he was showing the price being paid emotionally. After a home game I would sometimes stop by and join him for a Jacuzzi in the backyard of his house on Valparaiso Street in Menlo Park, California. Although by then he had won Super Bowl XVI and was on his way to more championships, his mind-set was not what you'd expect.

Late at night, we would sit there in that hot tub, father and son. If the 49ers had won their game that afternoon at Candlestick Park, he would have a sort of blank look on his face; if they had lost the game that afternoon, he'd have the same blank look. I kidded him about it once. He said ruefully, "This is what happens to a man, Craig." He wasn't talking about fatigue from that day's work. I felt bad for him.

It happened in part because one manifestation of his creative abilities— the West Coast Offense (a name he didn't like)—was such a paradigm shift that most of the NFL elite, including other head coaches, were reluctant to acknowledge him as a true equal or admit that his system was a dramatic improvement, a giant step into the future. "Backyard football" Dallas rival and head coach Tom Landry called Dad's radical but successful offense. Others were similarly dismissive and sometimes explained a loss to the 49ers with some version of the following: "We just had a bad day. We were off our game." Rarely did they like to mention that the cause of their "bad day" was the great football team they had faced across the line of scrimmage. In fact, as the 49ers gained dominance in the NFL, he would sometimes motivate his players when, for example, Dallas was next on the schedule by telling them, "According to Landry, we've never beaten the 'real' Dallas Cowboys. They've always got some goddamn excuse: 'We had an off day, somebody was injured, the sun was shining.' Always some excuse for us beating the hell out of them." His speech was meant to motivate but was based on his own perception of being discounted.

For some, perhaps, dismissive comments and excuses for losing to their team would mean nothing. It was different for my father; it was personal.

As a young athlete, my father moved around a lot. Going to three different high schools, he never felt as if he fit in with the teams he played on; his friends were always changing. With average grades, he fell to the wayside. He grew up tough and had a left hook to prove it. Dad was an outsider; he wanted to be an insider.

What he found along the way professionally, starting in his days as an assistant coach, was an unwillingness by others to "let him in." He didn't have the pedigree—the athletic résumé from a big-name school or assistant coaching credentials from a big college program.

He told me this story about a dinner he attended with my mother while he was a quarterbacks coach for the Cincinnati Bengals way back when. Some of the other assistant coaches talked about where they had played football—Duke, Ohio State, Alabama, and other big-name schools were mentioned, as he recalled it. When it came his turn, he said, "I played at San Jose State." A woman at the table asked, "Is that in Mexico?"

Most of the head coaches at the major colleges and all but a very few NFL coaches had had stellar playing careers; many were already household names. In their eyes, he felt, Bill Walsh was the runt of the litter.

This is the reason that he hid from view—never included on his professional résumé—a brief but successful tenure as head coach of the San Jose Apaches, a semipro football team that he coached very early in his career. Dad feared that others would view it as a step down, "slumming" as a coach, furthering the image that he was not big-league material.

He gradually recognized that the old boys' network that defined the NFL management and ownership in those days considered him junior grade, not up to head coach potential, in part because of his lack of a pedigree, but also because his style was not traditional, not heavy-handed. It was more professorial or corporate in style than the shouting and screaming, intimidation and punishment that were the usual tools of old-school head coaches in the league.

Here's a very small example: In those days, one method of "toughening up" players was to prohibit them from drinking any water while they were on the field during practice. Bill Walsh allowed it, because he saw no gain in the policy. In fact, he felt depriving players of water during practice was counterproductive; it lowered performance. The "toughening up" approach, however, was the one owners felt comfortable with because it had been around since the start. In this and many other ways big and small, nobody had ever done it like Bill Walsh did it. His unorthodoxy put off owners who subsequently held him at arm's length.

My father found evidence of their bias at Cincinnati, where he consistently worked wonders with the Bengals' offense but didn't receive a single inquiry from any NFL owner in those many years about becoming a head coach. Even the Bengals' Paul Brown, the man for whom he was working the wonders, didn't hire him as his replacement when he retired. Brown chose another assistant, Bill "Tiger" Johnson, who fit the conventional mold of what a head coach should do.

Dad felt snubbed by the NFL, and his feelings didn't change much as he emerged as one of football's greatest coaches.

As San Francisco became the dominant team in the NFL, he recognized another kind of prejudice on the part of critics elsewhere—not just against San Francisco but against other teams from "way out west." The media, especially in the eastern media capitals, were loath to admit that the center of gravity for professional football had moved to the other coast; that "backyard football" had replaced brute force coupled with the occasional long bomb pass; that a guy who looked like he belonged in a boardroom or lecture hall was the top dog in coaching.

The other West Coast team that won Super Bowl championships during this era, Al Davis's Raiders, was given short shrift because Al was viewed by the league as a troublemaker, a renegade. Even though the Raiders had a more traditionally NFL style of football, they, too, were considered interlopers because they were on the "wrong" coast.

My father's irritation continued when the radical offense he created was dubbed the "West Coast Offense" by the media. The slight may have been unintentional, but perhaps not. *He* had been the sole creator of the brand-new offense that turned football on its head, and he hadn't created it on the West Coast but in Ohio with the Bengals. No writer, not one, felt it appropriate to call it the Bill Walsh Offense. Even now, after all these years, that seems either intentional or uninformed.

All of this bothered my father a great deal. Regardless of what he did, it seemed the powers that be would not accord him equal status, would not recognize the legitimacy of his approach and his leadership skills. Thus, he increasingly became driven by a simple but almost obsessive goal: to prove them all wrong. And he did.

This feeling of being discriminated against was part of the reason he created the Minority Coaches Fellowship Program while he was at San Francisco. He knew that smart, skilled black college coaches were not even being considered for head coaching jobs in the NFL because of race. He understood their plight because of his own experience of being kept at arm's length when it came to a head coaching position. He hated it and was the first head coach in the NFL to establish a formal program to address the problem by inviting talented minority coaches to observe how he did things at San Francisco. He showed them what they needed to know to operate successfully at the top level. Later, the league followed his lead with a fellowship program that expanded on what he had done.

In Super Bowl XLI, the Chicago Bears faced the Indianapolis Colts. Lovie Smith was head coach of the Bears; Tony Dungy was head coach of the Colts. Both are black. Dad enjoyed seeing those two great coaches running the show. (In fact, Tony had played briefly for Dad as a 49er.) In 2009, two years later, the Pittsburgh Steelers won Super Bowl XLIII. Their young coach was Mike Tomlin. By now, the fact that a black head coach was in the Super Bowl wasn't even a big deal. Times had changed so much. My father didn't live long enough to see that game, but somewhere, he had to be smiling.

You might think all assistant coaches in the NFL have the same level of desire to become a head coach that Bill Walsh had, but the magnitude of his aspiration is impossible to overstate. He was a perfectionist, and he saw perfection as being most likely achieved *only* if his ideas and decisions weren't filtered through and inevitably—in his opinion—misconstrued and misapplied by others. He had to be the one in charge.

Oddly enough, he came to this conclusion as head coach at a little high school near San Francisco in Fremont, California, during his first two years of coaching—the Washington High Huskies. In short order, he turned a perpetual loser into a big winner. My father saw what happened when he did everything himself (including driving the team bus to away games). As you've read in his own words, this desire to "do it all myself" eventually became an Achilles' heel for him.

From high school coaching he moved up by moving down: "up" to the college and NFL level, "down" as an assistant coach (i.e., secondary) position.

Subsequently, he often saw his well-thought-out and often unconventional ideas ignored, modified, or, on occasion, screwed up by others above him. This drove him to distraction and created a smoldering desire to be in charge of everything once again—just as he was at Washington High School. Now, however, he wanted to do it at the highest level of football, where the quality of talent offered him the possibility of achieving perfection: the NFL.

There were lots of guys in the motor pool of assistant coaches around the league, but not many developed Dad's all-consuming passion to run the show. It finally paid off when, after many years of working for and learning from Paul Brown at Cincinnati, one of the NFL's acknowledged great minds, Dad was put in charge of virtually everything by Eddie DeBartolo, San Francisco's young owner, the man who must be given all the credit for seeing something special in Bill Walsh.

Eddie was too young—thirty years old—to be part of the NFL's good-old-boy network (the DeBartolo family had only recently purchased the San Francisco 49ers) and thus wasn't concerned about Dad's lack of "pedigree" or put off by the intellectual disposition of his new head coach—he liked it, in fact. Eddie was rewarded for both his perspective and his perceptive choice: Three years later, his team achieved one of the greatest turnarounds in sports history when San Francisco went from worst to best and won a Super Bowl.

Bill Walsh loved military history, including the Civil War. He had read all of the books he could find about it, and when Dad took the family to Gettysburg one year, he conducted a tour of the battlefield for us that was detailed to such a degree a paid tour guide could have learned something. He used his knowledge of military history to motivate teams and often invoked battles when, against all odds, the troops—i.e., his team—had overcome the enemy.

He was a PhD-level motivator with a powerful ability to get people's attention and point them in the right direction. Military analogies were useful occasionally, but he had a full bag of other options. Some are amusing. As head coach of the San Jose Apaches, a group of cast-offs and wannabes who all felt they deserved to be playing at a higher level (specifically, the NFL), Dad made the following statement in his first meeting with the team: "Fellas, I want you to think about something: There's a reason you're all in this room today." He paused as his implied message—"Nobody out there thinks you're any good"—sank in. Then he continued with a solemn warning: "This is your last chance to prove you don't belong here."

And regardless of the approach he used, Bill Walsh would not degrade individuals. While he was very careful in handing out compliments (that is, he was a master of withholding praise), he constantly focused attention on the next level of commitment and sacrifice and performance. One of his tactics occurred during the team meeting the night before a game. He didn't give a big rah-rah speech but incited players with his own method: One by one, selectively, he called players out for commitment: "Keith Fahnhorst, if I call 90-O tomorrow, can we count on you to hold your block?" Fahnhorst was a tackle; 90-O was a play that needed him to block. "Can you promise you'll knock somebody on his ass if I call 90-O, Keith?"

He'd go through the roster like that: "Ray [Wersching, 49ers field-goal specialist], how long can we count on you for tomorrow? Can you deliver forty-seven yards at the end of the game if we need it? Don't say yes unless you're sure. I need to know absolutely I can count on you, Ray. Can I?" On and on, commitments, publicly to their team, of high performance in the coming battle.

He was also frank about admitting his own mistakes. After a game, at the next meeting, he would review what had gone right and wrong with the whole team. While he didn't pull any punches when reviewing their individual performances, he was also forthright when it came to his own work. He would tell them where he had made mistakes: "I should have done this instead of what I called," he'd say. There was no culture of seeking scapegoats, no failure and finger pointing. It was very matter-of-fact: We did this wrong; here's how we do it right. He would critique himself equally hard in winning and losing, always leaving room for improvement. Improvement was his obsession—always looking for ways to improve his coaching, his team, his organization.

Twelve O'Clock High, starring Gregory Peck, was one of his favorite movies and inspired him a great deal. Eventually, after his retirement, he described to me the similarity he felt between General Frank Savage (Peck's character in the movie) and his own situation and trajectory at San Francisco.

The film is about an American bomber group in England during World War II that is suffering extreme problems. Leadership is poor; casualties are high; morale is low; their luck is bad. General Savage comes in and, against long odds, turns the bomber group around, installing discipline, high performance, and good morale while leading raid after successful raid over Germany. But the personal toll is high as he sees friends killed and good men destroyed in various ways in combat.

The raids continue day after day, until one morning, as the crews of the bomber group—the 918th Flying Fortresses—are climbing into their planes for another attack, Savage finds that he is unable to lift himself into his B-17 bomber to lead them into battle. Having led his fliers to victory, he is emotionally gutted—a basket case who is taken to a hospital ward to recover.

Substitute the San Francisco 49ers for the 918th Bomber Group, football players for flight crews, Coach Bill Walsh for General Frank Savage, retirement for the hospital ward, and you get the idea. My father loved that movie because it told the story of what he did in football, and what happened to him as a result, in the context of something he loved—the military.

It is in the framework of this dichotomy, extreme success as a leader in the NFL and extreme distress as a person, that makes Dad's story so compelling, his lessons in leadership so valuable. His staggering drive to prevail—to "prove them all wrong"—his ferocious competitive instinct, and his singular brilliance as a strategist, organizer, and team builder produced historic results. The blueprint for his kind of leadership is revealed in this book.

The lessons he shares in *The Score Takes Care of Itself* are both a beacon for leadership and a cautionary tale—what to do and what *not* to do. But isn't that the subject all effective leaders dwell on? Isn't it the perpetual puzzle of their leadership?

My father was a complex man, but he had a simple goal. Although the price was high, he achieved his goal, and as the years rolled by following his retirement, he gained peace and pride, great satisfaction and contentment, within himself. No longer an outsider in his mind, he saw that his philosophy and methodology were held in the highest esteem; his radical system the norm; his approach to team building commonplace. And that many considered him the greatest football coach of all time. At the end, he was lecturing about his ideas on leadership for graduate students at Stanford University.

I've told people that my father didn't need a traditional family; his real family was football. And it was almost true. His commitment to the team, his organization, and its goals was total. Bill Walsh may not have sold his soul to the company store, but he leased it to the game he loved for many years.

My sister and I were there with my father on his final day. He was so weak, but still so strong in spirit. I whispered in his ear that it was okay to go, that the time had come and we loved him. Dad closed his eyes and was gone. He was brave as hell. I put my arms around him and my sister, Elizabeth, and I wept. His triumphs had been recognized for many years. He knew he was no longer an outsider.

My father is gone, but his hard-earned leadership lessons remain in place, perhaps more relevant now than ever before. I know he would hope that something in his own experience, as shared in this book, is of value in your own challenges as a leader. It would mean that once again he was able to do what he loved doing and did so well: teach others how to be as great as they can be.

Index